Guide to Wordplay and Word Games

From **acrostics** and **alternades** to **word chains** and **word squares** and calling in on **spoonerisms, clerihews, limericks, Scrabble** and the **crossword** along the way, this book explores the wit and wonder of word games.

The **One Hour Wordpower** *series*

WORD BANK
Expanding Your Vocabulary
WORD CHECK
Using Words Correctly
GOOD GRAMMAR IN ONE HOUR
THE NAME BOOK
THE SECRETS OF SPEED READING
GUIDE TO WORDPLAY AND WORD GAMES
CRISP CLEAR WRITING IN ONE HOUR
SPELL CHECK
1000 Most Misspelled Words

One Hour Wordpower

Guide to Wordplay and Word Games

GRAHAM KING

Mandarin
in association with
The Sunday Times

A Mandarin Paperback
GUIDE TO WORDPLAY AND WORD GAMES

First published in Great Britain 1993
by Mandarin Paperbacks
an imprint of Reed Consumer Books Ltd
Michelin House, 81 Fulham Road, London SW3 6RB
and Auckland, Melbourne, Singapore and Toronto

Reprinted 1993

A CIP catalogue record for this title
is available from the British Library
ISBN 0 7493 1526 1

Printed and bound in Great Britain
by Cox & Wyman Ltd, Reading, Berks

Acknowledgements

Word games and examples of wordplay are like jokes; they travel far and fast and in a very short time assume their place in the public domain. They are also apt to be recycled between one generation and the next, sometimes changed and sometimes not; some of the examples in this book have survived for many centuries. It is thus difficult to acknowledge accurately the source of much of the material in this Guide, some of it the result of hours of mental toil and anguish.

Where possible, however, sources are gratefully acknowledged, in particular, Willard R. Espy's *The Game of Words*; *The Guinness Book of Words*, Tony Augarde's *The Oxford Guide to Word Games*; Gyles Brandreth's *Pears Book of Words* and the American magazine *Games*, now regrettably defunct. In addition, the compiler has been assisted immeasurably by access to a considerable literature on words and wordplay, and other compilations.

If your verbal wits are stimulated after this brief but, we hope, stimulating dip into the wordpool, watch for other books on wordplay and word games in the *One Hour Wordpower* series which will lead you into deeper, murkier, wordy waters.

Introduction

From a very early age most of us indulge in seemingly useless, utterly frivolous pastimes best described as *wordplay* and *word games*.

A toddler learns to recognise words and sounds with nursery rebuses. A schoolchild is introduced to punning through Knock-Knock jokes, and to malapropisms and spoonerisms when someone drops a howler or spots a misprint.

Later in life we learn how best to deal with those difficult visits by relatives by rushing to find the Scrabble set, or by cringing in a corner with a Word Search. Some of us – millions, in fact – spend part of our daily lives trying to complete a crossword. People have been known to expire, mid-clue, doing *The Times* crossword. From womb to tomb in one move, that's the life of humans as wordplayers.

Apart from the more ubiquitous forms of wordplay there is a rich ferment of verbal amusements from *acromonogrammatics* to *univocalics*, with *double dactyls*, *kadigans*, *mnemonics* and *qwertygrams* in between. The *Guide to Wordplay and Word Games* not only lists the most interesting of these but explains, with examples, what they are and, in many cases, sets a puzzle, with answers at the back of the book. Peep if you dare!

Messing about with such nonsense, at whatever level of difficulty, is always fun. It also leads, inevitably and quite painlessly, to a greater appreciation of and familiarity with the English language. Lewis Carroll, that Prince of Word Gamesters, would approve.

Acrostics

An *acrostic* is a puzzle or a poem in which the first letters of each line spell out a word, phrase or sentence. Where the last letters of each line form the message, it is called a *telestich*; and where both the first and the last letters of each line are used, it is a *double acrostic*.

The device goes back to Biblical days but was especially popular during the Victorian period. One of the chief exponents was Lewis Carroll; here are the first five lines of a little poem which spells out the name Alice Pleasance Liddell:

> A boat, beneath a summer sky
> Lingering onward dreamily
> In an evening of July –
> Children three that nestle near,
> Eager eye and willing ear . . .

Here is a *double acrostic*, adapted from the puzzle supposedly invented by Queen Victoria to amuse her children:

> An Italian city
> A river in Germany
> Capital city of the US
> A large city in the US
> Capital city of Holland
> Turkish name for Constantinople
> Capital of Albania
> An African country
> Pertaining to an eclipse

The first letters of each answer form the 9-letter name of an English city, while the last letters of each answer spell out two words, in reverse, which will tell you one of the products that made the city famous. If the Royal children could solve it, so can you.

(Answer Chest, page 61)

Alphabet Games

Games based on the alphabet, or *alphabetics*, appear also to date from the Old Hebrew, judging by the number of times a character named Abie makes an appearance:

> AB, C D FEG?
> L M N O FEG!
> O S A R N FEG.

A distant cousin, the comic alphabet, was invented in the 1930s. It has many variations, but goes something like this:

> A for 'orses; B for lamb; C for th' Highlanders; D for ential; E for brick; F for vescent; G for police; H b'for beauty; I for the engine; J for oranges; K for de Paris; L for leather; M for sis; N for a penny; O for the rainbow; P for relief; Q for a song; R for mo; S for Rantzen; T for two; U for nerve; V for la France; W for a quid; X for breakfast; Y for Gawd's sake!; Z for breezes.

The most common alphabet games are those that attempt to use all the letters of the alphabet in a sentence, saying or poem:

> A Big Collie Dog Eats Finely Ground Horsemeat In Jellied Kale. Little Mutts Nibble On Pickled Quince. Resting, Satisfied, They Undoubtedly View With X-Rated Yawning, ZZZ-zzzzz.

The poetic version is slightly more challenging:

> An Angular Anarchist Angrily saw a
> Bandy Baronet Batter a Boar
> and so on.

Another variation sets out to compose a statement that uses all the letters and makes sense using as few words as possible, like the familiar:

> A quick brown fox jumps over the lazy dog (33 letters) or, Pack my bag with five dozen liquor jugs (32 letters), but better still: Quick wafting zephyrs vex bold Jim (29 letters).

With the alphabet's 26 letters providing several million combinations, surely it is not beyond the bounds of human verbal ingenuity to construct a sentence using only those letters. Like to try?

Alternades

An obscure game in which the alternate letters of a word are separated to create two new words, as in:

T R U A N C I E S = T U N I S and R A C E

Anagrams

A versatile and durable diversion in which the letters of a word, phrase or sentence are rearranged to form an appropriate new word, phrase or sentence:

Waitress	A stew, sir?
Contaminated	No Admittance
Clint Eastwood	Old West action
Florence Nightingale	Flit on, cheering angel
Adolf Hitler	Hated for ill
Western Union	No wire unsent
HMS Pinafore	Name for ship
Margaret Thatcher	That great charmer

The longer the anagrammed sentence and the wittier the riposte, the greater the achievement, as when 'A stitch in time saves nine' becomes 'This is meant as incentive'.

There are numerous variations. *Anagram verse* incorporates anagrammed words, as in this example by the American wordsmith Willard Espy:

Sweet Molly MacDougal, in labour,
Warned her sister, 'It hurts like a **sabre**.
Sin **bears** a high price,
So a girl should think twice
What she **bares** on the **braes** for a neighbour.'

A different version has the anagrammed words hidden in the lines of the verse:

Your little canoe will surely tip,
If you take it on an ocean trip.

The anagrammed words here are **canoe** and **ocean**. There is also a lot of fun to be had by playing around with the titles of well-known books, films and plays. In this case, one word of the title is anagrammed, with amusing results:

DAS TOOB (The history of German TV)
TARZAN OF THE APSE (The jungle man is finally ordained)
A LA RECHERCHE DU TEMPS PRUDE (The dirty bits left out)

Antigrams

An *antigram* is an anagram in which the rearrangement of letters in a word produces a word or a phrase having the opposite meaning to the original:

Evangelists	Evil's agents
Funeral	Real fun
Festival	Evil fast
Violence	Nice love
Astromoners	No more stars

Anagraphics

These are visual anagrams, where the word and its anagram are represented by drawings or photographs. Thus the anagraph of a lemon would be a picture of a melon.

Apt Adjectives

An amusing diversion which aims to match proper names with wittily appropriate adjectives. Here are some attached to political personalities:

> The well-tempered Mr Steel
> The Achillean Mr Healey
> The big Mr Benn
> The crusading Mrs Knight

Charades

Although charades are usually thought of as a Victorian parlour game, they originally were – and still are – very much word games. The traditional form usually began: 'My first is . . . My second is . . .', each giving clues to each syllable of the mystery word, and concluding with, 'My whole is . . .' which would offer a final clue:

> My first I hope you are,
> My second I see you are,
> My whole I know you are.

This is an example from 1810, and the answer is WELCOME. Here is another, more modern charade by Hubert Phillips:

> No hard decode. And, in this case,
> A solid answer you can claim.
> It has (I'm told) a different face
> For every letter of its name.

If you anagram the first three words and pay particular attention to the statement in the third and fourth lines, you'll have the answer.

(Answer Chest, page 61)

Chronograms

Chronograms are mini-games played with the letters used for Roman numerals: I (1), V (5), X (10), L (50), C (100), D (500) and M (1000). A bit of cheating is sometimes permitted by using V as U, and two V's to form a W. The form goes back several centuries; for example:

> My Day Closed Is In Immortality

or, MDCIII – 1603, the year Queen Elizabeth I died. Another early chronogram is 'LorD haVe MerCIe Vpon Vs', which is rather clumsy Roman for LDVMCIVV or 1666, the year of the Great Fire of London.

Clerihews

The *clerihew* was invented around 1890 by – reasonably enough – Edmund Clerihew Bentley, a student at St Paul's School in London. One day, while studying the works of Caesar, he idly wrote in an exercise book:

Sir Humphrey Davy
Was not fond of gravy
He lived in the odium
Of having discovered sodium.

Having originated the form, which became the rage, the originator was quickly eclipsed by other, more skilled practitioners, and the best of these little biographical ditties come from their pens. For example:

Billy the Kid
Never did
Apologise
For killing those guys.

and

How odd
Of God
To choose
The Jews

together with the inevitable riposte: Why odd / of God? / His son / Was one.

Conundrums

The best *conundrums* are riddles that turn on puns. Like, 'Why is the letter N like a pig?' Answer: Because it makes A STY NASTY! Conundrums in verse were popular in the 19th century; this example dates from 1890:

> My first is a Spanish (or college) grandee,
> And in doors especially my second you'll see.
> My whole, if you can't guess this riddle,
>   you'll be!

You will have noticed the similarity to charades.

(Answer Chest, page 61)

Crosswords

An American once observed that if all the intelligence expended upon *The Times* crossword could somehow be channelled into more gainful pursuits, Britain could become a great power again. For, unlike the more straightforward American crossword puzzles, the British version is a wicked compilation of anagrams, homophones, abbreviations, cryptic and hidden clues, double meanings, puns and more besides. An addict, though, will quickly work out that HIJKLMNO is *water* (H-to-O); that 'a seed you keep in a garage' is *caraway*; and that orchestra is an anagram of carthorse.

The world's first crossword puzzle – or 'word cross' as it was called then – was dreamt up by American newspaperman Arthur Wynne and appeared in the *New York World* Sunday Magazine in 1913. It took a while to cross the Atlantic and at first was rebuffed; in 1924

The Times called the crossword 'a menace because it is making devastating inroads on the working hours of every rank of society'. Six years later, however, *The Times*, following several other British newspapers, bowed to the inevitable and introduced its daily puzzle which is now, arguably, the finest and foxiest in the world. The record time for solving it is 3 minutes 45 seconds, established by a civil servant, Roy Dean, in 1970. The record still stands.

Very few newspapers and magazines today are without their crossword puzzles, which are tailor-made to the tastes and demands of their readers; some are flatteringly simple, while others are diabolically difficult. If you are a beginner (and everyone has to begin some time) your best plan is to choose a publication which has a relatively simple or 'quick' crossword. After a couple of weeks you will have got the hang of it and can move to more challenging puzzles.

The clues to these puzzles will probably be cryptic, designed to make you think. To help you understand them, John Grant, Crossword Editor of *The Times*, offers some helpful tips on the various types of clues:

The Build-up. Clues are given for the components of a word; for example, 'Warning sound and light in tree'. There are three clues here: one for the first part of the word, one for the second part, and one for the whole. The answer is HORNBEAM (sound-light-tree). Be careful, though; clues aren't always given in the right order.

Anagrams. The clues are jumbled words or phrases which when unjumbled form the required word. For example, 'Missing epic reaps sad toil'. Missing epic? How about PARADISE LOST? 'Reaps sad toil' is an anagram of Milton's great work.

Double meanings. With this sort of clue the compiler gives two meanings, often contradictory, for the required word. For example: 'Not enough butter? What a predicament', The answer, which fits both clues, is SCRAPE.

Hidden clues. Here the answer is concealed in the clue, which also contains its definition. The hidden clues are usually indicated by such words as 'in' or 'part' or 'some'. Here's an example: 'Some hurricANE Winds again' for which the answer is ANEW.

Cryptic clues. With these, the compiler gets very wily by describing the answer in a misleading way. A good example is 'Handled glasses (10)', which cleverly conjures up a vision of a jolly barmaid pouring pints. In fact, the answer is LORGNETTES, which are reading glasses which have handles.

Homophones. These are words with different spellings or meanings but which are pronounced the same. Their use in clues is usually indicated by 'we hear', 'they say', or 'by the sound of it'; for example: 'Bad driver had piggy back ride, we hear (4, 3)'. The answer is ROAD (rode) HOG.

Abbreviations. Very common in clues. Typical are 'about' = C (irca); 'that is' = i.e.; 'gold' = Au; 'Outsize' = OS, etc.

Try your hand at the 'word cross' puzzle overleaf which was launched into an unsuspecting world on 21 December 1913.

(Answer Chest, page 61)

THE WORLD'S FIRST CROSSWORD PUZZLE
December 21, 1913

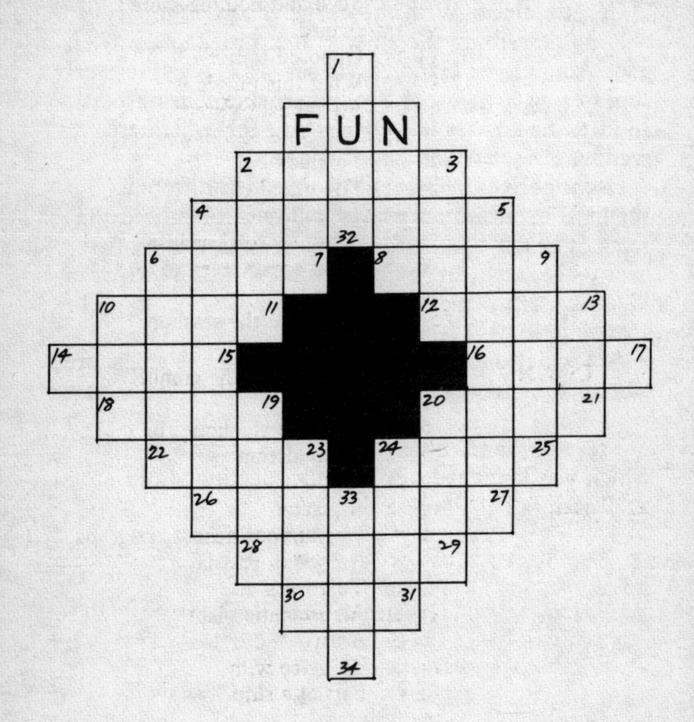

CLUES

ACROSS

2–3. What bargain hunters enjoy
4–5. A written acknowledgement
6–7. Such and nothing more
10–11. A bird
14–15. Opposed to less
18–19. What this puzzle is
22–23. An animal of prey
26–27. The close of a day
28–29. To elude
30–31. The plural of is
8–9. To cultivate
12–13. A bar of wood or iron
16–17. What artists learn to do
20–21. Fastened
24–25. Found on the seashore

DOWN

10–18. The fibre of the gomuti palm
6–22. What we all should be
4–26. A day dream
2–11. A talon
19–28. A pigeon
F–7. Part of your head
23–30. A river in Russia
1–32. To govern
33–34. An aromatic plant
N–8. A fist
24–31. To agree with
3–12. Part of a ship
20–29. One
5–27. Exchanging
9–25. To sink in mud
13–21. A boy

(Answers, page 64)

Cryptograms

Or, more cryptographically, DSZQUPHSBNT! This *cryptogram* has been achieved by the simple expedient of substituting the following letter for each letter of the word 'cryptograms'.

Cryptograms are coded words, phrases or, more commonly, messages. Most cryptograms are meant to be decoded into the letters and words of a language; in English, this is facilitated by a usage table of the most frequently used letters of the alphabet: E T A O I N S R H L D etc. If, in a code or cryptogram, we note that the most common character is the letter Z, then we begin cracking the code by assuming it stands for the letter E, and so on.

Try this cryptogram, in which C is a consonant and V is a vowel. Each of the 6 answer words begins with the letter C, and no word contains the letter Y. All the words are common ten-letter English words, and none is a plural:

1. C C C V C V C V C C
2. C V V C V C V V V C
3. C V C V V C C V C V
4. C V C C V V C V V C
5. C V C V C V V C C V
6. C C V C C V C C V V

(Answer Chest, page 61)

Double Dactyls

The *double dactyl* is a relative of the *clerihew*, a verse form of two quatrains in which the last line of the first rhymes with the last line of the second; the first line is a nonsense line (like 'Higgledy-piggledy', by which this word game is known in the US), the second line a proper name, and at least one of the lines is a single word. Here's an American example:

Tweedledum Tweedledee
Alice in Wonderland
First she was tiny and
Then she was tall

Argued with animals
Anthropomorphical,
Didn't accept their
Conclusions at all.

Doublets

A word game (also known as laddergrams, word chains, transitions and transformations) attributed to Lewis Carroll, in which the player changes a word, letter by letter, into another. That sounds simple, but there are rules: first, both words must be related in some way, and second, every step must be represented by a real word. The idea is to accomplish the task with as few moves as possible.

HEAT – HEAD – HERD – HERE – HIRE – FIRE
LEAD – LOAD – GOAD – GOLD

Now try to turn HATE into LOVE in three moves.

(Answer Chest, page 61)

Enigmas

Enigmas are riddles, usually in verse form, and have been around for nearly 500 years. Here's an example from the 19th century:

> I boast four syllables my name to make,
> Yet but eight letters for that name I take;
> In fact I actually require but four,
> If I may double each I ask no more;
> By Simon's land seek these letters out,
> I am a lake; you know my name, no doubt.

The answer is Lake Titicaca, bordering Peru and Bolivia. Simon refers to Simon Bolivar, founder of Bolivia.

Here's a non-verse enigma, set by Voltaire; the answer is a single word:

> What, in all the universe, is the longest and shortest, the fastest and slowest, the most divisible and the most protracted, the most neglected and the most regretted; without which nothing can be done; which consumes all that is small and exalts all that is great?

(Answer Chest, page 61)

Headline Game

It is difficult, if not impossible, to make up newspaper headlines that are funnier than the real thing. Try beating these: EIGHTH ARMY PUSH BOTTLES UP GERMANS; YOUTH HIT BY TRAIN RUSHED TO TWO HOSPITALS; CHIP SHOP OWNER BATTERED MAN; DEAF MUTE GETS NEW HEARING IN KILLING; FLAMING TOILET SEAT CAUSES EVACUATION AT HIGH SCHOOL; TRAFFIC DEAD RISE SLOWLY. No, you simply cannot, but you can have fun trying.

For example, set yourself the task of inventing a headline that incorporates self-defeating logic. Some examples:

MARCH PLANNED FOR APRIL
BLIND BISHOP APPOINTED TO SEE
INJURED UPHOLSTERER RECOVERS
LINGERIE THIEF GIVES POLICE THE SLIP

Or you could set your sights on the job of the tabloid sub-editor who invents those really outlandish headlines:

ELVIS'S FACE APPEARS IN WASHING MACHINE WINDOW
TWO WOMEN GIVE BIRTH TO SAME BABY
DOG BORN WITH WHEELS FOR LEGS

Homonyms and Homophones

These can be the source of much embarrassment, but can also provide a lot of fun in word games of your own devising.

A *homonym* is a word that has the same sound and the same spelling as another word but which has a different meaning. A *homophone* is a word that is pronounced the same as another word, but which has a different spelling and meaning. For example:

HOMONYM – BAY (geographical term); BAY (laurel tree); BAY (a section in a library).
HOMOPHONE – HEIR, AIR, AYR

Isomorphs

Isomorphs are pairs of words that have the same sequence of letters:

```
1 2 3 1 2 3 4 2 5
M U R M U R O U S
B A R B A R I A N
```

Kadigans

Recently, a correspondent asked *The Times* if readers could suggest a name for the hand-held device that changes channels, volume and picture on a television set; in the interim, he and his family were referring to it as a 'whatsit'.

What the writer was seeking was a *kadigan*, or vaguism, or a vague adjective. Some familiar examples are 'thingummy', 'gadget', 'thingummybob', 'whatchumacallit', 'doodad', 'doodah' and 'gubbins'. None of these, however, conveys any sense of the purpose of the handheld TV gizmo. Would you like to make lexigraphic history by inventing a suitable kadigan for the 'doowillie' under discussion?

Limericks

May 12 is Limerick Day, and to celebrate it the American novelist Erica Jong penned the following:

A bespectacled artist called Lear
First perfected this smile in a sneer.
He was clever and witty;
He gave life to this ditty –
That original author called Lear.

It could have been the ten millionth limerick written since Edward Lear published his first batch in 1846 in a *Book of Nonsense*, rather dated and wan whimsies that copped out by repeating first and last lines.

Since then, limericks have moved to the popular front of versifying, providing a form that was melodious to the ear and appealing to the intellect and into which practitioners could cast off their witty, ribald, libellous, rancorous asides to an eager world.

More than anything, limericks are firmly associated with eroticism and bawdiness – 'the dirtiest thing to happen to literature since graffiti was found in Pompeii'. The writer G. Legman, in a serious study of the art, published a two-volume collection containing almost 5000 limericks, almost all of them unprintable elsewhere.

> The limerick form is complex
> Its contents run chiefly to sex;
> It burgeons with virgins
> And masculine urgin's
> And vulgar erotic effects.

Still, the form allows plenty of scope for clean, healthy wordplay:

> There was once a girl from High Wycombe,
> Men? She just couldn't stycombe.
> If they ventured to kiss
> This most virginal miss,
> Up the backside in fury she'd kycombe.

More good clean sport can be had by setting the subject matter for a limerick, like ending it with the name of a household product:

> Despite matrimonial pledges
> The bride almost always on edge is;
> 'He watches TV,
> Or he gardens,' says she,
> 'But his real love is Benson & Hedges.'

Or compose a limerick on certain topics – literature, movie stars, place names, personalities; or if you really enjoy a challenge, on an arcane subject like mathematics:

> It's a favourite project of mine
> A new value of *pi* to assign

I would fix it at 3
For it's simpler, you see,
Than 3 point 1 4 1 5 9.

The form of the limerick is difficult to alter without spoiling its purity. Nevertheless there is a variation which delivers a shock last line which doesn't rhyme, as in this example by the Rev Patrick Brontë, father of the famous sisters:

Religion makes beauty enchanting
And even where beauty is wanting,
The temper and mind,
Religion-refined,
Will shine through the veil with sweet lustre.

And inevitably Ogden Nash, that master of abbreviated verse, invented the four-line Limick, in this case improved by Anthony Burgess who included an internal rhyme in the third line:

Two nudists of Dover
When purple all over
Were feasts for the beasts
Who mistook them for clover.

Lipograms

A *lipogram* is a literary composition which omits a certain letter of the alphabet. As the letter *e* is the most commonly used letter, its omission in a verse or a novel is considered to be the ultimate linguistic challenge.

A fifth-century Greek poet named Tryphiodorus, apparently an expert on lipograms, composed an epic poem on the voyages of Ulysses which ran to 24 books. Each of these books omitted, in turn, all the letters of the alphabet: in the first there were no alphas, in the second no betas, and so on.

Lipograms have survived to recent times. In 1939, Ernest Vincent Wright, a Californian musician, wrote a 50,000-word novel entitled *Gadsby*, without using the letter *e*. Thirty years later the late French author Georges Perec repeated the feat in another work of fiction, *La Disparition*, again without using a single *e* except for his name on the title page. (He also wrote another book limiting himself to a single vowel, *e*, which is discussed under Univocalics.)

Variations on the lipogram include verses which omit one letter but contain every other letter of the alphabet, a sort of *pangram*, as in this anonymous poem in which each stanza omits the *e*:

> Bold Nassan quits his caravan,
> A hazy mountain grot to scan;
> Climbs craggy rocks to spy his way,
> Doth tax his sight, but far doth stray.

Logograms

A *logogram* is a sign that substitutes for a word, for example # for *number*; & for *and*; < for *less than*. A logogram is also a word puzzle: I ♡ U is a simple example. There now exists a very large range of symbols – mathematical, scientific, road signs, abbreviations – that can be brought into play to create puzzle messages and verses.

Logogriphs

Logogriphs are riddles in which the players are given clues to find a word; each of the clues consists of that word with certain letters removed. Here is a 10-letter logogriph:

10 You squeeze it
9 You avoid them
8 You peel them
7 You pour from them
6 It's the most suitable
5 Suddenly, a lot
4 Over and done with
3 You drink from it
2 Preposition
1 First letter

(Answer Chest, page 61)

Another form of logogriph supplies the clues by suggesting certain words formed from letters of the answer word; this example is adapted from a Victorian book, *Excursions into Puzzledom*:

My 8, 6 and 5 is melancholy; my 2, 4 and 3 protects my skin; my 3, 6 and 5 is a boy; my 3, 4 and 5 fits on a jar, and my 5, 6, 7 and 8 should all be happy.

The answers (SAD, OIL, LAD, LID, DAYS) point to HOLIDAYS.

Malapropisms

If you hear someone languishing praise, searching for the bluebeard of happiness, dying interstate or admiring the flying buttocks of an old church, you are hearing a *malapropism* – a mis-applied word that resembles one that would, in the same context, be used correctly.

The term derives from Mrs Malaprop in Sheridan's play *The Rivals* (1775), the matron much given to the verbal confusions to which she also gave her name: malapropisms (from the French *mal à propos*: not appropriate). One should suffice: 'If I reprehend anything in this world, it is the use of my oracular tongue, and a nice derangement of epitaphs.'

Malapropisms occur naturally, but it can be fun making them up: 'He was hoist with his own leotard'; 'He keeps a revenue of servants'; 'He's at his wick's end'; 'She's doing her Arabic exercises', and so on.

Not a million miles removed are schoolboy howlers ('King Charles was condommed to death'; 'put the solution in a test tube and heat over a Bun St Bernard' . . .); Goldwynisms ('A verbal contract isn't worth the paper it's written on'; 'We have all passed a lot of water since then' . . .) and the sporting foot-in-mouth disease sometimes known as Colemanballs ('One mistake here could win or lose the match either way'; 'she has really plummeted to the top' . . .).

Metagrams

The *metagram* is a virtually defunct Victorian word puzzle in which the clues are usually given in rhyme. Here's one surviving example:

A vessel, when empty that makes a great sound	CAN
For frying it's used, in shape it is round	PAN
A lady carries it around in her hand	FAN
All the boys did it when they heard the band	RAN
God's great creation, he's proud of his race	MAN
A girl's name tho' it's short it's still no disgrace	NAN
The sun shines on your face and tints it with glee	TAN
Where the brave soldier stands who never would flee	VAN

Mirrorwords

Mirrorwords are words that when spelled backwards result in different words. Examples are:

Evil	Live
Desserts	Stressed
Lived	Devil
Reviled	Deliver
Straw	Warts
Rewarder	Redrawer

Mirrorwords are sometimes called *Semordnilap*, or palindromes spelled backwards. Does a nine-letter mirrorword exist?

Mnemonics

Mnemosyne, mother of the Muses, is the goddess of memory, and *mnemonics* are neat little sayings or verses that serve to help remember lists, facts and formulae, a sort of mental string around the finger. 'Every Good Boy Deserves Favour', sexist though it may be, has served for generations to remind music students of the lines of the treble clef: E G B D F. Students of mathematics remembered the value of *pi* to ten decimal places with 'But I must a while endeavour to reckon right the ratios'; the number of letters in each word gives the values: 3.1415926536. A more complex mnemonic exists that gives the value to 32 places; the problem is to remember the mnemonic! Many others exist: 'Nights Grow Darker After August' supplies the Latin declensions (nominative, genitive, dative, ablative and accusative); 'Camels Often Sit Down Carefully. Perhaps Their Joints Creak. Early Oiling Might Prevent Permanent Rheumatism' prompts the names of the geological periods from Cambrian and Ordovician right up to Pleistocene and Recent. History, with all its kings and battles and dates, positively begged for mnemonics, of which this one, listing in correct order all the English kings, is typical:

> William the Conqueror long did reign,
> William his son by an arrow was slain;
> Henry the First was a scholar bright,
> And Stephen was forced for his crown to fight.
> Second Henry Plantagenet's name did bear
> Richard Coeur de Lion, his son and heir:
> But Magna Carta was gained from John,
> Which Henry the Third put his seal upon . . .
>
> . . . Henry the Seventh in fame grew big,
> While Henry the Eighth was as fat as a pig.

Monograms

Monograms are stylised combinations of the alphabet, usually initials, but they can also be made into puzzles like the Victorian examples below.

Monosyllabics

This is writing or rhyming using only words of one syllable. It's not all that easy; the first sentence in this paragraph, for instance, simple though it is, uses more multisyllabic than monosyllabic words.

Many of the great poets in the English language, however, used monosyllabic words like musical notes. Here's a stanza from *A Red, Red Rose* by Robert Burns:

> Till a' the seas gang dry, my dear,
>   And the rocks melt wi' the sun:
> I will luve thee still, my dear,
>   While the sands o'life shall run.

Not the *Oxford*

About half a century ago a Boston writer named Gelett Burgess felt that the English language had failed him. 'Where,' he asked, 'is the word that paints the mild, faint enjoyment of a family dinner with your wife's relations?' He considered the cases of Edward Lear and Lewis Carroll, two enthusiastic inventors of new words; their technique, he concluded, was too hit-and-miss, with the result that very few of their words (Jumblies, Jabberwocky, chortle) have survived. He resolved, therefore, to confine himself to words required to 'fill a long-felt want' in his dictionary of future language. 'It will solidify the chinks of conversation, express the inexpressible,' he wrote. 'I shall create them from instinctive, inarticulate emotions, hot from the depths of necessity.'

Burgess's words of tomorrow included such imaginotions as '*Gorgule* – a splendiferous, over-ornate object or gift'; '*Uglet* – An unpleasant duty too long postponed'; '*Jujasm* – An expansion of sudden joy after suspense'; and '*Edicle* – One who is educated beyond his intellect'. Of his 100 original words, however, only one has irrevocably entered the language: *blurb*.

Inventing words is a popular form of wordplay; one recent manifestation has appeared under the name of '*Sniglets*' – quirky, ought-to-be-but-aren't words like *Exaspirin*: *n*. Any bottle of pain reliever with an impossible-to-open cap.'

Anyone can play at creating words that haven't made the *Oxford English Dictionary*, supplying new definitions, whimsical etymologies or derivations for existing words, of which the following are a mere sampling:

WORSTED – To lose a game of wits against a sheep.
WATTEAU – French unit of hydroelectric power
WIGWAG – A bald comedian

Number Plates

Obviously a word game of recent vintage, car number plates, real and imagined, can provide welcome light relief from the trials of traffic. Americans have the most fun because of the availability of all-letter plates: one driver drove his spanking new Chevrolet out of the showroom with the number plate YRUNVS; another driver named Robert Vowell has AEIOU; yet another has OWLBCNU. But the most popular plates, it seems, are those that announce the car owner's calling; a New York doctor has SAY-AH, and a Scarsdale dentist owns CAVITY. Here are some others reported by American plate-spotters:

EIEIO	–	A truck owned by MacDonald's Farms
LOQSHON	–	A speech therapist
4ZNUFF	–	A family planner

Oxymorons

An *oxymoron* (from the Greek, meaning pointedly foolish) is a statement that is self-contradictory, like pretty ugly, the situation is clearly very confused, it's a little big, act natural, and, it's not an optical illusion – it just looks like one.

Oxymorons are often used deliberately for effect, as in 'conspicuous by his absence', and similarly in literature, as in Act I of Shakespeare's *Romeo and Juliet*:

> Here's much to do with hate, but more with love:
> Why then, O brawling love! O loving hate!
> O any thing! of nothing first create,

O heavy lightness! serious vanity!
Mis-shapen chaos of well-seeming forms!
Feather of lead, bright smoke, cold fire, sick health!
Still-waking sleep, that is not what it is!
This love feel I, that feel no love in this!
Dost thou not laugh?

Here the oxymoron is aptly used by Romeo to try to describe the paradoxical nature of love.

You can amuse yourself oxymoron-spotting, as they are created, consciously and unconsciously, every day: Do I strike you as a violent person? You must stop taking advice from other people! May I ask a question? We're alone together at last . . .

Some oxymorons have an ironic twist, like Military Intelligence; Business ethics; science fiction; moral majority. They are, as you can see, everywhere. As a little training exercise, try matching the words to form well-known oxymorons:

1 plastic	shrimps
2 perfectly	silence
3 thunderous	host
4 spend	awful
5 jumbo	glasses
6 guest	thrift

(Answer Chest, page 62)

Palindromes

One of the most ubiquitous of all word games, the *palindrome* is a word, sentence or verse which reads the same forwards as backwards. Examples of palindromic words are level, deed, repaper and madam; palindromic names are Eve and Hannah. The longest palindromic word in English is the nine letter 'redivider'; and the longest place name, according to the *Guinness Book of Words*, is Kanakanak, in Alaska.

Common palindromes most people know include Adam's greeting in the Garden of Eden, 'Madam, I'm Adam'; Napoleon's lament, 'Able was I ere I saw Elba'; and the admirably succinct 'A man, a plan, a canal – Panama'. More recent palindromes include: 'Sums are not set as a test on Erasmus'; 'Was it a car or a cat I saw?'; 'Some men interpret nine memos'; and an extended palindrome from Godfrey Smith in *The Sunday Times*: 'Doc, note, I dissent. A fast never prevents a fatness. I diet on cod.' T. S. Eliot often had it pointed out to him that his name was an anagram of 'toilets', but it was also the subject of a palindrome: 'Was it Eliot's toilet I saw?'

The longest palindrome is supposed to run to 100,000 words, and a New Yorker, Lawrence Levine, wrote a palindromic novel of over 30,000 words entitled *Dr Awkward and Olson in Oslo*. In France, Georges Perec (of Lipogram and Univocalic fame) rattled off a 5,000 word palindromic epic in 1969. More recently, to celebrate the palindromic date of 19.9.1991, Mr Roy Dean, holder of the world record for completing *The Times*' crossword in the shortest time, composed a 72-line palindromic poem about a scholarly drunk reminiscing in a waterfront bar. Each of the lines is a self-contained palindrome, of which these, with their Joycean flavour, are typical:

Sleepless evening, nine. Vessel peels,
Sleek cats yell at alley, stack eels . . .
Rerack sack, can snack, cast carer,
A rare Medoc! O demerara!

To add piquancy to this considerable feat of palindromic nonsense, the poem was set to music by a group called Panama whose speciality is playing their compositions – backwards.

The palindrome has spawned numerous variations: the *Mirror Palindrome*, a word which if held to a mirror reads exactly the same (A TOYOTA; TOOT TOOT); *Picture Palindromes* (picture of surprised man with a party hat on his head and with an exploded cigar in his mouth = PARTY BOOBY TRAP) and, of course, *Number Palindromes* (10.9.1901; 17.9.1971).

Try your palindromic skill with these:

Twelve o'clock (4 letters)
Strictly on the . . . (5)
The Peacock Throne was the . . . (5)
Makes a peep . . . peep . . . peep . . . sound (5)
A beetroot compared with an orange is . . . (6)

(Answer Chest, page 62)

Pangrams

The quick brown fox jumps over the lazy dog is a *pangram*: a sentence, saying or verse containing all the letters of the alphabet. Like The Hunting of the Snark, the search for the perfect pangram has occupied the minds of many people over many years, but so far a 26-letter sentence that uses each letter just once, does not use proper names, and makes sense, has proved elusive. Here, though, are some worthy attempts, starting with a notice affixed to the castle bulletin board:

> Queen: Joust over by six PM. Wizard for lunch. King.
> Six plump boys guzzled cheap raw vodka quite joyfully.
> Quick waxy bugs jump the frozen veldt.
> Foxy nymphs grab quick jived waltz.

The nearest any pangrammist has got to scoring the perfect 26 is with near-meaningless statements that use foreign and archaic words, proper names and initials:

> Veldt jynx grimps waqf zho buck
> J Q Schwartz flung D V Pike my box

So the jury's still out on the perfect pangram.

Piano Words

These are words containing only those letters representing the notes in a musical octave that can be played on a piano: a, b, c, d, e, f and g. In 1986, Anthony Burgess published *The Pianoplayers*, the first novel to provide a piano lesson and a piece of original music. But that's another matter.

Puns

When you come across an antique shop with the sign, 'Den of Antiquity'; or a van delivering pastry goods adorned with the sign, 'Love and Quiches'; or a newspaper story about Albania's economic upturn headlined TIRANA BOOM TODAY – you're being got at with a pun.

A pun is simply – perhaps too simply – a witty play on word meaning, and the practice of punning can become addictive. 'A punster should be drawn and quoted', quipped the American comedian Fred Allen; likewise, a pun should always be greeted with a groan: the better the pun, the louder the groan. Here are some to make a groan man cry:

> The general mustard his troops at Cressy.
> 'Who was that piccolo I saw you with last night?'
> 'That was no piccolo. That was my fife.'
> The Texas Chainstore Massacre.
> Though he might be more humble, there is no police like Holmes.

Not to mention this superb cliff-hanger, a prizewinner in the Bulwer-Lytton Bad Writing Contest:

> 'Dawn crept slowly over the sparkling emerald expanse of the country golf course, trying in vain to remember where she had dropped her car key.'

Punning is a gloriously ancient art, and Shakespeare, Wilde, Swift and Joyce were all inveterate *paranomasiacs*. But even as punning nowadays reaches for new heights of sophistication, few punsters will ever approach the elegance of Sir Charles Napier, who led the British Army in India and captured the city of Sind. He sent a telegram to his headquarters which simply said *Peccavi* – which is Latin for 'I have sinned'.

Punny variations include paragrams, which are puns

created by substituting a letter or letters in a word or name ('An XXXploitation movie'); Knock-Knock jokes ('Knock, knock. Who's there? Howard. Howard who? Howard you like a punch in the nose?'); and Adverbial Puns ('Let's chop the tree down,' barked Bill; 'Do you like my new knickers?' asked Jo, transparently; 'Let's go camping!' suggested Bill intently.)

Qwertygrams

QWERTYUIOP is the display of letters on the second from top bank of a typewriter or wordprocessor keyboard, and the *qwertygram* obviously derives from the keyboard letters and symbols. The more inventive and cryptic the combinations, the more apt the qwertygram. Brevity counts, too. Some examples:

> No pa% un– paid 4 in +vance
> Turk eee R in h& not in pantry

(Answer Chest, page 62)

Rebuses

A *rebus* is a puzzle that uses combinations of letters, words, numbers, symbols and graphics to create a message. Here, for example, is a rhyming rebus from the schoolyard:

Y Y U R	Too wise you are
Y Y U B	Too wise you be
I C U R	I see you are
Y Y 4 ME	Too wise for me

Another clever rebus which has been around for a long time is:

If the B mt put :
If the B . putting :

which turns out to be: 'If the grate (great) be empty, put coal on. If the grate be full stop putting coal on.'

The pictorial rebus uses combinations of drawings and letters to form a message, in which, for example, a drawing of an eye, a drawing of a saw, the letter T beside a drawing of a hat and a drawing of a cat would mean, 'I saw that cat'. At the other end of the scale is the literary rebus, which demands a little more thought:

stand	took	to	taking
I	he	throw	this

reads, 'I understand he undertook to overthrow this undertaking'. This device of positioning letters and symbols, when combined with brevity, has surfaced recently as a game called DINGBATS, with puzzles like these:

		M
1. ORORO	2. 12AKER	3. GU

The answers are: 1. Double or Nothing
2. Baker's Dozen
3. Stick 'em up!

Here's a rebus you can try yourself; the answer is the name of a flower.

4 – U 01 – N + G 10 – T + M S – W

(Answer Chest, page 62)

Rhopalics

A *rhopalic* is an expression or verse in which each word has one more letter than the word that precedes it, as in 'I do not want words deftly written longhand, flaunting exhibitory attitudinal stubbornness'.

Riddles

I say, I say, I say! Epimenides the Cretan said, ‘All Cretans are liars.’ Was he telling the truth or a lie? That one is known as the eternal riddle. Others, more flippant, are meant to be solved:

> Which candles burn longer – wax or tallow?
> Neither. Both burn shorter.
>
> What wears shoes, but has no feet?
> The footpath.

Here are some genuine antiques:

> Why does a pretty bonnet lose its identity?
> Because it ‘becomes’ the lady who wears it.
>
> Why is a naughty boy like a postage stamp?
> Because he is licked and put in a corner to make him stick to his letters.
>
> What is the difference between an auction and seasickness?
> One is the sale of effects, and the other is the effects of a sail.
>
> What word is shorter by having a syllable added to it?
> Short.

Scrabble

For millions of families, a 'night on the tiles' is a game of Scrabble. Since it was invented in the 1930s, approximately 100 million sets of the game have been sold worldwide. Among its devotees are the Queen Mother, Joan Collins, Michael Jackson and ex-President Nixon.

Scrabble is played with a hundred letter tiles on a board with 15 × 15 = 225 squares. Each letter of the alphabet has a value, the highest being assigned to Q and Z, which score 10 points when used to make a word. The game is played by 2, 3 or 4 players (although there is a solitaire version) with each player receiving seven letter tiles at the start. When a player uses his tiles to make a word on the board he replaces them with the same number from the pool, ready for his next turn. When a player forms a word he adds up the values on the tiles used for his score, but the real excitement of the game occurs when players manage to position their letters over certain squares on the board which double or triple the values of letters or, in some cases, whole words. Nina, the wife of Scrabble's inventor, Alfred Butts, once soundly beat her husband with a score of 234 points for the single word, 'quixotic'.

End-game scores of over 2,000 are possible, but in championship matches, expert counterplay keeps scores below 400. You do not have to be incredibly literate to win at Scrabble, however. Good players need to learn all the two-letter words in the dictionary (in the UK *Chambers* is the authority; in the US it is Funk & Wagnalls *Standard College Dictionary*), all 106 of them, and how to use words with the letters Q and Z or both. In the 1982 National Scrabble Championships in London, one player achieved the highest-ever word score for his placement of 'caziques' (a West Indian native chief): 392.

To Scrabble your opponent, therefore, it is simply a matter of playing words like 'ree' (a bird); 'ewt' (a variety of newt); 'coho' (a Pacific salmon); 'el' (a New York elevated railway, or, if there is an objection, the 12th letter of the alphabet); and 'dzo' (a Himalayan type of cattle). It's as easy as that.

Spoonerisms

'It popped on its little drawers'; 'The Lord is a shoving leopard'; and 'It is kisstomary to cuss the bride' are examples of a rare condition called *metathesis*, or the transposition of sounds. The phrases are also called 'spoonerisms' after Dr William Archibald Spooner, one-time warden of New College, Oxford, who was given to these curious utterances.

The probable truth is that Spooner (b.1844) tripped up a few times during his lectures, but the transpositions provoked such mirth among the students that they lost no time inventing more – and better – spoonerisms:

> 'You have tasted a whole worm. You have hissed my mystery lectures. You were found fighting a liar in the quadrangle. You will leave immediately by the town drain.'
>
> 'Which of us has not felt in his heart a half-warmed fish?'
>
> 'I say! Who is occupewing my pie?'

Also probably apocryphal is the story of Spooner wandering around Greenwich looking for a pub called

The Dull Man, when he should have been in Dulwich looking for The Green Man.

It is possible to play a word game based on spoonerisms. Here are two columns of spoonerised words (i.e. DIVE and LEAD are spoonerised from LIVE and DEAD). Simply match the pairs.

WEST	FAST
HOLD	BURST
LIE	POLE
PALED	HOE
HEART	LEVY
HEIGHT	COT

(Answer Chest, page 62)

Shrink Words

A straightforward game in which players are asked to reduce a given word to a single letter in the fewest steps. A step consists of either deleting a single letter to make a new word, or substituting a letter for another to create a new word. For example:

A C C E P T	
A C C E N T	(substitution)
A S C E N T	(substitution)
S C E N T	(deletion)
S E N T	(deletion)
S E T	(deletion)
S A T	(substitution)
A T	(deletion)
A	(deletion)

Thus the word ACCEPT was 'shrunk' to one letter in eight steps. Now see what you can do with the word STRAGGLED. It has been done in 11 steps.

(Answer Chest, page 62)

Tongue Twisters

Alliteration, the repetition of stressed consonant sounds, is the compost from which tongue twisters spring. Even the Anglo-Saxons knew a thing or two about alliteration; typical is this line from the *Anglo-Saxon Chronicle* for 1083: 'In many matters he misruled the monks –'

The alliterative art, which predates rhyme, was thereafter widely practised. Here, centuries later, is a verse from the Gilbert & Sullivan opera, *The Mikado*:

> To sit in solemn silence in a dull, dark, dock,
> In a pestilential prison, with a life-long lock,
> Awaiting the sensation of a short, sharp shock,
> From a cheap and chippy chopper on a big, black block!

A tongue twister is merely an alliterative statement or verse with a difficulty factor multiplied by ten, and thus a verbal challenge. This was recognised long ago by teachers of speech and elocution; here's an exercise from *Peter Piper's Practical Principles of Plain and Perfect Pronunciation*, published in 1834:

> Oliver Oglethorpe ogled an Owl and Oyster:
> Did Oliver Oglethorpe ogle an Owl and Oyster?
> If Oliver Oglethorpe ogled an Owl and Oyster,
> Where are the Owl and Oyster Oliver Olgethorpe ogled?

This ditty, by today's schoolyard standards, is tame stuff, like the traditional 'She sells seashells by the seashore', and 'Peter Piper picked a peck of pickled peppers. If Peter Piper picked a peck of picked peppers, how many pecks of pickled peppers did Peter Piper pick?'

No, today's youthful chomping apparatus is made of sterner stuff, able to handle such twisters as:

Cheryl's chilly cheap chipshop sells Cheryl's cheap chips.
Half a pound of best mixed biscuits and half a pound of next best mixed biscuits.
Can you imagine an imaginary menagerie manager imagining managing an imaginary menagerie?
I'd rather have a full bottle in front of me than a full frontal lobotomy.

And, for good measure, a tongue-twisting limerick:

A tutor who tooted the flute
Tried to tutor two tutors to toot.
Said the two to the tutor,
'Is it harder to toot, or
To tutor two tutors to toot?'

Univocalics

When the late French author Georges Perec was composing his novel, *La Disparition*, he wrote it without using the letter *e*; these he must have saved for a subsequent work, *Les Revenentes*, in which he used no vowels *other* than *e*. The former work is called a *lipogram* while the latter is known as a *univocalic*.

An entire novel is a bit much, but you can have fun composing univocalic sentences, couplets and verses. Here is a well-known univocalic verse:

> Eve, Eden's empress, needs defended be;
> The serpent greets her when she seeks the tree.
> Serene she sees the speckled tempter creep;
> Gentle he seems – perverted schemer deep –
> Yet endless pretexts, ever fresh, prefers;
> Perverts her senses, revels when she errs,
> Sneers when she weeps, regrets, repents she fell,
> Then, deep-revenged, reseeks the nether Hell!

Try this simple exercise in univocalics. The clues below refer to words or phrases which contain no vowel other than *e*. Each answer word includes three or more *e's*. For example, 'Bar under canvas' would be 'Beer Tent'.

1. Heavy slumber
2. Protects food
3. Deaf and dumb educator
4. Extremely small
5. Just right (saying)
6. Character in *Alice in Wonderland*

(Answer Chest, page 63)

Word Search

Word Search, which goes under many names including Word Maze and Word Finder, is a very popular pastime in which the required selection of words (animal names, pop tunes, movie titles, etc) are hidden – horizontally, vertically or diagonally – in a dense grid of letters.

Here's a Word Search puzzle in which the common names of 33 flowers, plants and herbs are hidden.

Parsley, Poinsettia, Peppermint and thirty more plants are hidden in the undergrowth of this puzzle. Can you find them all? *Warning*: One plant name consists of two words.

```
N G P S H A C T N I M R A E P E
N A A G U I E A I G L M Z E P Z
P P R B F T D T H X G L A V E A
G L S C J T C C Y Z L C L P D Y
D Q L I I E B A H M O N E H O H
Z R E I K S G S C R X Z A P R Z
G A Y C T N S V L T I A V E R D
D F V L E I D U B F N L E N N T
I U S I E O J A S M I N E O A N
H C U L W P R D A T A P Q R A C
C H R Y S A N T H E M U M P S N
R S Z M R R Z Y K S Y C A A L C
O I L D E P M L O V N N P R I M
Y A P F T E I R I L L E O D W A
B G M H T T S Z L P S S P V X R
A S N O I F W A N D E R I N G J
L I B L B Q C D G A D N L E F O
C R L L I J Q H M I D R U N E R
E I H Y A C I N T H A E T T O A
D A F F O D I L S P Z F E N B M
```

(Answer Chest, page 63)

Weird Words

The English vocabulary is a goldmine for philological trivia: unusual words, unlikely combinations, grammatical gems, droll dolichologia. Could you write a sentence which contains the word 'had' eleven times without a break? Here it is: 'William, where John had had "had", had had "had had"; "had had" had had the examiner's approval.' Or a sentence with the word 'and' repeated thirteen times without a break! This one needs to be introduced with a little story, about a signwriter who was asked to paint the shopfront belonging to a firm called WELLAND and ANDERSON. Unfortunately, his sense of spacing left a lot to be desired, prompting the owner to complain that 'the signwriter had left too much space between 'WELL' and 'AND' and 'AND' and 'and' and 'and' and 'AND' and 'AND' and 'ERSON'.

Here are a few more curiosities to think about:

1. The longest one-syllable word is commonly used. It has more than 10 letters.
2. Few words contain all five vowels in their correct order. One is 'facetious'; what is another?
3. A fairly common human condition also has the most synonyms to describe it. What is the condition?
4. Amazingly, there is a perfectly valid English word in which the letter 'i' appears no less than seven times and which contains only one other vowel. What is the word?
5. Millions of Londoners see this word every day. Its middle letters are ERGRO, while its first three letters and last three letters are not only the same but in the same order. Can you identify the word?

(Answer Chest, page 63)

Word Squares

Word Squares are sets of words that read the same from left to right and from top to bottom – horizontally and vertically. An example explains:

H O P E
O P A L
P A L M
E L M S

You can either compose Word Squares yourself, or solve those created by others. Inventing four-letter squares is considered easy; five-letter squares are intriguingly difficult, while those consisting of six, seven and more letters generally require the use of proper nouns and obscure words. Word Squares of ten letters have been compiled but you would need a library to help you solve them.

Here, though, is a seven-letter Word Square, with clues to help you:

1. They can help companies grow
2. Forever
3. A display of sailing craft
4. Newton knew all about it
5. Sanction
6. Noisy reptile
7. The Vikings were reputed to be

(Answer Chest, page 63)

The Wonderful World of Words

Is there no limit to the ingenuity of playful philologists and gamesome grammarians? Decidedly not! Take a pencil, an inventive frame of mind and the English alphabet, and there's always the chance that something new will be added to the already awesome warehouse of wordplay. Like these examples:

Words within words It is strange, but true, that the names of things often conceal related words. Here's a list of American car makes, just those beginning with the letter *C*: Capri, Cavalier, Charger, Challenger, Cougar, Corvair and Camaro. What's so strange about them? They all contain the word CAR. And, as one wag has suggested, The White House contains the word TWITS. So there's an interesting territory for exploration.

Add a letter Which letter can you add to these five words to create five new words: OTHER, ORES, UTTER, ARROW, EMBER? Well, the letter M, of course. Easy, but can you make a list of 26 × 5 words, each of which will make 26 × 5 new words, going from A right through the alphabet to Z?

Word chains Here's a short word chain: WHERE/EVER, MORE/OVER, HEAT/ER, GO/ING – in other words, a series of compound words in which each syllable forms a new compound word with its neighbour. How long a chain can you make?

Contractions Here's a peppy little puzzle that should inspire many others like it. What do these six words have in common: SHED, WELL, ID, WED, ILL, SHELL? (Answer Chest, page 63)

Garbage Computers and word processors are in the habit of unpredictably spewing out verbal garbage, as all operators and owners know. But, even among this unlikely tangle, a game is to be had. Translate the following:

Perfect letter quality printing is ob?ain½d from ?6½ buil?-in [>in?½#, w6ic6 c!n 6!n£(½ "6½½? o# c+n?in]+]" [![½#!"w½((!"[½#mi??in% "im](?!n@+]" @£i?in½£i?in%!n£[#i@?i@%.

Match play This is a word game which demands speed and a loud voice to succeed. First, invent a series of three words that can be linked in some way, like RIVER – SLEEP – WOOL. Then ask the players to provide single words to link them, in this case, RIVER (BED) SLEEP (SHEEP) WOOL. As you will guess, there can be plenty of alternatives, but the first player with appropriate links wins the round. Here are a few more:

ARTICHOKE – BLOOD – ORE	(heart, vein)
LUGGAGE – ELEPHANT – KEYS	(trunk, ivory)
BLUSH – CLOCK – FIRE	(face, alarm)
MOVIE – NIGHT – HORSE	(stars, mare)

Homage to Lewis Carroll It is only fair to conclude with a salute to that master of puzzles, Lewis Carroll. As Charles Lutwidge Dodgson, he was a mathematics don at Christ Church College, Oxford, so unsurprisingly many of his posers were of an arithmetical persuasion. However, as the creator of *Alice's Adventures in Wonderland* and other stories, he was also a gifted wordster. Here's just one of dozens of word games he left us, a sort of daisy chain in which the last letter of each word is the first letter of the next, beginning with *a* and ending – with persistence and luck – with *z*. Like: AraBardiCrackeDinElFlinG . . . don't stop! KEEP GOING!

Answer Chest

Acrostics

NapleS
ElbE
WashingtoN
CincinnatI
AmsterdaM
StambouL
TiranA
LesothO
EclipticC
Thus, reading down from the top you get NEWCASTLE, and reading up from the bottom, you get COAL MINES.

Charades

DODECAHEDRON, which is an anagram of 'No hard decode'; which is also 'solid' and has 'a different face for every letter of its name' – 12 letters.

Conundrums

Donkey (Don – key).

Cryptograms

1. Chloroform 2. Courageous
3. Camouflage 4. Circuitous
5. Comedienne 6. Chimpanzee

Doublets

HATE / HAVE / LAVE / LOVE

Enigmas

Time.

Logogriphs

10. TOOTHPASTE 9. OSTEOPATH
8. POTATOES 7. TEAPOTS
6. APTEST 5. SPATE
4. PAST 3. TAP
2. AT 1. A

Oxymorons	1. Plastic glasses 2. Perfectly awful 3. Thunderous silence 4. Spendthrift 5. Jumbo shrimp 6. Guest host
Palindromes	1. NOON 2. LEVEL 3. SHAHS 4. RADAR 5. REDDER
Qwertygrams	No paper sent unless paid for in advance Turkeys are in hampers and not in pantry
Rebuses	4 (FOUR) – U = FOR 01 (Ten backwards, ie NET) – N + G = GET 10 (TEN) – T + M = MEN S (2–two–backwards, ie OWT) – W = OT ie, FORGETMENOT
Spoonerisms	West / Burst = BEST / WORST Hold / Cot = COLD / HOT Lie / Hoe = HIGH / LOW Paled / Fast = FAILED / PASSED Heart / Pole = PART / WHOLE Height / Levy = LIGHT / HEAVY
Shrink words	STRAGGLED STRANGLED (substitution) STRANGLER (") STRANGER (deletion) STRINGER (substitution) STINGER (deletion) SINGER (") SINGE (") SING, SIN, IN and I.

Univocalics	1. Deep sleep 2. Deep freeze 3. Helen Keller 4. Teeny weeny 5. Bees knees 6. Tweedledee
Word search	Ivy, Tea, Dill, Lily, Iris, Rose, Fern, Tulip, Holly, Cactus, Azalea, Fennel, Orchid, Jasmine, Verbena, Fuchsia, Gloxinia, Hibiscus, Hyacinth, Primrose, Parsley, Lavender, Marjoram, Evergreen, Narcissus, Spearmint, Thyme, Poinsettia, Peppermint, Bittersweet, Daffodils, Chrysanthemum, Wandering Jew.
Weird words	1. Strengths 2. Abstemious or arterious 3. Inebriation 4. Indivisibilities 5. Underground
Word squares	M E R G E R S E T E R N A L R E G A T T A G R A V I T Y E N T I T L E R A T T L E R S L A Y E R S
Contractions	Each of the six words can be used as colloquial contractions, as in she'll, I'll, we'd, etc.
Crossword	For solution, see over page.

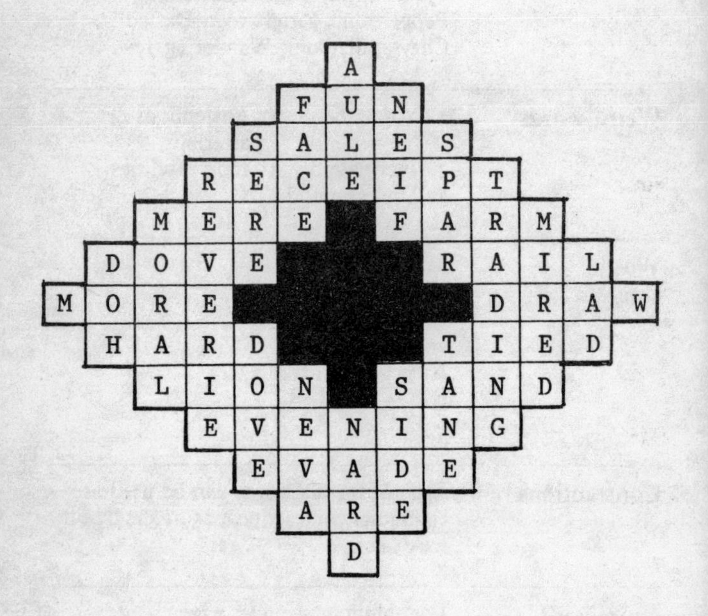
A
FUN
SALES
RECEIPT
MERE FARM
DOVE RAIL
MORE DRAW
HARD TIED
LION SAND
EVENING
EVADE
ARE
D

The Caring Church

Other books by Maggie Durran

Hello, I'm a Person Too
Dear God, Most of the Time You're Quite Nice
Single Parent
The Wind at the Door
Children of the Troubles
Understanding Children
All Age Worship
Festive Seasons

The Caring Church

Maggie Durran

British Library Cataloguing in Publication Data

Durran, Maggie
The caring church.
1. Pastoral theology
I. Title
253 BV4011

ISBN 0–947697–26–8

 Typeset in Britain for MARC, a division of Kingsway Publications, Lottbridge Drove, Eastbourne, East Sussex BN23 6NT by Watermark, Hampermill Cottage, Hampermill Lane, Watford WD1 4PL and printed by Richard Clay, 47–48 Bastwick St, London EC1V 3PS.

Contents

With thanks to all the churches and individuals who gave their time to tell me about their life and ministry:

St Luke's Church and St Luke's School, Holbeck, Leeds
Community of Celebration and Fisherfolk, Bletchingley, Surrey
Brother Bernard of Hilfield Friary, Dorset
St Oswald's Church, Shipton Oliffe, Gloucestershire
Church of the Good Shepherd, Wolverhampton
Christ Church, Bayston Hill, Shropshire
St Agnes' Church, Burmantofts, Leeds
Church of the Redeemer, Edgbaston, Birmingham
Cambridge University Mission, Bermondsey, London
Steve and Cathy Burgess, from St Mark's Church, Malabar, Australia, and now with Church Missionary Society
Church of the Redeemer, Houston, Texas, USA

FOREWORD

A recent poll enquiring into religious beliefs held by people in Britain revealed that over eighty per cent of those questioned believed in God. A majority of these also assented to the main doctrinal affirmations of Christianity. Yet when other surveys of attendance at church worship have been taken the percentage has proved very much lower. On average only about fifteen per cent of the population attend any church for worship and in many of the great urban areas of the country the proportion is probably nearer five per cent.

Why is there such a gap between professed belief and the committed practice of such belief in attendance at worship and church membership? One major reason would seem to be the deeply-ingrained idea in the minds of millions of ordinary inhabitants of our cities, towns and villages that the institutional Church in its different denominational manifestations is at best an irrelevance and at worst a hollow sham.

A popular image of churchgoers is that of a bunch of hypocritical do-gooders eager to denounce the sins and shortcomings of their 'pagan' neighbours but unwilling to engage in the demanding business of helping those around them who are in some form of need. Of course we protest that this is a caricature, and the real situation is very different, as indeed it often is. But there is sufficient truth in the accusation to give us pause for thought and (more importantly) prayer that the Spirit of God would renew our churches and transform them into dynamic cells of mission and minstry for the Gospel.

The report *Faith in the City* published by the Archbishop's Commission on Urban Priority Areas in December 1985 called for churches to be 'local, outward-looking and participating'. Only churches which are structured in this way can hope to exercise their function of being salt and light in the larger community where they are placed. As the dimension of caring becomes integral to a healthy pattern of spiritual activity embracing worship, prayer and teaching so we may expect God to bring all kinds of needy people within reach of this love and power flowing out through this church.

Maggie Durran presents for our reflection and encouragement the stories of people in need—unemployed, bereaved, handicapped mentally or physically—who have found acceptance, help and healing through the caring ministry of a dozen local churches or communities whose story is recounted in these chapters. They illustrate the activity of the Holy Spirit at the grassroots of local church life. They do not constitute an alternative or rival strategy to the shaping of programmes and policies at national level in church or society designed to promote care in the community. But unless such statements are complemented by practical involvement with individuals in need the witness of the Church to the life of the Kingdom of God will remain ineffective.

Patrick Dearnley

INTRODUCTION

The caring church is neither a new nor an innovative element in twentieth-century church life. Already in Old Testament times, when the people of Israel began to be formed into God's people, laws and instructions were written down whose main concern was an approach to family and community relations that could best be described as caring. When the prophets exhorted the people to return to God's way for them, the message was directed at the ways in which they failed to care. Jesus picked up the theme himself, pointing out that while the Pharisees were scrupulous about tithing such things as mint and cumin, they failed to care for their own relatives, and as leaders to care for the people.

The Early Church was noted for its caring—holding all things in common so that no-one went without the necessities for daily life. Stephen was chosen as the disciple to take care of the distribution of food to the widows and orphans who were dependent on the church for sustenance. In later years the Christians were known to collect discarded babies from town rubbish dumps and to raise them as their own.

The early Church expected that wherever it gathered there would be caring among its members and that whoever came to them for help would always find generosity. The disciples remembered Jesus' teaching: 'The poor you will have with you always.' 'If a man asks for your coat give him your cloak also.' The Church was to be like the mustard tree in the parable, whose life consisted as much of giving shelter to birds and other creatures who pass through, as of being a beautiful and fruitful tree.

Historically the caring quality of the Christian life has found expression in the local church, in religious communities and in missions. In the local church, caring is often of the Good Samaritan kind. As people go about their daily work and family life they care for each other, for their neighbours and for those who pass through or come to them with requests for help. Caring consists very much in being the salt and light of one's own neighbourhood. Just as salt is invisible once on the food and yet adds distinct savour, so the local church is often invisible to the neighbours and local community, yet the flavour of the active local congregation touches many aspects of life.

Religious communities have found their identity in specific callings that could not so readily be expressed through the local church structures. For some Christians the call to prayer could not be met in the midst of the cares of family and local community life. Groups such as the Fransciscans found it impossible to minister to particular people within the local church; lepers were excluded, yet Francis chose to associate closely with them, expressing a peculiarly different kind of love and care for the needs of specific, impoverished people. Missions and similar organisations have over the more recent years formed a collective response on behalf of the Church to the needs of others—spiritual, practical, and often medical needs—without replacing the local church; these have been missions funded and staffed by people specially trained and employed in such work.

In each age the nature of the caring church has developed and been reshaped. The dynamism of the Spirit has adapted and fitted the Church in all its expressions to the needs of each new generation. As times have changed, the needs within each society, nation or culture have varied. Within the twentieth century the advent of a National Health Service in Britain relieved the burden of many missions who existed to care for the health of the very poor. Similarly, Social Security payments decrease the need to provide food and clothing.

Yet the caring concern of the Spirit in each age and variation in human life is like oil in an engine, seeping into all the pressure points and providing ease for the tensions and stresses with which ordinary people struggle. The Spirit leads God's people to be the human vessels for ministering the restoring, affirming, redeeming grace of God.

In the twentieth century the Church has gone through as much rapid change as society itself. Through the task of redefining itself to meet the needs of contemporary society the Church has sought to be revitalised with a relevant gift of caring and a contemporary prophetic message. Despite much criticism the Church has been at work in quiet and deep ways: reaching the powerless, keeping alive ongoing good neighbourliness, stimulating a new look at attitudes to the Third World, ministering nearer home.

The sixties saw a major outpouring of the Spirit through the charismatic movement, which has now become rooted in the life of many local churches. The Holy Spirit refreshed many Christians who had become like the proverbial bruised reeds or the dimly burning wicks, giving them new energy for the work of the Gospel, so that they might lay down their lives for the world. This was often expressed in a zest for community patterns of living, parallel to the commune movement of the hippies, as Christians were called into a new sense of caring for one another, sometimes even choosing to hold all things in common as the Early Church did. The movement too led into a fresh sense of being called to look to the good of neighbours, nearby and around the world.

That work of the Spirit brought vision, drive and motivation, and brought together the skills necessary for today's work. The religious orders, though decreasing in numbers, have met new and contemporary needs: Mother Theresa and the Sisters of Mercy have located themselves in places where human misery is at its most extreme: in the Ballymurphy estate in Belfast, in Calcutta slums, in famine-racked Ethiopia. The Franciscans—now less often brown-robed—are looking afresh at their ministry as they study the South American base communities with their roots in liberation theology, and as Brothers live with the down-and-outs in cardboard boxes on the streets of London. The local churches are meanwhile establishing new expressions of caring for the new housing estates and the decaying inner cities, for dying communities and for those so new there is scarcely any pattern to community life at all. Missions and missionary organisations have redefined their roles and functions to accommodate the way that the twentieth-century media have brought the Third World to our doorsteps, working to exorcise paternalistic and out-dated attitudes in the face of new understanding of human dignity and human rights.

The stories, testimonies and reflections in this book are a window into these developments. They represent churches, communities and missions in varying stages of change and development, seeking to be the caring church within the spheres to which the Spirit has led them. With stories from Africa, America, Australia and Britain the people tell of their calling, how they heard God, where they find hope and sustenance, and how, in the midst of following that call to serve others, they have themselves changed and matured.

1
Who Cares?

In an article in *The Spectator* on 16th August, 1986, Stan Gebler Davies argues that it is 'The Caring State That Ruins Us'. After exposing faults in State systems of legislation, education and welfare, he asserts, 'The doctrine of love which is contained in religion is the only true doctrine. By loving-kindness we may provide for the unfortunate. To delegate responsibility for charity, for the welfare of our neighbours, to the State, is an offence to God and the certain destruction of ourselves.'

Through the political and social awareness of the present century, this theme is echoed by many, from socialists to the most conservative; each presenting his own slant for his own reasons. Yet each makes the point that whatever the structure, caring exists at the local level where love, compassion and good neighbourliness can be found. That is the place where we express the love of God for our fellow human beings. Justice and concern for human rights are issues for the State, but within an established system, only the daily concern of ordinary human beings can add that quality of caring and being cared for.

Throughout history the Church has carried a dual identity: an institution with structures that support caring, and one in which the individual members are exhorted, inspired and encouraged in their love for one another. When we see the fullness of Christ's instruction, 'Love one another as I have loved you', then we will see an expression of a caring society in which there will be little need for State intervention to care for the unfortunate. But we live in a society where the Gospel is neither the dominant, nor the most present motive. Thus the Spirit works through churches, missions and communities to introduce God's goodness to people whose lives are damaged by societal and individual sin, as well as to inspire and encourage the expression of quiet, deep, family and neighbourly caring among members of the local community.

Within a fallen humanity the Spirit is constantly at work to reform and remake his servants into people who can more fully express the love of Christ. The ingrained hardness of heart, destructive patterns of behaviour, defensive barriers, prejudices and stereotypes, are remoulded and remade whenever individual and church meet with God. Daily prayer for use by the whole congregation is a traditional expression of this renewing encounter with God. Often, however, a pattern of daily, corporate prayer is followed only by religious orders, and most congregations look to Sunday services or weekly Bible study to renew them. But reforming prayer has a contemplative element to it, a listening to God without precondition or prior assumption, a readiness to let God take charge. Otherwise the very patterns of which we wish to rid ourselves would of necessity come between us and God, as our own, natural tendency is to turn away from that which may be painful to hear and readily continue in old, familiar ways.

A church is rooted in and inseparable from the society around it, absorbing attitudes and prejudices, subject to the same pressures and forces that come from work and home and the catastrophes and joys of everyday life. To live as the body of Christ in the world, we need a regular cleansing—our 'foot-washing', a function that is essentially one of worship and of the Body gathered in the presence of God to pray and praise. Hence the healing and renewing that has happened in Fisherfolk worship; hence the cleansing that Jane Tupper from Christ Church, Bayston Hill, knows when with her church on Sundays.

The quality of compassionate servanthood that is necessary for the work of Christ is built on a foundation of human experience that has itself been touched and healed. When we suffer and find the love of God sustaining, healing and upholding us, we also find that God brings into our path others who will receive hope as we have empathy and compassion for the suffering. Only those who have experienced pain and discouragement and have been reconciled to God in these experiences can offer affirmation to people whose lives are broken; in essence this is a recognition of our common weakness and common humanity, a common need for redemption.

Should the caring church adopt a particular political stance? So many caring churches find themselves struggling with principalities and powers that oppress; many Christian reformers working for human rights eventually change those systems. Capitalism has a hard-edged, survival-of-the-fittest aspect that does not concern itself with those who are pushed out by the competitive system. Combining competition with an inherent status-orientation, capitalism cannot reflect a Gospel life. But Phil Shiner from Edgbaston is right: you cannot legislate caring, and socialism, too, needs the Gospel qualities of love and compassion added to it. Since it is obvious that despite all the benefits of the Welfare State many millions of people in Britain still suffer, we can conclude that no system, in itself, holds the answer. A full acknowledgement of the foundational need for *love* is necessary.

It is remarkable that so much caring is happening in so many areas of our daily lives. There again, perhaps it is not remarkable, for the goodness of God is in humanity to the extent that we are 'in his image'. Where deceit, dishonesty and mistrust predominate, or where people are oppressed by systems and authorities, then the Spirit may call together a body of people who can be the salt of the earth, affecting and changing the quality of life, the lot of the people.

Close fellowship, accepting and forgiving friendship, openness and above all a knowledge of being the people of God, who serve him, are the qualities that are evident in the caring church. As the skills, resources, and personalities are drawn together, moulded and made into a tool to serve the local community, the Spirit refreshes and inspires the congregation to follow the call on their lives. It may find expression in daily caring as they go about the ordinary tasks of going to school or to work, but also in the more specialised call given to particular individuals and churches: to care for groups of people in society who will always be left to the last, pushed out first, ignored, neglected and forgotten. There are many to care for, many to weep with, many who look for a place to be joyful and laugh. The calling into which we enter is Christ's, and the empowering and planting of the vision is the work of the Spirit, and God himself will bring to harvest the seeds he plants.

The inspiration and grace to continue faithful in a discouraging environment, or when times are hard, lies in our worship together. God calls, directs, corrects, and empowers his people when they meet together with him. God does lift us up, giving us a taste of resurrection hope; but he never denies our daily lives and the harsh realities with which we live. In churches where worship enables those present to bring the whole of themselves to God, the healing Spirit is at work reassuring and affirming. Where the hardships of abused children, of debts and desparation will still be there after the service, the tired limbs are strengthened to carry on. When we know God has met us, given life to us in the sacrament of the Body, listened to us and received us in and through our sisters and brothers, we may continue to walk our daily path of serving him with the knowledge of his presence with us.

2
Listening to God

St Luke's, Holbeck, Leeds

God is concerned to call people together to be his Church in any particular place or area. Recognising that call when the area concerned is depressed or run-down can be hard, for that call may be contrary to personal expectations and aspirations. The call to be the Church is also never static, just as society around the Church is constantly changing. To be the Lord's servant requires constant listening and paying attention, both to the foundation and the ongoing shaping and developing of church life.

The charismatic renewal oiled the wheels by refreshing both understanding of and sensitivity to the voice of God. This enabled Christians to adapt and follow God's voice more easily and with greater joy. Unfortunately, sometimes renewal and the gifts of the Spirit have become an end in themselves, with the dangerous result that they have become reduced to mere injections of energy that provide temporary thrills. But the gifts of the Spirit are for the Church, for its whole life and ministry. There are occasions when churches and fellowships become blinded by the excitement of renewal, not realising that they are no longer hearing the word of God. To be led by the Spirit, then, is to be led into a life of constant and continuing change.

John Holmes arrived at St Luke's Church, Holbeck, in Leeds, as a socially aware Christian who had a concern for the local community and neighbourhood, but who was without a very clear vision. The vision became more apparent when he came into renewal, and the possibilities more obvious. John and his wife Rosemary have a common commitment to what they are doing and from the earliest days he says, 'There have been people around me to whom I have been committed and who have been committed to me.' This meant that John was sustained both by his personal spirituality, and by the sense of partnership that came from being part of a church that had a reciprocal commitment. He affirms, 'Although it has had its heartaches, suffering and problems, it's been an exciting place to be in, to see God at work and to see what he was doing. It has never been dull.'

From the start John had a strong sense of God's call, drawing him always further on towards whatever God himself was seeking to establish. 'Even at the worst times we always said we could never go back because God was always going on ahead of us. In the verses in Matthew 28—"He is going ahead of you into Galilee."—the God of the resurrection is the God who has gone before us, always bringing forth the new.'

With that sense of the moving Spirit, an individual or a church can never think he has the situation fully under control. Listening to God requires openness to God's leading in a new direction in the ministry, or a new way of dealing with a familiar situation. There is a sense in which the Holy Spirit is like a moving light; following it can never be predictable. When St Luke's Church found itself saying, 'What's going to happen next?', the church grew to realise that God was present and would bring good out of the chaos, for that was the nature of the God the members served. When challenged as others deserted Jesus, the disciples responded 'Lord, to whom shall we go? You have the words of eternal life' (John 6:68).

Early in his career John had been an ambitious man, with a will to succeed in the path he chose for himself. In the midst of the stress of ministry, when God intervened, John came to the point of saying, 'Lord, all I am interested in is what you want me to do—whatever that is.' As he later found out, neighbouring clergy had watched the growth at St Luke's with interest, thinking at first that John was the reason for the development; later they became aware that the truth was different: God was at work. John comments, 'But we had to go that way anyway because God was leading us. God beckons us on—that still has the same sense of risk and uncertainty of new paths. It's exciting because of the nature of the God we serve.'

At a Fountain Trust Conference at Reading University in 1976, as he reflected on Ezekiel 36:27, Juan Carlos Ortiz taught on the compelling nature of the voice of God: 'And I will put my Spirit within you, and move you to follow my decrees and be careful to keep my laws.' An inner voice urges obedience to the will of God, as the Spirit inhabits the church. St Luke's discovered this truth as the Spirit called more and more people to its fellowship.

Answering the Call

Moving to Holbeck, an area characterised by the problems of the inner city with that pervasive air of poverty and decay, may not be an attractive proposition. Certainly, most families, thinking of bettering their life for the sake of their own and their children's futures, would gravitate towards more pleasant surroundings. So what brings people here, and what holds them here?

John accepted the post as vicar here. 'My mother thought I should have been added to the Dictionary of Saints. She thought I was crackers.'

The area was very different from his own background, which was upper-middle-class. John's father was a wealthy and successful businessman, and John was brought up first in a large house, and then in an even more luxurious bungalow.

But God's calling to John was a calling to minister among people historically alienated from or at least adrift from the Church. Both his curacies were on large housing estates. Holbeck was the first traditionally working-class neighbourhood in which he had lived, but was far preferable to a Council housing estate because Holbeck had retained a sense of community. For all its deprivation, John found the area actually had a more human feel about it.

There were problems. As John says, 'It wasn't easy for my daughter in the early days when, if someone had an axe to grind with me, they would take it out on her in the playground.' There were problems, too, with an endless string of people knocking at the vicarage door. Some were friends he was delighted to see, but many brought with them stress and problems. Since the family lived just up the road from Shaftesbury House, there was—and still is—a regular stream of people wanting sandwiches, money or other form of help.

When John and the family arrived the children were 6, 4 and 2 years old. They have now spent the whole of their growing lives in a working-class community which still has a good sense of community and of caring about one's neighbours. Some may call this being inquisitive or gossipy, but it is all part of belonging together. John adds, 'It's certainly been the happiest time of our lives.'

While the location was strange at first for John, it was less so for Rosemary, whose father was a fitter in Sheffield. As a family they were a little different from the others Rosemary's father worked with, as they bought their own home, but they were still working-class. So she found Holbeck quite congenial, and felt at home more quickly than John did.

For the caring ministry that was to come, the Spirit drew others into St Luke's Church. Eve Oldfield has been a member of the church almost as long as John. Eve grew up in a tiny country village. As a child she was familiar with the missions at the Methodist Chapel to which she went, and Cliff College students who came to lead them. When she went to college in Liverpool, Eve decided that the Lord was telling her not to work in a rich area but in a poor area. Eve turned down a job in Harehills, Leeds, and was then offered a teaching job at St Luke's School, Holbeck. She knew nothing at all about the area. She walked up the road to where the school stood, a stone's throw from the church. She says, 'It was really like the place where I had worked in Liverpool, and it was a church school, so I thought, "Right, this is it."' That was the beginning of Eve's involvement with St Luke's.

Eve did not live in Holbeck, she worked and worshipped there but lived across the city. She had decided that since she worked in the school she did not also want to live where all the parents and children were close by. When she married, she and her husband continued to commute across the city until she heard the Lord saying that she should live in the parish where they worshipped.

Later, when her marriage broke up and she was left alone with a small baby, she thought, 'For Rupert and me, this is our family. We are close to many people here. When we meet we share our joys, our problems and our worries, and we pray for each other.'

John Leckenby, who is paid by the church to be on the staff part-time, remembers his own arrival here to become a member of the original core group, after John Holmes became vicar. He and his family used to live on a pleasant Council estate in north-west Leeds. They had a house with a big garden, not ten minutes from the country. They had been looking for another house for some six months when his wife phoned him at work one day and said, 'There's a house for rent. Shall we go look at it?'

'Where is it?'

'In Holbeck.'

'*Where's* that?'

They went to look at the house in Holbeck. John responded adamantly, 'No way am I going to live here!' But his wife was equally determined that they should.

For the first year John found the area unbearably depressing, but St Luke's Church saved the situation for him. Holbeck became a place where he saw that God was present, and this changed his whole outlook. Despite the everyday problems—such as the negative effects of local culture on his children—he has come to love Holbeck, in part at least because wherever he goes he finds the fellowship of the Church.

The Church's Calling

Shared ministry at St Luke's is based on shared lives. The crucial moment came when John Holmes opened himself to other people—the core group of the church—in the early days.

On a weekend visit to another church, Barbara, a fellow church leader, said, 'The most significant moment for me in the renewal of our church was when John asked for help. Up to that point it was understood that he was there to help us.'

This was a key step towards the group (lay and ordained) taking responsibility for listening to God together. As John has discovered, God really does provide people with whom the minister can share his leadership. Now, as the church grew, he was able to stand back more, seeing as part of his job a continual assessment of where the church was strong and where it was weak. Such an assessment is God's, so the task was primarily one of finding out what God had to say about each particular situation. The church also wanted to hear God's word. John describes this longing for God's word after he was invited recently to move to another parish in Leeds: 'We had an exciting Church Council meeting after the announcement of my departure. God does speak to our Church Council; we wait on him and we expect him to speak. People knew this was right for us as a church, not just for me and for Rosemary; God was moving us on.'

One or two people were afraid about John's departure, but during the meeting there was a word of prophecy, 'Be full of faith not full of fear.'

Afterwards someone came up to John and said, 'That word was for me. I was beginning to be afraid, and the Lord was telling me to trust him.'

That kind of dynamic creates life, a living church serving a living God. It is exciting, even if at times disconcerting to those who would enjoy a more orderly and comfortable life.

Open to One Another

A shared ministry can only develop out of an atmosphere of honesty and openness, out of a readiness on the part of everyone present to share strengths and weaknesses, insights and prejudices.

The leadership team learned, through teaching given by David Watson, that if personal relationships weren't right, a meeting's agenda could go on all night and get nowhere. If, on the other hand, the relationships were right, there would not be the same difficulty. David Watson had talked about leadership being both pastoral and relational.

At one St Luke's leadership meeting, John found himself saying, 'What is happening? We have a simple thing to deal with, but after talking for three quarters of an hour we still haven't got it settled. Surely someone here must have some personal, unspoken agenda? So let's be quiet for a moment and hear what the Lord is saying.'

So they stopped talking and were quiet.

Someone then said, 'I'm sorry. I had a wretched day. I had more than I could take, and I have come and unloaded it all on you.'

Someone else said, 'I've got an axe to grind because ...'

The meeting began to flow more easily. A special quality of openness enabled that to happen.

John relates this to other experiences when he goes to committee meetings, board meetings and diocesan meetings and can spot the same dynamics there. The problem may, for instance, stem from the disappointment of a middle-aged priest who thinks he should have been made Chairman instead of the man sitting opposite him. Every time the Chairman opens his mouth, the other man is going to interject, 'That's not right. I don't agree with you.' The chairman then becomes very tentative and can't say what he really feels for fear of upsetting the applecart.

But at St Luke's people do share their weaknesses and hurts. The leaders have become mature enough to do that, and the results have permeated the church. Unity in relationships is built on reality, not on what's artificial or masked. With unity, the leadership becomes a sacrament, or a gift through which life comes into the church.

Hearing God through the Needs of the People

Holbeck is an old city working-class area. Houses are packed back-to-back in closely knit, straggling lines up the side of the hill. The motorway to Manchester channels endless streams of traffic along a swathe cut through Holbeck, just two hundred yards to the north of the church. The edge of the parish nearest the City Centre is marked by the link-up between the M1, the key motorway for all traffic to London, and the city centre by-pass. In the last ten years some of the housing around the church has been demolished and the old houses replaced by neat new terraces, which are still Council owned. Yet the older houses still dominate. Back-to-back houses are literally that: two rows of terraced houses are built with a common back wall, so most homes have neighbours on three sides. On the fourth side there is normally a tiny patch of yard or greenery and then the street. The front door is the only possible outside door. Some modernisation has taken place. Council policy in the last few years has provided grants for homeowners to put in bathrooms and for modernising many of the dwellings that have not been demolished to make space for new housing. However, up until the last few years, many of St Luke's church members, and not only the older members, lived in houses where the bath was in the kitchen and the toilet outside. Holbeck is categorised as an urban priority area.

Hearing the voice of God in such a neighbourhood can be especially hard, though essential if the church is going to become the church of and for the people—a caring church—which is its biblical mandate. Often there are ordinary cultural and language barriers to this. For example, those who go to church often have more mobile and middle-class lifestyles than those who do not. Their manners, their concerns, their language, and their values owe as much, if not more, to their background culture and education, as to any essential Christianity. So it is easier for such people to listen to fellow church members and meet God in them than in the 'unchurched' people on the streets.

The core group of the church came mostly from more comfortable settings than those in which St Luke's is surrounded. As a group they found that hearing God not only involved recognising his concern for the parish but also realising that they would not automatically know exactly what needed to be done. To begin with, one or two people wanted to start up an unemployment project, out of a worthy concern for the well-being of their neighbours, but there was disappointment as idea after idea failed.

Each time the desire to do something was present, but it wasn't really matched to the needs of the neighbourhood. The leaders wanted to listen to two questions at once: 'What is the Lord saying to us, and what is the neighbourhood saying to us?' Eventually a man from the neighbourhood came along with the idea of involving the long-term unemployed in a programme to help the elderly. John and others realised that here was something different. In this project the two key strands came together.

Really listening to what the neighbourhood is saying takes time, and some people—often those from outside—have to acquire a different perspective. As professional people who have committed themselves to the local church, they may think they have many answers, but they must first hear God speak—and then things begin to come together.

Salt and Light

John has always been very impressed with the images in Jesus' teaching of the salt of the earth and light of the world. When he came to Holbeck in 1973 he was conscious that he had only an embryonic vision, that he believed utterly in the church being involved in serving the neighbourhood, but that this perspective was very different from that of most church members at that time.

In the church council minutes John found references that clearly demonstrated this. One recorded that the council felt it a pity that the recent redevelopment of the area had increased vandalism. The congregation had felt disappointed and threatened by what was happening around the church. At that stage, the housing was being pulled down or boarded up. The possibilities and opportunities that the redevelopment offered to the church were not yet being considered. The electoral roll gave the impression of a loyal congregation who owed a loyalty to the church primarily because they had been brought up in the neighbourhood. Most of them, however, had moved up the road to higher quality housing and better neighbourhoods.

John had the vision of the church becoming more integrated with the neighbourhood. But first, a lot of spiritual changes had to happen in him, to make this possible.

Since then, to a very significant extent St Luke's Church has changed so that now more than half of the parishioners live within the parish boundaries. Of the other half, the vast majority live within ten or fifteen minutes' walking distance from the church, like Eve Oldfield, who now lives opposite the parish boundary. The congregation has become much more 'indigenous'.

John is unsure which of two strands came first. As the church focused on its own neighbourhood, more people came in because they saw it to be a caring church. Or perhaps it was inevitable that as local people came into the church, it would become more concerned about the neighbourhood. Both had happened in a stream of caring ministry going out into the locality while the local people come in for that caring.

The scriptural basis for such ministry is in the powerful images of the church as salt and light, emphasised quite recently at St Luke's rededication service. The church is there, everyone believes, to throw light into the neighbourhood.

God's Creation, Children of God

Self-worth and recognition of the worth of others have proved to be the most crucial issues, both theologically and in the practical development of the church's ministry. John wrote a paper that he presented to a gathering of clergy, in which he talked about the powerlessness of people that stems from their own views of themselves, a powerlessness which is more than political and social.

John talked about how people felt alienated from all structures of government, of whatever kind. The attitude to Labour councillors, traditional representatives of the working class and trades union voters, was, 'We'll vote for them, but they won't do anything for us.' John discovered there was also a deeper, all-pervasive sense of worthlessness, expressed as, 'We're no good. We are going to be treated as no good. That's who we are.' Problems became overwhelming, and there was a downward spiral of despair.

It was exciting actually to see people change their perception of themselves—an effect which is profoundly Christian—as they came to realise who they were, that they were God's creation, children of God. They discovered their value in his eyes. Renewal began to be seen and felt when the members started affirming one another, both in their own friendships and in their conversations with newcomers; they were no longer the has-beens, the misfits or the failures, they were actually precious. Having grasped this theological truth intellectually, that this was who they were in Christ and also who all the local people were, they put it into practice; it became a strong thrust in the teaching and the pastoral work of the church.

John recently shared leadership of a housegroup with two women, one of whom was a single parent who had been left on her own with five children. She is now becoming one of the most effective leaders in the church. The other woman was young, married with two children. She came from an unhappy home background, with a poor opinion of herself, and expected to get little out of life.

Over the last four or five years, she has changed and grown tremendously. What has been crucial to her has been the way she looks at herself, the way she is, and what her potential is.

The importance of an environment in which individuals discover their worth is the reason why St Luke has so many leaders. Many people who can take responsibility in this congregation were earlier in situations where they were given no opportunity. They were told, 'You couldn't be a leader, you haven't got the right qualifications. You didn't do well at school.' People so often have the potential but the social and cultural system does not allow that potential to grow.

Developing Potential for Leadership

In those early days, a little group of about fifteen people from the congregation was concerned to discover more of the reality of God. This group began to blossom, at first still under the control of the leadership, John and his curate. As people matured and grew as Christians, they were trusted to exercise leadership. In the last three or four years this has come to include more of the local people, with a conscious shift of leadership away from the professional people, even though these still play a part in leadership. John looks, 'not for fresh professionals to come but at these folks who are of the neighbourhood and the community and therefore understand how people tick better than we will ever do.'

There are technical leadership skills that must be learned. St Luke's Church has an established training pattern where people are drawn into housegroup leadership. In each group there are three leaders. The first is the actual leader or teacher, the second is the assistant or pastor, and the third is the novice. In every new group this third person, the novice, may have been a Christian for only eighteen months or a year but may show signs of potential as a teacher or pastoral leader. By working alongside the other two, this third person is trained. This process has been deliberately used in the last couple of years, having developed more casually before that.

Eve was one of the original core group at St Luke's. Contacts through the school had brought her into the fellowship, and she remembers how her sense of self-worth and her potential for leadership were developed. 'You aren't in our church for long before John or somebody finds you something to do.' Very soon the newcomers are going out with more established members to tell others of their experience. The freshness of the story brings life as it is told. Eve was going through a particularly difficult time and thought herself to be hopeless, but John asked her to be a housegroup leader. She found herself thinking, 'He must think I'm all right.'

Members of the church go out in twos and threes, knocking on doors and talking to people. New members feel, 'Oh I'm not just a pew filler. I'm obviously someone important to the church; they believe in me.' Everybody becomes involved unless they individually choose not to.

The church actively reaches out to non-Christian people; it is not an exclusive group, nor is there one dominant age-group. No-one has to have status to fit in. Eve adds, 'It doesn't matter really how intelligent you are, or what sort of job you've got, or even if you have a job. It doesn't matter whether you are married or unmarried. We are a real mixture from all walks of life.'

Suffering Brings the Church Closer to God

In 1978 St Luke's was crippled by problems of broken relationships at the centre of its life. When 30 or 40 of the church people later went on a camping holiday together, John noticed the closeness and the quality of the fellowship and asked, 'What is it that all these people have in common?'

Rosemary responded, 'They've all suffered.'

There was a common faith in God's faithfulness. Also, everyone in that group, in one way or another, had been drawn deeper into the heart of Christ through suffering—whether through personal tragedy, break-up of relationships, or the suffering from pain carried throughout life.

Among those who were seeking to know God more fully in the close-knit core of the fellowship of the church were two whose marriages had broken up. Two partners had left. Eve had not seen her developing problem as others had, but suddenly, traumatically, she was left alone with Rupert, her small son.

On the night Eve's husband left, God spoke to her particularly. It was a profound revelation that God loved Eve as a person, in spite of the trauma that was happening. She could look at life a different way. She became more involved in the church, despite the fact that she had earlier been the sort of person who sat back and let things happen.

The crisis also pointed to a problem in the stability of the church. They were like a tree with shallow roots, with lots of flowers on the upper branches, and in the first flush of renewal they had leapt about and enjoyed it. But even then some were a bit sceptical; it had all happened so quickly. Suddenly there was the shock wave of broken relationships and the tree started to sway as if it might fall. God used the situation, and the church began to stabilise.

The relationship of both church and individuals to God changed. He looked after them and pulled them through the crises, but the church now also began to look more closely at its roots. Eve summarises, 'It sorted the people who were really committed from those who had merely hung on to personalities in church. Sceptical members were saying, "Renewal can't be happening if we're having all these problems. It is supposed to be lovely..." But the Bible never says that. As the pain and the hardship began, it was a bit like separating chaff from wheat.' The church turned through teaching and pastoral care to the biblical basics: putting their roots firmly down into the teachings of Jesus.

As people began to say, 'We *are* going to listen to what God wants us to do,' there came a turning point, and growth through change began to happen. Some very important lessons were learned.

The church became an illustration of what David Watson

once said when teaching of Spirit and Word: 'The Word without the Spirit, and you dry up; the Spirit without the Word, and you blow up. With the Word and the Spirit, you grow up.'

St Luke's blew up! The church had been heavy on charismatic spirituality but not strong in putting down deep, individual spiritual roots. When problems arose, they started digging much deeper roots into Scripture, into personal spirituality and prayer. John himself became much more interested in silence and contemplation to balance the charismatic activity, and everyone concentrated on devoting time to listen to God.

The Fisherfolk led a weekend of ministry for the church and taught that worship is about the whole of life. John accepted their ideas, and the church has practised it to a considerable extent. A prayer time is vital to every Christian, but prayer must be carried further to enable people to pray in the whole of their lives, at work or at home, silently or out loud in groups. People are now much less self-conscious about prayer. It is part of their lives. The Fisherfolk showed the relevance of an integrated Christian life.

At a recent evening meeting in Leeds Town Hall the preacher said, 'You may have been having a tremendous time here tonight, but how many of you tomorrow are going to be able to make any kind of witness to this?' John saw that the church had been redeemed from having a WONDERFUL TIME which didn't actually relate to the rest of daily life. Through the problems and through the teaching they knew they had to bring together spirituality and ordinary human life until they were fully interwoven.

John read a passage from Isaiah that had been a significant support to the church. 'Which of you fears the Lord and obeys his servant's commands? The man who walks in dark places with no light, yet trusts in the name of the Lord and leans on his God' (Isaiah 50:10; NEB). The church was in dark places and learned to lean on God. God was the stronghold; people were not simply holding on to him, but he was holding on to them; God had a strong hold on St Luke's.

Somebody once said to John, 'These people are praying Christians,' and indeed so they were, ever since that rupture in the life of the church. They emphasised prayer—in its different aspects—and being people of prayer. The church had always been committed to intercession as something to focus on at certain times: praying for a church renewal project, a campaign in the neighbourhood, the unemployment scheme. There had always been good attendance at a day of prayer. But contemplative prayer was needed to build a foundation for becoming a prayerful people. Now many couples and groups of friends are quite accustomed to having a chat and then in a very natural way allow the conversation to become a prayer. So prayer permeates the life of the church and is very much practical prayer, linked with what people are doing and not put in a separate compartment. It expresses the practice of the presence of God.

The deeper spiritual foundations for the life of the church have set the ministry in this very needy neighbourhood on much firmer ground. Some have been enabled to cope better with failure—an essential ability in this locality. Not all go on to a mature and fruitful Christian life, but the church members help, sitting with people, listening and talking as long as they can—and sometimes the Lord brings about a change in them. Sadly, though, some—given the difficulties they bring with them into the church, and the chaotic nature of their background—cannot handle or sustain the change and go back to old life patterns.

At first the church found this crippling, having spent time and money trying to save a marriage, for example. The neighbourhood is tough and difficult and is always going to provide major challenges to ministry, and Christians are not always going to succeed—humanly speaking. Coming to terms with suffering and failure has been part of the maturing process, and the church is now a much stronger source of help than before.

The foundation for an outward-looking ministry in a local church, one that cares for a host of needy and despairing people, must be founded firstly on the word of God. Listening for that word—in Scripture, in teaching and preaching, in prophecy, in the stillness of prayer, in the needs of the people and circumstances—is essential. The problems of ordinary life, whether stemming from human failure or from immaturity in discipleship, are often the circumstances through which a church grows in stability. In urban priority areas there are particular lessons for professional people, whether lay or ordained, for they tend to assume that they know the answers. In reality, a taxing environment can bring a new sense of God's presence because solutions are not obvious and every member has to look to God for direction.

Church after church has discovered that an essential element of any evangelism and growth is a theology which gives human worth to all people. The friars at Hilfield Friary (Chapter 6) call everyone Brother to make just that point. Only in an environment of mutual respect and affirmation can people in depressed and decaying neighbourhoods discover the truth of their own worth, especially when their circumstances and previous experience have taught them otherwise.

Professional middle-class people who come into the church in inner-city working-class areas may have an additional handicap in ministry: that of being easily identifiable by accent, manner, appearance, and roles, with the kind of authority that has denigrated the local people in the past. They may only learn humility the hard way, through discovering by experience that what is offered rarely seems to be adequate or right for the situation. Compassion is most fully expressed by those who have themselves suffered. Paul writes that God comforts us all in our affliction so that we may comfort those who are themselves in affliction, with the comfort we have received (II Corinthians 1:3–4). It is a sign of the presence of grace in a caring church when, like Christ, his people suffer with those among whom they live, and with whom they share a common humanity.

3
'We Have Hope to Offer'

St Luke's, Holbeck

In the changes from decade to decade, from area to area, God's Spirit is constantly active to make all things work together for good. We often hear reference to 'the spirit of the age', a term that refers to the principal characteristics of that age; in Western society today we would recognise elements such as individualism, competitiveness and hunger for power. Whatever the spirit controlling the patterns of society, there will always be people who lose out, who don't possess the characteristics necessary for success, and become marginalised. Nowadays, with aggressive competition and a limited market, unemployment is a major and apparently insoluble problem which sets many people on one side. The Church's interest in tackling unemployment, wanting to give worth to those who have been made the losers, is apparent on many fronts: the interest of the Archbishop of Canterbury and other bishops, the report *Faith in the City*, and many individual initiatives undertaken by local churches and missions. This is the work of the Holy Spirit, always bringing marginalised people to places where they will find sustenance and hope.

Some years ago Graham Pulkingham, then Rector of the Church of the Redeemer, Houston, Texas, said, 'It's easier to find a leader and make him a Christian than to make a Christian into a leader.' The human attributes of each person who gives her life to God are taken and redeemed, and often new gifts are discovered that were not known before. But God doesn't add gifts and attributes entirely distinct from those he gave that person in the first place. Conversion doesn't make a concert pianist of a person who has been tone deaf all her life, though an affirming environment may enable her to relax and hear a little more clearly. Often when God has a particular work to be undertaken in any one locality, it is necesary for the Spirit to draw people with appropriate gifts together as they make themselves open to him. Until those skills are available, the work cannot proceed.

St Luke's Church, Holbeck, in Leeds, has twelve leaders, each looking after a different aspect of the life. Bill Burch took the lead in the group concerned with social responsibility in the neighbourhood.

Two things struck him as essential for Christians to be doing in the local community. The first was to take risks, as illustrated in the parable of the talents. The only man who was criticised was the man who had one talent and buried it. The second thing was to be salt to the people. Jim Punton, of Frontier Youth Trust, taught the church about salt, for salt in biblical times was used as a cleanser.

Bill says, 'That's what we are here for, to be right up against the dirt and squalor of the world. We are here to be Jesus to people who are living desperate, broken lives.' He continues, 'We need evangelism, to show people the Good News. The Lord believes in wholeness. Therefore the healing he give us in our lives and to other people is vital. Then there's social justice; we are called to that, as the Old Testament prophets urged.'

The unemployment figures were very high in the parish, with one in five people out of work. In calling together a small group of church members, Bill felt they should take some form of action, but didn't know what would be relevant or helpful. After deciding that the group should listen closely to God, little progress was made, as a variety of ideas and proposed projects never came to fruition. This was a waiting time, during which more resources had to be brought to bear on the problem.

From Bystander to Disciple

The task of affecting unemployment positively needed particular people and resources. God began to call those together.

Keith had been a member of the Church of Jesus Christ of the Latter Day Saints, the Mormons. He enjoyed the company. He enjoyed the fellowship but there was always something he couldn't put his finger on, something missing. Eventually the family simply stopped going to the meetings.

His sons were getting to school age, so Keith and his wife began to look around at different schools in South Leeds, and found that for the primary age-group the best was St Luke's Church School. After Darren had been there a couple of years, the question arose of where he should go next. Quite a few of the children went on to St Michael's at Headingley, reputedly an extremely good school. But the only way to get children into St Michael's from other catchment areas in Leeds was with the vicar's recommendation. After a momentary hesitation, the family decided to begin to attend the church and so get the vicar's recommendation.

Keith went to church on Sunday mornings and was always relieved when he could leave at the end of the service. His wife quite liked it, perhaps because she knew several of the mothers from seeing them at the school. With two other men, Keith used to stand in one corner, talking and waiting for the wives to finish chatting over coffee after the service so they could go home.

Keith was eventually confirmed, and then the curate came along and talked him into going to a housegroup. Keith spoke of the change, 'I'm not sure what happened, but at the end of it I came out walking on air, a totally different person. From that time onwards I felt God was calling me not just to be a churchgoer but to be an active member of that church.'

Keith's active membership led him into Bill's group, where he began looking more closely at service in the neighbourhood.

The group planned a co-operative that never quite came together. They looked at knitting and sewing projects, then at a cleaning co-operative.

Whereas other people on the leadership team were doing well with their projects, Bill saw himself doing badly. 'I was getting a little despondent. Two years had passed and nothing had really happened. Then one day the Lord sent this man, John.'

A Man for the Job

During Mission England Keith had been given a list of names of people to visit, who had been told that the nearest participating church was St Luke's. To meet the needs of the new Christians, St Luke's decided to start up nurture groups, and Keith was asked to be a leader.

John Grieves was put into his group. The first night the group simply set about getting to know each other, meeting each other and saying what they did for a living. John told the group what he did, and the more he talked, the more Keith became aware of the implications. 'My ears went up,' he later said, 'like a donkey's ears. Everything he was saying was what I knew we were looking for.'

When Keith came out of that meeting, at about eleven o'clock at night, he rang Bill and said, 'Bill, there's a fellow in this housegroup. He's working on this scheme that's something to do with Manpower Services. You must meet him.'

Until five years before, John Grieves had considered himself extremely well off, working as a training officer for a television company. However, the company was taken over by another that already had a set of training people. Inevitably John was made redundant.

John had run training courses on how to get jobs, how to sit interviews, how to write CV's. But nothing came up. He went to interview after interview, and short list after short list. When people he knew read the adverts for the jobs he applied for they all used to say, 'It's tailor-made for you. If we were to sit down and write something you can do, this would be it.'

John went along to the interviews and got nothing. This situation went on for four years.

John went into Leeds one Friday afternoon and saw a job advert in the paper saying, 'Supervisers required for Community Programme—Leeds City Council'. Despite being dressed in a pair of jeans and a teeshirt, with video films under his arm, he decided to pop in to fill out the necessary application form. He not only filled in the form—he was interviewed and offered a job.

He had been in Leeds for only twenty minutes and couldn't believe it, so asked, 'Is this a joke?'

The interviewer said, 'Don't you want the job?'

'I've been searching for four years; of course I want the job.'

On the following Monday morning when John started, he had to interview other people, to take on his own crew.

John ran a painting and decorating crew, until seven months later when there was a job advert for Bicep Community Programme in Bramley. A painting, decorating and gardening programme was being started. John applied and became assistant manager.

The scheme started with twenty people. It went remarkably well, and in the second year the project leaders kept taking on more people. John comments, 'I knew at the back of my mind that something was going on, as everything was going right, and it shouldn't have done. We are not that clever.'

The Billy Graham Mission came to Sheffield and John said 'No' to the friends who invited him to go with them. So they asked him why he refused. 'Because the man sells religion like washing powder, and I don't think religion should be sold like that.' He hadn't been to church for 20 years.

As it got nearer and nearer to the Billy Graham meeting somehow John found he wanted to go. He was still rebellious, and says, 'I didn't like the idea of sitting with all those born-again Christians singing all those stupid songs all the way to Sheffield.' But he did go. Those on the coach were singing out of the *Good News Hymnbook*, and he asked the friends, 'Why don't they sing proper hymns?'

When he listened to Billy Graham, he was amazed that Billy Graham was so quiet. John almost wanted him to start ranting and shouting, but he didn't. John's respect grew. Billy Graham had had the opportunity to pressurise people, and he hadn't used it.

When Billy Graham asked people to go forward, John thought 'No'.

Then the thought came into his mind, 'You're very good at joining video clubs, John.' He thought, 'Yes, I'm brilliant at joining video clubs.' If John drove down the road and saw free membership to a video club, he would stop and go in. He had eight or nine video cards in his pocket.

The voice said, 'Well, this is free,' and John said, 'Yes?'

So the voice said, 'Well, what about it?' John couldn't argue and found himself walking out onto the field.

When John drove to St Luke's Church, he started crying as he saw the church on the hill, not at all what he had expected of himself. He walked up the steps, feeling that he was going home. Later he explained, 'Everything that I ever really wanted had been wrapped up and put in that church. They were all talking to each other, and the vicar came out and talked to me. I started crying again.'

John met Keith and they started talking about what they did for a living, and John discovered the church's concern for the neighbourhood. John saw no future in the groups' ideas for sewing and knitting machines. 'Why are you going that way? Why don't you run a Manpower Services Scheme?' Keith looked at him blankly. 'They'll give you money, lots of it.'

Bill and Keith were interested in the suggestion, though sceptical, so John went away and copied the Bicep material. He put St Luke's name in place of the Bicep heading and brought back the papers to show the others. They caught their breath when they saw £115,000 written in at the bottom. 'Is this man a lunatic, or what?' was written all over their faces.

Serious discussions got under way in the group as John

pointed out, 'Now this would help not only the unemployed, but also people who are old age pensioners or disabled.' Within Leeds, two areas—the City and Holbeck—have the highest number of old age pensioners living alone.

John talked more about his experience on the Bicep scheme and helped the group with the grant application. A proper request was put in to Manpower Services. John alone was confident, and he speaks of his experience, 'I know it sounds strange, but people talk about speaking in tongues, and I have never been able to do that, but I realise I must have been doing that in a way, because I was talking the right language, and Bill wasn't. Because I had been with the scheme for two years, I knew the right things to say to them, and if you say the right things it's like pushing the right button.'

The application was accepted. The St Luke's Holbeck Community Project could get under way, funded by Manpower Services and involving mentally handicapped people working on a part-time basis, undertaking gardening and decorating for old age pensioners and disabled people in the local community. The premises were to be in the St Edward's Community Centre, in a basement that needed much clearing out, cleaning and redecorating before the scheme could begin.

The staff were to consist of twelve mentally handicapped people, the part-timers, and eight full-time able-bodied. In addition, there was to be a manager, a supervisor and two assistant supervisors, a secretary and a wages clerk.

Finding the Manager

John had ambitions. He had found working with the Bicep scheme very rewarding. But he was second in command, and though he and the manager had a good relationship, nevertheless at the end of the day it was not quite his own scheme. He dearly wanted to run the St Luke's scheme. John had begun to realise that God had been with Bicep throughout his time with that scheme, helping its progress. He was even more enthusiastic about what might be achieved in a scheme that was rooted in the church and so obviously drawn into being by the Holy Spirit.

In his prayers John kept asking, 'Can I run this scheme?' but kept hearing 'No'. He didn't even want to ask the next question, 'Who's it going to be?'

Then one night after about a week he asked, 'Who's it going to be?' The name Keith Bardsley came to mind.

The group had agreed noboby should give up a job to do this, so management continued an unanswered problem with John asserting, 'I still say it's Keith,' adding each week, 'Something will happen.'

Being Unemployed

For several months Keith had been unemployed since the firm he had previously been working for had suddenly gone bankrupt. With John Holmes, he looked at various possibilities. They prayed together, and Keith realised he was to wait for God's timing.

He applied for several jobs but nothing came up.

For the first month the family had no income at all. The man he had been working for had not only lost some £300,000, but had also not been paying Keith's National Insurance contribution or income tax. He was therefore not entitled to unemployment benefit. The Supplementary Benefit Department said Keith needed a letter from his employer before it could process his claim. The problem was that the employer had left his home, and nobody knew where he had gone.

Keith and his wife managed to pay the bills at the end of the first month. Then came a second month, still with no income. Keith's pride stopped him asking for help, even from his friends. The mortgage payment was due from his bank account, plus a few other Standing Orders; they needed a large sum of money and were panicking. There was only one person they would ask, so both Keith and his wife got down on their knees and prayed. 'God, you know the position we are in; give us some advice. What do we do? God, can you help us? You know how much we need;

here are the bills and the Standing Orders.'

Then Keith and his wife sat back and looked at each other and he said, 'Well, it's in God's hands now.'

Before half an hour had passed they had a visitor. He came in and sat talking for a while before saying, 'I've got to go now, but I've got an envelope here for you. I don't want you to open it till I've gone.' As he walked out of the gate someone else drove up.

The second visitor was more direct. 'Are you all right?'

'Yes.'

'Are you all right financially?'

'Yes.'

'I've got something for you, though it's not from me.' He put down an envelope and went.

Keith and his wife sat down and opened up the two envelopes. There was a cheque in one and cash in the other. They needed just under £200. When they added up the money it came to exactly what they needed to pay the outstanding bills. Not a penny more and not a penny less. They looked at each other and burst into tears of joy. Keith knew from that day that no matter what happened, everything would go well eventually. During the following six months they learned to live on what they had coming in; they learned to eat and live differently. Christmas drew nearer, and rather than panicking about what to buy the children, they were praying, 'God, can you help us out here? We'd like to buy the kids something.'

A company Keith had worked for previously found out he was looking for work and rang him up, saying would he like to go back. With overtime pay, his wages became reasonably high in a short space of time, and life settled down more comfortably.

Then one Tuesday morning Keith was called into the manager's office. 'I'm sorry, but we are making you redundant. Can you go home now?' Keith was thoroughly shaken and very upset.

John and Bill were together that evening at a church meeting when Keith approached them.

'Guess what? I've been made redundant.'

When John's response came back quickly, 'I told you something was going to happen,' Keith saw the situation in a new light.

Keith looked at what the job involved with the community project—working with the mentally handicapped, working with old people—everything he had felt for over a year that God had been calling him to do.

He was still a bit puzzled and worried. Would he have the ability to do the job? Yet everything was coming along according to a pattern; each step was smooth. He decided to accept the job as manager.

With a key member of the team now brought into place in this way, Paul's words in II Corinthians are again appropriate. It is when we have experienced suffering that we can be compassionate and understand the response of others in their own suffering. God was bringing good out of Keith's own traumatic and distressing experience of unemployment, for he had found the comfort of God in the midst of it. Now he could comfort others.

Becoming an employer brought its own problems. When Keith and Bill went down to the Job Centre, they were told, 'The supervisors—you may have trouble getting them, but labourers—we can provide as many as you want. How many do you want us to send you for each job?'

Bill answered, 'Just send enough for the job.'

'Oh, no. We'll send you four to one.'

The St Luke's Project men wondered about this, but were told that normally some of those referred fail to turn up, sometimes as many as twenty per cent. Not in this case—only one of their sixteen referrals failed to arrive for interview. The selection was heart-breaking.

The Gift of Equipment

The scheme adopted a man of about seventy-four, Peter, who goes round with an old barrow picking up bits of wood and anything he can find on the trading estate. He helps firms by tidying up their grounds, and then asks them for any old wood or scrap that's lying around.

Keith told Peter that the scheme needed desks, and the following day Peter came back saying, 'There's a firm on the estate that's closed down. There are desks all piled up. You might be able to find one or two good ones.'

Keith went with Raymond, one of the newly-employed lads, and spoke to the caretaker. They told him about the scheme and what they needed, so he said, 'There are the desks; take what you want.'

They dug into the pile and found two reasonable desks. Keith asked the price, and the caretaker responded, 'If it's for the project, you can have 'em.'

Work with a Purpose

If work is going to be helpful to the lives of individuals then they must find value in it, find personal affirmation and a sense of worth and have opportunity to take responsibility. Underlying principles for the scheme had been well talked over by the men. 'Jesus never was a soft touch, and we are not called to that either,' Bill comments.

John points out from his own experience in management that everybody likes order. They like to know how far they can go and have defined boundaries. If they can't find those boundaries, they have to keep pushing until they do.

Keith had a growing sense of what he wanted to see achieved through the project. 'Each man will be given a job in the morning, and then there will be another one waiting when it's finished. He is not going to be standing around. Most people like gardening; they like to see the end product. They love to see God at work, even though they don't realise he's there. They plant a seed, and in a few weeks' time they'll come back and there'll be something beautiful growing. They have faith in that seed.'

Keith was looking for additional facilities to use in wet weather so that the men could grow produce and be taught to grow plants ready to put in gardens. Then they would not only do gardens for old people but be able to put something in those gardens—lettuce, bedding plants or cabbage.

The main pattern of the scheme was to go around every four or five weeks so that the gardens in their care always looked nice. There were many old people who loved to potter in the garden, but could no longer turn over the soil or cut their hedge. But if some men came in to do the hard work for them, then they could themselves do the light work and end up proud of their gardens.

John talks of giving his men responsibility, an essential ingredient in life-giving ministry. 'We give each man the responsibility for sorting out his own work. On the gardening side we have made teams, each with a full-timer and two part-timers, and given them twenty gardens in a block. We give them a set of tools, and they go round and work on these gardens on a regular basis. After a monthly cycle they are back at garden number one again. Nobody is telling them how fast to go, and we find that because they have that responsibility, they set their own levels: 'Let's get this one finished, because we want to do so-and-so tomorrow in Mrs Jones's.'

A Gift to the Neighbourhood

The advantages of such schemes to many local residents are obvious. Unemployed and disadvantaged young people, who are not Christians, are becoming part of church organised programmes. Many old people never leave their houses, having become too infirm and isolated. Friendship grows between old and young during the regular gardening schedules and the occasional visits to do redecorating. Additionally, those who are church members have opportunity to make contact with the old people: 'Do you go to church? Would you like to come to church? We could collect you. If you don't want to come out, would you like Communion at home?' As Keith says, 'You can make contact with people over a cup of tea.'

John speaks vehemently for both himself and the others when he says, 'I will say loud and clear: this scheme is not just about church people or Christians being employed. It's to do with *people* being employed.' The last thing that St Luke's project wants to know is whether a person is a Christian, or whether he goes to church. Their business is to make sure that the scheme runs properly and that they employ whoever walks through the door. That has required faith—to believe that God will lead people to them.

Building a Future

The concern expressed by St Luke's project draws together Christian concerns for justice and for being the salt of the earth. The aim is to make life more tolerable for their neighbours, with the kind of evangelism that spreads the Good News through what is done. If there is talk of God—and there obviously is—it takes root in ground well dug and fertilised with the Gospel in action.

John continues, 'It is easy to touch some people; they'll listen because they have nothing better to do. But we are talking about somebody who is unemployed, who has been sent an electricity bill and a gas bill—though he doesn't know where the next meal is coming from! How can you touch people with burdens like that, which the majority of people are carrying round now? The answer is that our role as Christians, and as the church especially, is to go out and relieve those burdens as best we can.'

Relieving people of their most pressing burdens opens the way for God to speak to them—a lesson John learned from his own experience.

Until he began working with Bicep and had joined St Luke's Church, John felt the world was in a desperate plight. Now he looks at the economic climate and can actually thank God for it, because in it there are such opportunities for Christians to show what they are worth. Without the crisis, would he and fellow Christians have got involved with people? He concludes that they probably wouldn't, 'We would probably all have sat in our churches and done nothing.'

At a meeting entitled 'Faith in the City' John heard it said that those gathered should go out into the city and find out what God was doing. God had always been there and had always been working, but they might never have seen him. God had always been at the school, working away, and local Christians had only just noticed. But because God *was* working in these places, people had come to the church.

John sees a parallel in the St Luke's project, of which he says, 'You don't have to browbeat people. All you have to do is say 'St Luke's Community Programme', and give them a job. After they have worked there a while, met the old people and worked with the handicapped, if they have anything alive inside them at all, they'll be coming to church as well. You've given to them, you've solved a problem, and you haven't required anything in return.'

Bill, Keith and John summarise their own experience of taking up the Gospel mandate to care for their neighbours. 'We can't change people's lives; only the Lord changes people's lives. All we do is say, "This is what we have found. Why don't you give it a try?" If they say they don't want to, that's okay.

'We show people by the things we do that we are just like them. We are not religious freaks, but ordinary people who have found that God loves us.

'We have found the power of God among us. There are churches with a lot more money than we have, in much better areas, who haven't latched on to the fact that the Spirit of God can actually move the church. If you are open to him, he can do all sorts of wonderful things.'

The security and future of the scheme can only, however, be seen to be fragile. The experience of the Church of the Good Shepherd in Wolverhampton (Chapter 8) has shown this. A change in government or local Council policy may wipe out such schemes with very little notice, by turning down application for further funding. The St Luke's project is concerned that the Church nationally put its words into action. Will *Faith in the City*, they wonder, find expression as anything more than hot air?

Changes in government policy could result in a re-look at Community Programmes; they might well be discarded altogether. It is therefore already time for those who lead the Church to look at this question and answer positively, giving a lead to churches such as St Luke's and the Good Shepherd, and giving hope to the employees and recipients of the community schemes who would like such programmes to be more than just a temporary stop-gap.

The hope one holds is that the attitude of the Church authorities, who spoke with such discouragement to Dave and Lin in Wolverhampton, will change. The saddening fact is that schemes such as St Luke's employ—albeit for a year only—handicapped people who may never get work in the competition of the open market place. Thus they face a future of unemployment again. Even with full employment, many handicapped people prop up the numbers at the bottom of any unemployment list. They have a permanent need for such schemes even as their clients, the old and disabled, have an ongoing need for their friendship and the fruit of their labour.

4
Arteries into the Community

St Luke's, Holbeck

The Church in Britain in Victorian times played a major role in the provision of education for all children. Throughout the nineteenth century thousands of children received an education through church schools whose aim was to provide enough basic training for each child, particularly of the working classes, to read the Bible and receive a minimum of Christian education. By the time the State had prescribed compulsory education in the latter half of the century, the majority of school places were in those attached to the parish church in each neighbourhood. A Christian foundation was as much emphasised in the State system as in church schools.

The balance of provision has now changed, the finance being provided by secular authorities, and the aims of education have similarly transferred into the public sector and broadened considerably. In a multi-racial and multicultural society the church school often finds itself in a peculiar position, reflecting its roots but under the authority of a system that is increasingly alienated from the Church. However, such schools are still partially financed by the Anglican Church and often maintain close links through the involvement of the local clergy in the school's assembly and religious education programmes.

Where such opportunity can form the basis for contact and exchange with the local community, a strong artery into the local community can be established. Through the school, members of the church have involvement in the quality of education given to their own children, can participate in serving the neighbourhood and can meet and make friends with other families.

St Luke's School, in Holbeck, with its relationship to the church for which it is named, has such an opportunity. The relationship between the vicar and the headteacher has been creative and lifegiving, and the means of many local people finding help and care.

Eric Whitehouse is the present headteacher. He is a committed Christian and had worked in other areas of Leeds before coming to St Luke's. He says, 'People use the term "ethos" in all sorts of airy-fairy ways, but nevertheless we have a Christian ethos in the school.'

Eric talks of little things that are signs of that ethos: welcome signs on the doors, parents being allowed to come in and share in school assemblies, teachers and children going to church, invitations to the vicar or the curate to come in on Friday to lead assembly. Each Tuesday John Holmes, vicar of St Luke's Church, and Eric have lunch together, and Rosemary Holmes is a member of the school staff. The governors have a policy of employing committed Christians, or certainly people who are quite happy to work in a Christian school. All these things are signs of the faith that is the strength of this school.

Leeds, like most larger cities in Britain, has become home to people of other races and religions. Could this be a point of tension in a church school that is openly and candidly Christian? Apparently not, for many of the Asian community in Holbeck choose St Luke's school particularly *because* it is a Christian school. The school does keep the major Christian festivals and does emphasise Christian values, and families want these standards for their children. (According to various reports in *The Guardian* and *The Church Times*, throughout the country church schools tend to be high on the list of preferred schools, regardless of the religious beliefs of the parents, because of the caring quality and high standards often found in them.) Of the many approaches from parents who want their children to come to this school, Eric says, 'We open our doors to everybody and say, provided we have got places you can come. We are a Christian school; you can take us or leave us. Most people come and take us as we are.'

There are people who came to the school as non-churchgoing families who have now become staunch members of the church through contact at the school. They come in, experience the atmosphere, meet Christian teachers and find fellowship with other parents. An open-door policy gives the parents access to the classroom, and many come in to help with the work.

St Luke's School serves the community; it is not just a school for Christians. That is significant, showing there are two possible ways the school could look at itself.

Church and School Working Together

Eric talks about the partnership between church and school from the perspective of the school and its image in the locality. St Luke's, both church and school, stand for being alive in every sense, alive and growing. Like an octopus, the church has its feelers out. Eric gets favourable reports back through parents and colleagues as well as through the popularity of the school. The academic standard of the school may be no better than that of others nearby, but undoubtedly both St Luke's School and St Luke's Church are seen as a family. They have a strong forward drive and are doing things for the community, and for the children.

When Eric meets with John Holmes, he tells John of anybody he is worried about, parents or staff. A couple of years ago a young boy whose father died, came to the school. His was a Catholic family. Eric told John, who arranged a visit to the family.

Eric tries to sort out many problems which have no direct connection with education, e.g. social problems. The school, like the church, is a place where people feel able to go and say what they feel. When I spoke to him, he had just spent three-quarters of an hour with one family.

Though the meeting wasn't constructive in practical terms, it was still very helpful in giving the parents opportunity to talk over the problems.

The church is not just concerned for fund-raising reasons about the people who come to it, but are concerned for the wider community. When once there was a car accident at the cross-roads near the school, the church family rallied round the woman. Parents from school, and the curate, all converged on the accident scene. The woman lay in the middle of the road, with the ambulance coming. They reassured her that she didn't have to worry about her kids; somebody would look after them for her. She didn't have to worry about getting in touch with her husband; that too would be done—all by this church family. John Holmes, then, has sought to make the church grow in such a way that it does involve everybody—including the school—in partnership with the church.

Eric concludes, 'I am very committed to church schools, but not to those attached to a church in name only. If you have a Christian ethos in the church and it spills into the school, and vice versa, you're on to a winner.'

Making Contact

Anne Smith started attending St Luke's Church through School Sunday, when the children from St Luke's School were going to take an active part in the service. Her son Dean was reading a lesson. He asked if his parents would come to hear him, and they did.

Anne—among half a dozen others—found herself wanting to go back to the church because of that School Sunday.

She went to a housegroup. It was there Anne realised she knew of God, but she says, 'I didn't *know* him. I *know of* the Queen, but I *know* my friends. All at once, God was real and close and something I experienced. It was amazing, I now had a completely different outlook. It was like an open door. One that I didn't know whether to go through, or wait for him to come through to me.' One of the passages Anne was reading was 'Knock, and the door will be opened to you.' For the first time Anne was aware of God speaking to her.

Anne went on to an evening housegroup and now helps to lead it. Because she was at home during the day, the church leaders asked her if she would lead the daytime housegroup. At first she thought there was no way she could give to these others what she had received from the first group. Then she realised, 'No, I can't, but God can.' As she says, 'It is an onward going thing. I'm always learning.'

Monday Break

St Luke's had a Pram Special—a monthly service that was a follow-up to baptisms. Families were visited and invited along. The service took the form of two or three songs, a prayer, Bible reading and a testimony or talk. That worked quite well for a couple of years, when numbers fell, so Anne and the other leaders reassessed whether this was the right form, or whether the Pram Special had outlived its usefulness. Some people were put off by it being a service in church. Newcomers were looking for fellowship and friendship as much as for worship.

Two years ago the church therefore started Monday Break in the church hall. Anne says, 'We didn't want to put people off. We hoped they would see the way we were with one another, and they'd be seeing something of God through our lives.' The group aimed to bring God to the newcomers through friendship, without putting pressure on them to come to church, leaving individuals to make up their own minds. They knew Anne and other leaders were Christians, as they were known to be part of a St Luke's group.

A few women came and in turn brought others. News spread by word of mouth, and meetings were quite well supported. The local Health Visitors recommended Monday Break. When they visited homes and found a young mother under pressure, they would ask if she knew about Monday Break.

A committee arranged a varied programme and contacted outside speakers. On some afternoons there would simply be an opportunity to sit around and talk, or on other occasions there might be a swop shop for children's clothes, with no charge. One of the first outside speakers was a Health Visitor.

There were speakers on children's interests, then on women's interests, such as Well Woman Clinics. This came at a time when one of the group had found she had cervical cancer, and everyone quickly put down her name to go for a smear. They were scared. One woman in her forties had never had a smear test because she had always been frightened, but because a group were going together she went as well. There proved to be nothing wrong, but the experience helped her overcome her fear. The leaders also invited a woman called Irene, who had written a book, and who had been a prostitute, to give her testimony.

The group provided contact and an avenue into church life. There were some whom the members knew locally—well enough to say 'hello' to in the street. They started coming to Monday Break, and the friendship grew. They were invited to go to a housegroup. Some were friends who would say, 'Oh, if you are doing it, I'll go with you.' These women went on to be confirmed, and they still come to Monday Break. There are also those who have been coming to the group meetings for the last two years but who don't want any involvement with the church; they are quite happy just to come. The group is just as friendly and open with them.

Mothers' Union was a bit too churchy, as the need was for contact outside the church building. Members of Mothers' Union came and wondered about prayer at Monday Break. Each week now, three or four people go into a room at the side of the coffee area before the meeting, to bring it to the Lord. They pray for the planning, the outreach and for friendliness.

Most of the Monday Break members have children at St Luke's School, and that brings other contacts. Last year a couple of Indian girls came. One of them had marital problems. Anne discovered it was really taboo in her religion for her to speak about them. She lived near Maggie Hewson, a church member who had told her about Monday Break. At first she felt conspicuous, being the only dark-skinned girl there, but she was welcomed and said she found people friendly. At a previous place where she had gone to Mums and Toddlers, they hadn't asked her name or her little boy's, just put them down as visitors. Anne reflects, 'That borderline between being friendly and being pushy—you've got to know where it is.'

In some churches it would seem that only the clergy are blessed and gifted. But the ordinary people can be used by God in just the same way as clergy. It is a question of recognising their gifts and using them. One girl was the godmother to a little boy who was ill with eczema. She felt that the group should meet and pray for him. The group knew that God could work when they prayed together. The little boy began to improve, his skin looking pink as a baby's should. The group has met again to give thanks to the Lord for the healing.

Families under Pressure

The children are all an integral part of the church family on a Sunday morning and at other times. At the daytime housegroup they are there. Anne says, 'It is not always ideal, and we may say, "Is this what you really want, Lord?" But we know it is, because the women who do come wouldn't have a fellowship group otherwise; they can't come out at night.' Some are single parents, or perhaps the wife goes to church and the husband doesn't.

Monday Break has initiated fund-raising for the lone parent families. Lone parents felt that they were not really supported through the church, and that nobody really understood their problems. If there were evening meetings, they couldn't get to them, as they couldn't afford to pay for a baby sitter. Some were really struggling financially and the church outings were expensive for them with their children. In conjunction with the pastoral leaders, Anne was therefore asked to get the single parents together and see what would be helpful to them. For instance, there are times when parents are desperate over the need for a new pair of children's shoes, so the group has a fund to lend money until it can be paid back.

The young teens in the church have undertaken baby sitting. One person in the church lent her caravan so that one of the single mums could have a holiday. One girl had her electricity cut off, so members of the congregation kept the children for her. Another of the mums was decorating, so some of the young men went to help her. Anne was impressed that one couple at Christmas freely gave some money to be shared out among the single mothers.

Susan, another leader of Monday Break, grew up in a back-to-back house, with no bathroom and an outside toilet. The bath was built into the kitchen like a work unit, level with the top. The same was true of her home in Morley when she married. She says, 'The bath was filled from the geyser (boiler) with a tube. And there I was squeezing myself down between cooker and draining board for a bath, when I was nine months pregnant! So when we moved down here, it was quite posh after where I'd lived.'

Susan started to go to church after a church member, Andrew, had come knocking at the door to sell magazines, and they started talking on the doorstep. Susan had been to another local church once, but said, 'It didn't seem friendly, and they didn't bother.' Andrew responded, 'Come down to St Luke's, there's always someone friendly there. There's always somebody waiting to greet you.' So she went, and the friendliness fired her curiosity.

Julie, also a leader at Monday Break with Anne and Susan, moved into Holbeck. When her family circumstances became difficult, someone from the church visited her, hearing about her through the school. She had five young children; only one had reached school age. She remembers, 'Somebody took the trouble to come and see if there was anything he could do to help in the situation. It had a big effect; I was feeling extremely hostile towards everybody. Yet somebody came out of the blue, and that somebody did care.'

Not only did that person care, but when she got to the church, the church as a whole cared. She wasn't treated as somebody odd. Her earlier experience had been that because she had a big family, people would look at her and say, 'Oh, there she is, the one with five kids.' But the church really impressed her. She says, 'I had such a big hang-up, but they accepted me and my children just as we were.' People saw them coming and said, 'Oh, here is Julie and her lovely kids.' It didn't matter what the age-group was: the church treated Julie as a sister in a family.

Until she began to go to Monday Break, everywhere she went Julie had the five children trailing along with her. At Monday Break someone had come up and taken the four pre-school children and said, 'You go and have a cup of coffee and forget about them for an afternoon.' For Julie that was the attraction, an opportunity to let someone else look after the children while she sat down with a cup of coffee and a chat, or to listen to what was going on. 'A young child will drive a parent to despair, no matter if there's one or five.'

Julie comments on the value, not just to her but to other young parents, in having a place such as Monday Break for friendship and fellowship. A lot of mothers get fed up with sitting at home looking at four walls. Even though nowadays one anticipates more freedom to go out and do things, people in fact don't. An isolated person has less incentive to go out, and many retreat into their own houses more and more. When Julie was a youngster, it was the neighbourhood that was her family. Her family was around her, and there was Mrs So-and-so next door whom she always called auntie, and families used to share the children. There was not so much call for Monday Breaks then.

Monday Break mixes people who go to the church along with people who don't. July says, 'That lets them know the church isn't full of old fuddy-duddies and that we are not people walking around with haloes round our heads. We are just the same as they are, except that we have found Somebody. We have found something in the church.'

A church that is constantly looking outward with a caring concern for the neighbours finds avenues of contact. Very often the most effective contact comes when someone from the church is helping a neighbour in the context of the pressure of daily life. Where a church and its outreach becomes fully rooted in the neighbourhood, becoming the salt on the food, the local community will have a sense of that family quality that so many people experience in Holbeck.

Most of the caring in Monday Break happens in the course of ordinary human friendship. It is in the context of family and friends that individuals can normally find help and encouragement. Professional help from Health Visitors, doctors, and social workers has an element that is similar to a medicine that treats symptoms. But in the loneliness that is experienced by such a large number of parents, friendship is both the preventative and the curative medicine.

The effectiveness of these local people in reaching their own neighbours goes far beyond what could be achieved by professional people coming from outside, even the clergy. When local people have matured in discipleship through the church, they are able to give themselves to the caring ministry and build ongoing friendships with those whom they meet at school, in the clinic or in the street.

5
Worship—Christ Among Us

St Luke's, Holbeck;
The Community of Celebration

Worship in its every dimension is the foundation for the caring Church. The ordinary good neighbourliness that is inherent in human life reflects the goodness of God in creation. The church which seeks to live as the Body of Christ in its daily work and worship, to live out Kingdom values, finds that the encounter with God in worship gives context and perspective, grace and energy to the sacrifice of caring. Truly caring for others is a costly process—eased in a body of people where it is reciprocated and supported, but nevertheless a sacrifice.

The particular experience of being present in worship can be a breakthrough for many people, a contact with the intangible, a sense of being touched by the presence of God. On many occasions, the weary, the hopeless, and the despairing have an encounter with God that is as life-changing for them as was Saul's encounter with God on the road to Damascus.

Such worship is not a coincidence, or easily established. Such transforming worship, which leads on to real maturity, is founded in costly integration, between joy and suffering, between ordinary human life and the transcendence of Spirit-filled worship. In this the Church is standing with Christ in the divide between the glory of God, the resurrection hope, and the terrible chaos of a Godless world. In the Church's choosing to worship God while holding hands with ordinary human life with its sin and misfortune, humanity is renewed and transformed. The Church is not lifted out of its humanity, for humanity that is inspired with new life is a constant witness to God's creativity rather than to chaos, so that creation may also have hope.

Paul writes:

> I consider that our present sufferings are not worth comparing with the glory that will be revealed in us. The creation waits in eager expectation for the sons of God to be revealed. For the creation was subjected to frustration ... in hope that the creation itself will be liberated from its bondage to decay and brought into the glorious freedom of the children of God. (Romans 8:18–21)

During worship this mystery is often perceived, not clearly but enough for people, with that inner urgency to find what is real, to be suddenly touched by the grace of Jesus Christ, and the love of God.

Led by the Spirit: St Luke's, Holbeck

Leading worship that enables and serves people in their relationship to God is a particular gift among a congregation.

Tim and Jane are fairly recent members of St Luke's Church, Holbeck. Tim had lived in that area as a student; though as Jane said, it would be very hard living there if they didn't have the church.

Tim and Jane arrived at the church at a time when a guitarist was desperately needed. Even more swiftly than usual, St Luke's had their new arrivals taking responsibility, and Tim began to play the guitar for worship. His gift is very apparent, having an intense sensitivity towards the other musicians as well as towards the congregation. As he has led for a while now, he is able to put his understanding into words.

'People are moved by worship,' he says. His thoughts are therefore always with the meaning of what he is doing and how that relates to the congregation, what's happening with the mood and what the Spirit is saying. In the midst of all this he is also thinking of the youngsters in the music group, whom he is teaching and guiding. He often feels he is spread very thinly.

There is inevitably a difference between contemporary and traditional music. Music involves personality, too, so that as musical differences come close to the surface, leaders can create tension, if they are not careful. Some churches have conflict between the old and new, between pianos and guitars. The music at St Luke's is good because the church has both hymns and more modern choruses, which go together perfectly well. For the whole congregation there is harmony in both styles and the way they are played. It is not a case, as Tim commented, of the north aisle having all the hymn singers the other aisle having the hand-clapping chorus singers, with a four-pew gap between them. Instead, there is a blend of the two. People are willing to sing, and when they worship it is together.

In the evening someone else leads the service, and Tim leads the music alone. There are times during a devotional song when he can feel the Spirit move through the worship. He then puts inflection in the music, going through the song again very softly. Or he may shape the music the other way round, with a quiet start and build it up, as he feels the Spirit moving among the people. All this serves the worship, though there are times when it feels flat to Tim, and there hasn't been any obvious movement of the Spirit.

There are occasions when the words of a particular song fit to worship and identify with God, as for instance in 'Abba Father'. Tim may think of the song, and the Spirit may prompt that the words are for him or for someone else for whom the group is praying. Sometimes there are long silences that Tim finds exceptionally beautiful: time to listen to what God is saying.

The Presence of Christ

The report of the Archbishop of Canterbury's Commission on Urban Priority Areas has gathered together a presentation of Christian experience. This is of immense value because of its basis in actual experience. A substantial section concerns itself with the ongoing life of the church in the city, of its formation and the processes by which it grows. The sub-section on worship makes the following comment:

> The worship offered by the local churches is also an important means of evangelism. The stranger who comes into the services will make a judgement about Christianity on the basis of what he encounters there. Is the worship lively and participatory? Does it evoke a sense of the presence of God while showing a concern for the real things in people's lives? Much of this will depend on how the local congregation order their services.
>
> Worship is about good dreams: it needs to hold them alongside what is sometimes a harsh reality. UPA Christians want a beautiful service, but they may go home to domestic violence or a leaking roof. A Church life which has nothing to say about these things simply leaves people feeling inferior. They feel they must hide from the clergy and the local church their debts, their court cases, their sufferings at the hands of their husbands. Reality must be faced. There must be something to understand about God's will for a wife terrified of her husband, for a husband terrified of his gambling debts, for parents who dread that their son is out beating up Bangladeshis.
>
> Worship will put harsh realities into a new light. It may enable people to withdraw for a time from the pressures, but it will be 'withdrawal with the intent to return', not evasion.[1]

The balance between the knowledge of the presence of God and of living with grim reality, and the holding of these together, is relevant to St Luke's Church. People can come as they are, with the realities they face, not to hide from them but to bring them to God. A local woman had visited John Holmes, vicar of St Luke's, Holbeck; she was very distressed. Her daughter's children had all been taken into care. The situation was traumatic and the woman said, 'You know, only the church has kept me going.'

John said he would see if he could be of any practical help, but after one or two inquiries, it was obvious he could do nothing. John spoke to the woman again saying, 'I'm sorry I can't be much help.'

'But just coming to worship at the church and being aware that God was there helped,' she says.

John had also been talking to a young couple who were to be married at St Luke's. They'd been coming ever since they booked the wedding and had been struck by the worship. The worship the young man had been used to was rather staid. Coming to St Luke's had taken his breath away.

The conversation made John reflect. At St Luke's John found the worship had related more and more to the cultural life of the neighbourhood, as the informality, the simple songs and the sense of family—all part of this neighbourhood—had come together.

The charismatic renewal brought new energy and life into the worship. But because of the church's pastoral orientation, this was not a renewing worship in any abstract way. It was renewal in the neighbourhood as a whole, an expression of the unity of human reality and God's glory. It could not be transplanted; it was part of Holbeck. The way the church worshipped God reflects the sort of people who lived there.

In a very short space of time newcomers are caught up in the worship, often without the members really being conscious of it. Just recently a woman who had come to church for the first time, two or three weeks before, went forward for ministry, during the Communion. She came because she had heard it was a healing service. She asked those ministering to pray with her that her son 'may come to know the Lord'. Nobody had spoken to her directly about God but she had been caught up in the movement of worship with other people, with the life of God in such a way that it had spoken to her. Quite a number of local people have started attending church after bereavement or because somebody invited them, and very quickly they are touched and involved.

The fact that St Luke's worship is sacramental at its heart is important to John. The Eucharist has always meant a lot to him personally as a sign of God's unfailing love. When John saw himself to be a poor Christian, he nonetheless knew that there—in the bread and the wine—Christ was present.

The fact of the Eucharist at the heart of the worship is important in the same way to the ordinary folk of Holbeck, who form the congregation at St Luke's. Coming forward to receive the bread and the wine, sharing in the presence of Christ, sharing with their brothers and sisters: those things are at the centre of worship.

John was once in a group of clergy who were talking about worship and ritual. One man said to his curate, 'I don't know what you think, but I thought our worship yesterday was desperately bad. But the week before it was okay.'

John puzzled over the comment. Perhaps the previous day's service hadn't been as zippy, and perhaps it hadn't all come together in the way he expected, but—for John—every Sunday is meaningful when there is worship, when the sacrament is ministered and people can know the presence of Christ. That's part of the givenness of worship, something that ordinary folk can relate to because they do receive Christ.

Worship Touches and Renews: The Community of Celebration

Because worship can be a time of offering the *whole* of oneself to God, it often happens that tensions within the individual prevent a full offering of oneself to God. As the person offers herself to God, the pain of the past suffering may not only hinder but, ironically, seems to block the individual from feeling God's love.

In its calling to offer acceptance and belonging to others, the Community of Celebration, now living in

Bletchingley in Surrey, has found that its resources are stretched to the limit as many newcomers, families and single people, come to share the Community life. Those who come are treated with the respect and dignity appropriate to children of God. Those who are troubled are helped to pick themselves up, to make a renewed start on ordinary life. Those who are insecure are affirmed and given responsibility. Families whose ways of relating to one another damage and violate the members are given time and space to begin to appreciate and love one another, both as adults and children. I am a member of that Community myself.

Such renewal is not the result of institutional rules and disciplines; the healing and renewing are the fruit of love. In his first epistle, John says that we love because God first loved us. The Community of Celebration was called together by God to live out a quality of life, a faithfulness to the simple commandments of Jesus, to love God and to love our neighbours. That calling has continued to be expressed in others' finding and receiving the love of God in a measure that has enabled them to go on their way refreshed.

Fisherfolk

The Fisherfolk teams—members of the Community of Celebration known for their ministry in worship leadership, music and the arts—have been able to express to others in various churches the heart of their life. 'Worship is the whole of life', they would say, only to hear the immediate question, 'What do you mean?'

Christ defines worship for us. To worship is to love the Lord your God with all your heart and with all your strength and with all your mind—everything. Then you love your neighbour as yourself. The Community seeks to serve God with their lives, with their hopes, their ambitions, their trust, their despair, their humanity, their weakness and strength. So God is with each person when she is washing up, or in the bath. He is with someone who is bad-tempered, depressed or discouraged. 'Can we offer this to him?' you may ask. The Community would answer resoundingly, 'Yes!' Being able to give oneself to God and know acceptance is often limited by a sense of guilt and self-rejection, but never by any limit in God's love. To break that cycle of offering God only part of our lives—the part we think is good—there must be recognition that God loves each person totally. Only Christ has done that for us. While a Community or a church is as yet an imperfect reflection of Christ, as his body, members can together begin to offer a love mixed with acceptance. But it is never easy.

John, a member of my household, was knocking at my bedroom door. I rolled over and looked at the clock—1.15 am. I had been fast asleep. 'Could you come, Maggie? Your friend Anne needs you.' The friend had arrived in the Community just a few days earlier with her husband and two children. I had put flowers in their room as a welcome. Moving internationally to join us was, I sensed, going to be culturally and emotionally shocking for the family. We had quickly made friends. And now some of the despair that had attracted my new friend to the Community and had made her so unhappy with her marriage, was coming into the open.

When outsiders see a group of people who love one another in an accepting manner, they are drawn towards that love with a longing to be accepted themselves. But they hit a barrier almost immediately: their own self-rejection keeps them separate and unacceptable. They stay closed against love in case others, seeing the nasty side of their personalities, also reject them. It's a Catch-22 situation confronting many as they join the Community. There is no way to belong more fully without opening up the areas of weakness, sharing them, taking the risk of rejection. Many people who are trapped this way feel the pain most deeply when trying to sleep, and my friend was overwhelmed with despair. In that late-night conversation—and in many others that followed—she opened up her darkness and shared it. She was accepted by that body of people, to be renewed in her relationship with God. She could begin to worship with the whole of herself.

Another time, a woman stopped me in the hallway, where I had just gathered together a broom, dustpan and brush from the cupboard of housekeeping equipment. 'I have to be honest and tell you something,' she said. I leaned on my broom for a moment; she looked a bit upset. 'I am so angry with you, I can hardly speak.' I wondered what I had done. 'You smile at me, and say hello as if you care about me, but I know you don't. I'm not the kind of person anyone likes. I don't even like it when you say hello to me.'

Every day two people were meeting with this woman to help her get beyond the depression and self-rejection that was destroying not only her but her family too. The effect of coming into an atmosphere of acceptance and fellowship at first increased to breaking point her sense of unworthiness and hopelessness. The Community would stay close to her while she slowly dismantled the barriers and let God into the darkness and despair, till she came to receive his love into all of her being and could offer the whole of herself freely to him.

The Fisherfolk worship tradition expresses a gathering of the lives of the congregation in a corporate act of worship. Together they offer worship to God with the whole of their beings. The gentle atmosphere in which that worship happens enabled these two women to be touched by the love of God. At first with fear and trembling, then with confidence, they found a place to express that offering of themselves to God. Worship that heals and renews is that which gathers the people, with all their hopes and fears, all their despair and longing, and offers these to God.

In the early 1970s, The Fisherfolk were often invited to churches to lead services. In one particular instance, they accepted an invitation before hearing a specific problem in the church. A small group within the church, who had experienced something of the charismatic renewal, wanted The Fisherfolk to come to lead praise and worship, so the recalcitrant and conservative members of the congregation could be shown that being charismatic was 'acceptable', and could get converted to the style of praise and worship in which the renewed group found so much fulfilment.

'I don't want to be used by one part of the church to criticise another,' said one member of The Fisherfolk. 'It seems to me that God wouldn't want that.'

'I think that we should try to find a way to break down the barriers, and make the church one people for God and get them beyond thinking that renewal is a style of music,' said another.

Renewed worship is not about style, or form. Nor is it a question of spontaneity as opposed to liturgy; it is coming together in worship and finding God meeting us in hope, joy and love. Thus the team agreed that the task of worship leadership in that particular service would be to find ways that all those present could worship God and have laid open before them the possibility of meeting and hearing him.

But how should the team do that when one group adamantly requested up-tempo songs of renewal and another group felt so violated by the 'noise' that it withdrew from all participation? We decided that the group who knew The Fisherfolk, the more charismatic people, would trust that the worship was Spirit-led. We would worship and give ourselves to God, and in gentleness and quietness we would worship in such a way that the more traditional members would be able to participate.

We led Evening Prayer from the Anglican Prayer Book. It was one of the most beautiful experiences of all my years of visiting churches with The Fisherfolk. In the psalms and canticles we used modern settings, and for hymns we carefully chose both traditional and new, ones that we knew were both quiet and powerful. Our setting of the Magnificat and of the Song of Simeon were used by the Spirit to melt the hardness of division, in a common encounter with God.

Once I went as a speaker to a group of people who were training for ministry in the church. After a day of teaching and workshops we met for a final act of worship in a

Eucharist. Within seconds I realised that the musicians had not integrated their understanding of loving their neighbours as themselves into their worship planning. They used the opportunity to 'get in' some of their personally preferred style of worship, about which they had been trying to convince the rest of the group for some time. To 'love their neighbours as themselves' in planning worship, the leaders have to ask themselves, 'How can we stand where these people are and see God, meet God, and offer ourselves to God?' The worship leader is a servant who cares, at her or his own expense, that the congregation are enabled to worship fully. The hearts of the leaders must be offered to God, open to the Spirit and laid down for the people.

Frank Lake, founder of the Clinical Theology Association, brought influence and understanding of grace and caring through his close relationship to the Community of Celebration. Frank pointed to the symbol of the Cross to say that Christ himself identifies with people at the place of their deepest pain. He is with them at that place, and there is no blame attached to being there, though most people go around feeling guilty.

Christians are not healed of their humanity. They may overcome some tendencies, such as projecting their pain onto others, but they will always have their human nature. They are not going to become fundamentally different creatures, but may become more integrated, more balanced.

Integration with Everyday

Throughout the history of his people, God has expressed dissatisfaction with forms of worship that are not integrated with everyday life and the needs of others.

In Isaiah we read:

> The multitude of your sacrifices—what are they to me? says the Lord.
> I have more than enough of burnt offerings, of rams and the fat of fattened animals;

> I have no pleasure in the blood of bulls and lambs and goats.
> ... Stop bringing meaningless offerings! Your incense is detestable to me...
> When you spread out your hands in prayer, I will hide my eyes from you; even if you offer many prayers I will not listen to you...
> Stop doing wrong, learn to do right!
> Seek justice, encourage the oppressed.
> Defend the cause of the fatherless, plead the case of the widow. (from Isaiah 1:11–17)

Isaiah communicates with the same spirit as Jesus when he rebuked the Pharisees, whom he likened to white-washed tombs. Susan Abbott, another Community of Celebration member, observes, 'Denying your humanity is like always scrubbing away at your inward parts; you use a lot of effort without accomplishing a lot.' The incarnation of Christ—the ultimate integration of humanity with the spiritual—points the Church towards integrating its spiritual parts with the ordinary humanity of its members.

Phil Bradshaw is a member of the Community of Celebration. He came from a lively Baptist church some twelve years before joining the Community. In addition to functioning as Managing Director of the business that marketed Fisherfolk music and worship resources, Phil has also been a leader in the caring and pastoral ministry. He says that there is a connection between integrating humanity into spirituality and the way you look at the elements in the Eucharist. If one's spirituality is of an 'other-worldly' kind, the tendency is for the Communion—the Eucharist—to be a memorial, and no more. The Catholic tradition, on the other hand, has the teaching of the Real Presence. If a person lives out his spirituality in his humanity, the spiritual and the material somehow come together. This integration is not just in the body; it is in the bread and the wine too.

For Phil, the elements are a real source of grace, which he needs in order to make sense of his spirituality. In the churches Phil came from, the focal point of the service was always the sermon. That is a valuable tradition, in that one does need to feed on the Word in the Scriptures. Since he came to the Community, however, the sermon has diminished in its significance for him, compared to the focal point of the Eucharist. The congregation hears the Word in the readings and sermon, but receives the Word in the sacraments.

During the history of the Community of Celebration, from its beginnings in the sixties in Houston, Texas, the influence of the wide variety of people who have visited, lived with and affected the life of the Community has been apparent. The evangelical tradition has safeguarded for us the truth that the word of God is the living Word and the sermon is the ministry of the Word. From the Catholic tradition has come the understanding that the Word is present in the sacraments themselves. The fact that the Community has married the three traditions—Catholic, charismatic and evangelical—has been very important.

One weekend I was visiting friends in Birmingham, and went with them to a local Catholic church. As the service drew to a close and the congregation were beginning to move, I became aware of an old man, who from his manner and dress appeared to be poor. As he shambled out I sensed from his gait and posture towards others that he was an isolated person, alienated from them socially, too. He hurried out, but stopped at a small recess in the wall and dipped his hands in the holy water. There was a momentary stillness in him that spoke of spiritual as well as physical peace. The experience left me aware of more than the personality of the man. For so many people, the meaning and communication value of the spoken word is negligible. The power of communication through that which is touched and tasted is very much stronger for them. The word of God is most meaningful when touched as well as heard. That is the nature of the sacrament.

When church or community begins to serve both neighbours and the poor who come among them, the Eucharist takes on new meaning. No longer is the service a simple memorial; it takes on the added reality of being a means of grace to those who are present. When Christ is present among his people in a tangible form, every person present, regardless of her mood or state of mind, can experience Christ outside of herself and her own problems. If Christ were only present to the extent an individual felt that presence, many Christians whose lives are full of discouragement and suffering would never experience his grace and life for themselves. To know that Christ is present, that the sacrament can be touched and eaten, is a tangible gift from God to suffering people.

6
Caring and the Life of Prayer

Hilfield Friary, Dorset

The Anglican Franciscan community at Hilfield Friary is approached through tree-lined, single-track lanes in rural Dorset. So close are the sides of the lane that the trees touch overhead to form a leafy tunnel. Several houses cluster around a courtyard and the chapel. The Friary has been here since 1921, one of the many friaries scattered throughout the country. When we think of friars from an historical perspective, a picture comes to mind of brown-robed and sandalled Franciscans travelling from village to village and town to town, with a gospel mission of caring.

Though the travelling from town to town on foot may be less common now, the Franciscans are conscious of their history and their heritage. Their particular position within the worldwide church, as disciples whose life may be structured around their Christian commitment, has brought many people to them for refreshment and renewal.

Brother Bernard, besides being Guardian of the Hilfield community, is spiritual director and helper to many individual Christians and groups. His role within the community involves oversight of this ministry as well as the life of the Brothers.

For Bernard, caring is not a higher calling that belongs to some and not to others: 'Christians are not called to the poor who need help; everybody needs help, the poor may need less help than the middle class blind people. Caring is neither essentially beyond the calling of the least of us, nor are there two kinds of people, those who give and those who receive, all of us are both.'

Since the Friary began its ministry at Hilfield, it has been a regular stopping-off point for men of the road, that wandering population who for a multitude of reasons have turned their backs on the more conventional lifestyle of the rest of society, or have been pushed out. Just as every vicarage has several callers a week asking for money or sandwiches, the Friary offers hospitality (a bed and meals) to those who soon become familiar with its secluded location. The men stay a couple of days and then move on again to another town, another hostel, another refuge. Brother Bernard explained that there is in the Franciscan spirit a specific concern for the people at the bottom of the pile. Built into their constitution and their approach to life and ministry is helping homeless men. For the men who come, it is a passing through service, with the occasional possibility of the community's helping some of them beyond that. But a lot come—fifteen on an ordinary weekend, and twenty-three at Christmas.

There are men in permanent care at the Friary who are handicapped in various ways: one is blind, one is extremely nervous, another has a speech difficulty, another is an alcoholic. The Friary has a house for people who come with shorter-term needs, such as clergy who get into difficulties or younger men in need of rehabilitation. Then other people come in for the day or part of the day. Yet Bernard has to say 'no' a lot more often than he would like.

It was an ordinary Saturday morning at Hilfield Friary. A group of teenagers came from a Coventry school, young and inner-city born, who had never visited anywhere like this before. The Brothers have a long day's work and keep silence from after Compline at 9.45 pm till their conference at 8.45 am the following morning. This time provides space for reading and praying and just getting away from people for a while.

Various guests and men off the road were at the silent

breakfast, including some younger people, who were holding a whispered conversation between themselves. Among those staying in the house for men with problems was also a very damaged person, who comes for a week's holiday once a year. One of his difficulties is that he has little real judgement about the volume of voice to use when he speaks, so he always shouts. That particular day he felt responsible for the silence at breakfast; he turned round and spotted one of the teenagers talking in a very low voice to another about where to get something, to which none of the friars objected. The man yelled out, 'It's a silent breakfast and we don't talk here.' The adjustment to his behaviour for all the different groups there—friars, men of the road, other troubled men, and school children—was quite demanding. The teenagers were already over-awed about being in a house like this, and then found that they weren't behaving properly!

Such tensions become apparent when disturbed people are brought alongside others individually and in groups. Sometimes the group into which they come can be prepared, through conversation and teaching, but often the disturbed person in his unpredictable and uncontrolled behaviour affects and even frightens others. There are situations where the mixing may happen creatively, such as in sheltered housing or as here in a close-knit community, but at other times attempts to integrate mentally sick people into society generally has unfortunate results.

Ministry at the Lower End of the Scale

The life and ministry of the Franciscans have resulted in an awareness that in the Body of Christ there are different ministries within the one calling to be in Christ, because no-one can be Christ alone. Individuals may offer a variety of gifts, and in the same way different groups have different emphases, and the Franciscans work particularly with people at the lower end of the social scale.

Francis came to self-realisation when he kissed a leper, crossing the barrier of his own fear and inhibition, 'for the love of Christ's sake'. Francis subsequently served lepers and always delighted in the poor. He sat on the ground to eat food at banquets rather than at the high table, and witnessed very strongly to what mattered in life, as opposed to the false values of the affluence around him.

Francis would have preferred a life of solitude, as he was primarily a contemplative. Yet he was the first of the religious founders to put mission into the rule; he was a great enthusiast for preaching and mission, and—at a time when the Moslem nations were feared as much as the Communist nations are today—crossed the boundaries to preach to Moslems.

The primitive Franciscan ideal was the care for God's poor, and it has inspired Western Christendom since. It is not uniformly the focus of contemporary Franciscans—in the Roman Catholic Church a great number of Franciscans are parish priests or school teachers—but Bernard observes, 'Franciscans have that image of being of the people and popular'. We see this in literature in Friar Lawrence (who helped Romeo and Juliet), and even in Friar Tuck.

Brothers

When the Franciscans started, everyone was called 'brother', whether they wore a habit or not. They have always had a common table—always eating together. Bernard reflects on his own limitations made apparent by such a life style, 'I find myself so limited as a human being in the amount of myself I can share if I sit down to every meal with forty or fifty people. Some of them are school kids visiting for the first time, some are psychologically disturbed, some are alcoholics resting with us, and some are men of the road, I'm not Jesus—I can't lead the fifty, let alone the five thousand.' He continues to explain that within limitations the friars do treat the men as ordinary people, at least in their basic attitudes. The friars don't screen them, or hassle them or pry into why they are doing what they are doing, or try to change them.

The Christian motivation for caring lies in the theology of personhood. The friars had just kept the Feast of the

Ascension, when the Church recognises that Christ has taken humanity for all eternity into the Godhead. So every human being is potentially in God, and people are all at different levels of fulfilling that potential. The friars therefore treat everybody as a reborn person in God, however much he, or the friars themselves, may not show it. Bernard concludes, 'That's the theology and the vision, though I find the gap between the theology and the performance is alarming, both in myself and in other people, but that's the concept and the vision. We live in partial truth and see only partially. In the same way we all partially live out what we know to be the Gospel.'

A Caring Community

As they are structured today, Christian communities are able to offer different aspects of caring ministry from those local churches can usually undertake. The community is freer to organise its own day, normally having a timetable that revolves around prayer; whereas for most people in the Church the world around them sets the timetable, and they fit their prayer into their routines. Additionally, the local church lives as small family groupings—the nuclear family or friends sharing a house—generally with at least one member of the family having a full-time job outside the home, and the homes being scattered through an area or neighbourhood. The community, on the other hand, with its work and prayer life under one roof, has far more resources for offering residential help where it is needed; it is, however, more separated from the day-to-day good neighbourliness that is a common expression in the local church.

In their inner-city houses, as they tried to be more self-sufficient, the Franciscans have taken part-time jobs, nearly always of a caring nature. In addition they have maintained both their prayer life and their community life, but they usually also have some sort of voluntary caring work. This kind of pattern is more similar to the daily routine of the ordinary church member. Bernard comments, 'If you think of a local church as being its people, a local community, all of them are tremendously caring. They're going home to look after their sick mother, and bringing up their children. They're caring for one another in the family, in their marriages and at work.'

Places like the Friary are in some way signposts of caring, incarnating human values that are being expressed all the time in a variety of settings. The degree of caring among those living in cardboard boxes in London, for instance, is very high. They've become neighbours to each other. In addition, there are people who come round with hand-outs, with soup and other food stuff.

Though no human being is perfect and everyone has problems, the people the friars are dealing with are those who have gone wrong socially and whose problems have emerged in their particular way. For most people it is a matter of caring for each other, problems and all. One does have to distinguish between the congregation meeting as a congregation to plan certain caring tasks, and the congregation as human beings living the caring life to which all Christians are called.

It suits the world to think of the Church as interested only in itself, but that isn't true. Some churches act conspicuously to 'demonstrate' that they are the caring church, but in reality most churches are very caring.

If a person is using caring work as a justification for himself or the church, he may heroically attempt to do too much. There is a danger in the Church, if people overstrive to demonstrate that they are caring people, that part of the caring becomes a performance. The motivation for caring is therefore important. Bernard adds, 'A balanced motivation lies in knowing that we are not the Saviour. We have to accept that we do our two-pennyworth, and though it isn't enough, that is all we can do.'

Styles of Caring

The way in which we talk about caring as a ministry can in itself be a sign that our motives are patronising; is it possible to consider caring as a separate aspect of the Christian life and discipleship? Most of us who live in families, churches or lively local communities experience mutual caring, for that is a key to the existence of such groups. When we look upon caring as an extra to ordinary life, then we have to reassess the style in which we live. Have we heard criticism that has made us self-critical, unable to see the everyday caring that is going on? Have we valued some kinds of caring more than others? Is it of more value to care for down-and-outs than for our own family members? Have we got our lives so ordered and protected that we care for no-one and no-one cares for us, so caring has to be a conscious effort?

To Bernard, there are dangers inherent in any discussion of caring. 'There is something capitalist and middle-class about the concept of caring. "We are the ones who work hard and earn our living. We are the ones who have come to the top and now from our successful place we give peanuts away while we help ourselves." We've become professional so that people train themselves to be professional carers, but it actually comes from *above*.' The contemporary notions of self-help, group tasks and members contributing what they can and receiving what they need seems a healthier one in the end.

The Franciscans are looking at the base communities of South America (see p 4) where the poor are trying to adopt new values while subject to oppressive social structures, and so bring themselves into a new society. Helping and caring for them means being brotherly, and is not from above. The evaluation of the relevance of the principles learned there will take time, and in the meantime the Franciscans go on with their present ways of working, having discovered that the lifestyle of the carers does affect the quality of the caring that they can give, whether from a great height or from alongside. Ideally giving includes receiving. If the lifestyle says, 'I don't need anything from you' there is no opportunity for the other person to give. Bernard reflects the understanding that has grown in the last two decades.

The men who come into the Friary off the road are usually just passing through. They sometimes contribute their work, but the friars do not hold to the old workhouse idea where a man received a free night's board and lodging but had to do so many hours' work before he could go on. The friars don't *require* any work; the care is a gift, not a contract. But some of the men give a lot in their generosity. They share in washing up; they keep the house where they live very clean.

Just after the Friary opened its new house for the men of the road, two of the men asked if they could stay on and help, because the Brothers were going to paint the chapel on the following week. One of the men was a painter and the other was a steeplejack. So they worked all night and the Brothers worked all day and the work got done in a week. It was a pure gift on the part of the men.

The people that are handicapped all work according to their capacities, making some contribution, laying tables or clearing up the rubbish or working in the gardens. The friars couldn't run the Friary without those people, being dependent on them for their work.

There is a very fine line between opportunities for people to contribute, to give as well as receive—and actual requirements that people give in return for having received. Just as God gives to all people 'rain on the just and unjust'—those who serve him will give without condition. God gives, and leaves each free to choose whether to reciprocate that love, or not.

Real Values

A religious community is a signpost to a reality. One recognises the difference between the signpost and the reality, and the difference between the stereotype and the reality. Monastic vows are in themselves a reflection or sign of the commitment all Christians make in baptism—to renounce the world, the flesh and the devil. In commenting on the commitment to poverty, Bernard recognises the decrease in sharing with one another that is evident in richer nations of the world. 'You might say that we have given up everything, but we still have things. If we compare ourselves with the majority of people in the world, we are extremely rich in material things.'

Bernard had been to New Guinea where the Franciscans have a community, and one Brother recently returned from Tanzania. In those places, poverty isn't a sophisticated, cultivated matter of people simply having fewer things than they might have had. Such a life points to real values—'Don't be anxious, your heavenly Father knows you need all these things'—trusting in divine providence and living simply in confidence in God's world, and recognising a person can't meet his spiritual and emotional needs through material things.

Being Formed

What Christians try to do is show the same care for everyone else as the Lord shows for them. Christian caring does not put down, patronise or make others into permanent invalids. Loving that creates an environment where responsibility and maturity can grow can be very tough and demanding.

The daily prayer life of the Christian community is the means by which the mind of Christ goes on being formed in the members. It is a life-long process to perfect Christians in their discipleship, their way of offering the love of Christ to those they meet on the way. Bernard comments, 'One hopes that the listening to the word, the responding and praying, actually do nourish us towards the mind of Christ in our caring. In prayer we move over—God is after all God, and we can't be the Saviour to these people, just as we can't be our own saviour.'

The carer has to have one foot in the problem situation and the other outside it: it's only if he empathises and gets into the dilemma with the person that he is able to speak to them. And it's only if he has one foot outside that he doesn't get sucked into the emotional difficulties. That balance is very much strengthened by prayer.

That balance is also a sort of respite for Bernard, underneath the praying and in the praying, without this being a conscious thing. Bernard finds he is broken by what he can't do, more than by what he can do. A man had spoken to him, asking if he could stay at the community longer, because he had had his tools stolen. Meanwhile a job had come up which he couldn't get because he hadn't got the tools. After that he received a bit of money from the Social Services, but he was then mugged in the place where he was living. He was shaken up, angry and hurt about it all, and so asked if he could stay longer at the Friary. He was a man with a record of burglary and obviously a very disturbed man, so Bernard had to say to himself, 'If I had a bed, could the other members of the house cope?'—because there's nothing that destroys community more than thieving. Bernard didn't know if the man would settle down, or if his story was accurate, anyway. In the end Bernard had to say to him, 'You can stay over till Monday, but I'm afraid you can't stay any longer than that.' That was hard to do; it is extremely hard in winter putting old men back on the road at nine o'clock on a Monday morning.

Bernard believes there is so much wrong in the world that he has to bring the unmet needs into prayer. There is a ministry of word as well as a ministry of action, and there is a ministry of prayer undergirding both.

The prayer-life of a community enables its members to bring their own weakness and the pain of others before God, and in the stillness that is the heart of contemplation to know that redemption for it all lies in the cross. The inability to make all things good for everyone they meet can be resolved in the context of community, by acknowledgement and acceptance of the members' own humanity, by intercession for those who suffer, and by the corporate discipline of obedience. Through obedience, members of the community determine together what work and ministry each member should be undertaking; there is safety in this corporateness, which protects each member from the danger of trying to do more than is possible for any human being, from becoming proud, or from feeling he will be justified by the amount of caring he can do.

The long history and heritage of community living has also allowed a reflection and resolution of the tension of everyday human caring. The fellowship of a strong community helps the individual overcome the weariness or discouragement of daily ministry. Failure is a continuing factor in all caring ministry, but in the depth of prayer and in the support of fellowship, there is the peace of God's grace and redemption.

7
A Gentle Healing Spirit

Shipton Oliffe, Gloucestershire

Jeremy Hutton is vicar of a small group of Anglican parishes in Gloucestershire. Shipton Oliffe, where the vicarage is located, is a cluster of Cotswold stone cottages and old farm houses, a church and a village hall. The road that once dipped through a ford now bridges the shallow stream to lead past a picturesque farmhouse and on upwards out of the village; after the spur of a hill it descends into another valley and another of the villages under Jeremy's pastoral care.

There was a revolution inherent in the way Jeremy Hutton saw the Bible when renewal began to touch his life. 'I lost the General Ordinand's Examination approach and saw the Bible as a living book. I knew that Jesus intervened in people's lives in a powerful way because that was my own conversion experience—that he really does come into the heart of the situation. There's nothing that he can't change, and however intractable the problem might seem, Jesus can change it.'

Jeremy sees himself as a cautious person, but faced with the problems of parish and family, asks himself, 'Now, what would Jesus do? Jesus wouldn't have left a person standing, no matter what.'

Graham Pulkingham was speaking at the first seminar when Jeremy and Jane, his wife, went to Watcombe House, in Dorset, in 1973. During his talks about the Sermon on the Mount, Graham asked, 'What is a Christian?

What does he look like? What does he do? How does he think and how does he feel?' For Jeremy these opened up a new perspective on caring. Through the seminar Jeremy and Jane realised that ministry had to be all-encompassing. Caring is not an addition to daily life; it is a way of life that affects and integrates the whole of life, relationships and lifestyle.

Where Jeremy is reticent, Jane by instinct seems to be an out-going person. Jeremy observes, 'Jane can't hear of a problem before she rushes out to do something about it immediately.' Yet Jane cares, not just as the vicar's wife, but as a friend and neighbour. 'From the day we were married I have known that people have their own view of who the clergy and clergy wives are. I have made it my business in all these years to let everyone know that a vicar's wife is a perfectly ordinary, fallible person. First and foremost you're an ordinary person who bothers about another ordinary person.'

One of the parishioners rang up asking for help, so Jane leapt on her bike, thinking, 'Lord, you will have to tell me what to say as I have absolutely no clue what the problem is or what this person needs.'

When Jane went into the house, the woman said, 'You'll never know what a dreadful thing is going through my mind.'

Jane responded, 'Well the most dreadful thing I ever thought was such-and-such.' Jane's honest response portrayed a 'something' worse than what the woman herself was thinking. She grabbed hold of Jane, for in her she saw safety and sanity. Together, they talked and prayed over two or three days. She was anointed with oil when Jeremy and Jane prayed with her, and they held a Eucharist to commit various parts of her situation to God.

Jane adds, 'This woman has changed so that Jesus is no longer a person who goes along with her; Jesus is the whole of her life, and she goes along with him. So I have just been a vehicle in passing, to help her.'

Farming in Shipton Oliffe for nearly thirty years, the

Bailley Hamiltons, Angus and Prue, have seen great changes in village life during that time. Few people have been in the village longer. When Angus and Prue first came, most local people worked in agriculture in the immediate area; now such people form a tiny minority. Farming methods and lifestyles have changed, and most of the village folk now commute into Cheltenham or Gloucester to work, the village having become a dormitory. The community spirit has slowly evaporated.

A man in his sixties who made a commitment at a recent mission led by members of St Andrew's Church, Chorleywood, said that as a boy he learned to dance in the village hall, where there was a weekly dance. There is perhaps only one dance a year now.

Prue observes, 'There's no shop or pub for people to go to and meet others. People don't walk through the village and stop to chat; they drive. The bus service is probably one of the few ways to meet others. But fewer and fewer use it. People don't know each other, and there isn't the sense of community there used to be.'

Angus adds, 'There can be a negative side to pubs, but an awful lot of good goes on as people meet each other socially. And we lack even that point of contact.'

Such diminished channels of communication result in difficulty in knowing whether somebody needs any form of help or care. As the rector, Jeremy has more opportunity to meet the local people and is a person others naturally turn to even if they don't know him personally—part of his traditional role as a vicar. In the prayer group on Wednesday mornings it is Jeremy and Jane who know the people with specific needs for prayer. As a layman with a job, however, Angus finds it harder to get alongside many people, knowing only if any of his own employees or immediate neighbours need help, but on many occasions not hearing about others until after the crisis is past.

The structures of life have changed considerably. The social patterns that give more independence and freedom of choice have also separated people from the established patterns through which they cared for one another. Often such care was so much an accepted part of life that it was almost unconscious; now if the good neighbourliness is to be a quality of the local community, it requires conscious organisation, drive, and a common feeling of concern for its re-establishment. Such revitalisation of village life and caring for neighbours can come through the church.

Prue has seen the connection between the busy lives local people lead and the increased awareness that they 'keep themselves to themselves', and if they have a problem, they feel they have no-one to share it with. She has made attempts to establish communication links through the church and the parish magazines. A continuing effect of the church in Shipton Oliffe has been to create a network of neighbourly contact and caring.

Drawing People Together

Jane comments, 'In worship people taste something that brings them back next week.' On his arrival, Jeremy began the round of services, Sunday after Sunday. In each of the churches under his care the effect can be seen, because he has a profound understanding of the encounter with God that happens in a service. In worship the congregation enters into a different realm. Lives are affected, and non-Christians may experience their first encounter with God, while those who are already disciples gain a new sense of vision and power for serving others. Jeremy speaks of his understanding:

> Worship honours God, puts God first, lifts God up. In honouring God, putting God first, and lifting God up, we ourselves are lifted up; we get involved in God's plan and Kingdom. Worship is an inspirational time, when the vision comes and when the vision to follow through is renewed. So on a Sunday morning the prayers bring together the whole concern of God for his world. Without a vibrant worship, and above all a worship with great integrity, all the other caring would simply collapse and become prosaic, reduced to an ordinary, humanistic way of caring, which—

> while it gives some value—doesn't really value people as the sons and daughters for whom Christ died. This is the essential thing to remember: that everybody—every single person we work with— is also a person for whom Christ died; one is reminded of this time and time again in prayers and worship.
>
> The Gospel must come together in all its manifold aspects in the parish church on Sundays, not just in the spoken word, in the preaching of the Gospel, but in every other way. If the Gospel is not fully alive in the worship, then the church is not really alive.

Such understanding brings integration between worship services and the daily caring in the local community.

Jean Packer, whose husband Bob is a local postman, has lived in Shipton Oliffe for fourteen years, going to church very occasionally. When Jeremy and Jane came to the village she went along 'to have a look at the new people'.

At the time Jean had a feeling of dissatisfaction and found herself extremely critical of family and friends, yet underneath she was aware that she was the one with a problem.

Jeremy said something at that first service that Jean had never heard before, 'You have to ask Jesus into your life.'

Once home, Jean went straight into her bedroom, knelt down and asked Jesus to come into her life. 'I didn't believe in him at all, I just got up and thought "Well, nothing's happened" and carried on as normal.'

In the midst of recurrent bouts of depression she eventually prayed more determinedly and became more aware of the peace of God in her life. She went to church again and was invited along to a mothers' group. Jean had never been to anything like that before and found there was a choice between going to one meeting on childcare, and going to a nearby village where the group would be talking about God. She remembered thinking that it really wasn't her scene, but that if she was really going to go, she might as well go to hear about God. She went along but wouldn't ask any questions and so later went to the library. There she read lots of different books, and she kept going to the meetings.

Friends who Cared

A group from the church was meeting regularly to listen to tapes of Colin Urquhart teaching on the Holy Spirit. Jean went to the seminars, and as she came away one day, she asked Bet King, one of her neighbours, a question about what it meant to be filled with the Spirit. They prayed together, but Jean remembers, 'I had ten days of complete blackness. Then when I accepted the gift of tongues, that lifted.'

Over a period of two years Jean received regular ministry. Jane and Jeremy were always ready to help, and in the early days Jean often appeared on the doorstep, asking for help. In a growing friendship Bet and Jean found times to talk and pray together, and this helped Jean cope.

Her reading was also helping her, and in the Bible studies she found that one verse became very special to her, 'Do not conform any more to the pattern of this world, but be transformed by the renewing of your mind. Then you will be able to test and approve what God's will is—his good, pleasing and perfect will' (Romans 12:2). While at the time Jean did not understand the verse, through the fellowship and the prayer God was healing the source of the depression. She heard God saying, 'Keep going, it will all work out.'

Jean experienced God's healing grace in the life of the church. The persistent good-neighbourliness so readily offered brought life where there had been only darkness, isolation and depression; friendship blossomed, too, in the knowledge of God's grace. Jean continued to experience that grace when she was later pregnant and having problems—fearing that she was going to miscarry again. Bob, her husband, phoned Jane late one night to ask for help, and praying together was reassuring. At the hospital, however, Jean had a scan, and the placenta was found to be too low. After a week in hospital the doctor advised,

'Go home, as I can't do anything more, but do take it easy.'

The church was planning a mission led by members of the church of St Andrews, Chorleywood, and the mission team came to talk to the Church Council, so Jean went along that night. Ian Roberts talked about having been a surgeon before he became a clergyman. Jean explained her own problems to him and he prayed with her. She remembers:

> It was seven weeks from when I had come home from hospital and I was still having problems. After he prayed I had a real sense of peace, that everything would be all right. From that very night, I bled no more. At Christmas I had another scan. Everything had moved into place and I had a normal delivery, on St David's Day. My husband came in with the children, and said, 'Right, we'll call him David.'

Jeremy—knowing the grace and healing that is ministered this way—has a special Eucharist for those with particular needs. While being formal, this is an important opportunity for people to pray individually with others and through the sacrament to receive the grace of God. The use of the Eucharistic form identifies the one who prays with the Church in general, and it reassures the person that he or she is not peculiar, nor the only one who has ever come to the church and to God with very painful needs. In the context of the sacrament and prayer, God usually makes an enormous change in the individuals, and those who pray know this is God's grace because they have set out to seek God. These Eucharists have changed people's attitudes to Communion and to the life and work of the church.

Outside Help and Encouragement

During the years of the developing ministry in Shipton Oliffe, the church has been helped by other churches and ministries. A number of the people who have become committed members of the church were first challenged and encouraged by a group visit to the Lee Abbey

Community at Lynton in North Devon. This is a Christian conference centre, staffed by the members of the Community, which runs courses and seminars on many aspects of the Christian life. Through this visit the sense of fellowship deepened for the people from Shipton Oliffe, and their common understanding of the Gospel deepened.

Jeremy also says that the fellowship with leaders of the Community of Celebration in Dorset was pivotal in supporting and establishing the vision, and gave them confidence to press on without discouragement.

Within the parish in Shipton Oliffe, at North Farm, another fellowship had been established that brought encouragement to many Christians in the isolated Cotswold villages. Among the speakers Dr Dennis Ball was a regular favourite, and there were Bible studies and times of worship with a charismatic thrust. For the many people who visited, North Farm was the only place where they experienced renewal in the Spirit and training in leadership of their own renewal groups.

To small and scattered churches such as that at Shipton Oliffe the resources available for ministry are limited, and the resultant fruit may seem slight. But an increase of ten people may be a miracle, doubling the congregation. Without outside encouragement and fellowship, the ministry itself would be discouragingly small. Over some years, however, the investment of life and energy has borne fruit. Other people have joined Jeremy and Jane in the commitment to the caring ministry of the church, joining with them to pray for others and address the spiritual needs of the parish.

Betty Dodwell has seen change in the church. 'There has been a lot of preparation for caring for each other. There was always a tiny nucleus, and it has grown. For me the church has altered greatly, as I have heard the Lord speak to me about helping other people.'

From a fairly uncommitted beginning, Betty has seen member after member of her family become committed Christians. The influence of John Wimber's work has helped to guide and train her to be one who serves others in the church.

Attending the John Wimber conference in Sheffield, Betty was excited. She received the impression that she was to be given the necessary gifts at the time when they were needed. She knew therefore that she had to step out in faith, not knowing for sure whether she would be given the gift for that occasion, because it was *the Lord's* gift, not one to be for her exclusive possession. The teaching gave her the feeling that if she failed, she could say, 'Well, I'm sorry Lord', and that he would much rather she stepped out and failed than that she did not try at all.

Having enjoyed John Wimber's talk, Betty felt uncomfortable and restricted when the gathering split up into small groups for ministry, but then in the evening she saw the others ministering to one another, and saw how people had such peace afterwards, and felt differently.

That evening she was sitting near an old Yorkshire couple, and the man tapped her on the shoulder and said, 'Would you mind praying for me?' As Betty was praying for him, the man began to receive the Holy Spirit.

For Betty this ministry confirmed the significance and importance of the Church, that this is the Body, in the context of which gifts of the Spirit are expressed. Her determination—'There's no more going out on your own; how you serve or what you do is in the church'—reflects a strong sense of the local church having a ministry to the neighbourhood.

Sharing the Ministry

Over the years much growth has taken place in the life of the church. On his first Sunday Jeremy looked out at the congregation and prayed under his breath, 'Lord, you've got to help me out.' This was the service in which Jean gave her life to the Lord.

Now, with Jean and other people having come through conversion and matured in their commitment, they are themselves giving direction to Bible study and the mothers' group. Others—new contacts—see life in this second generation and are touched by it. Jean discovered that ministry meant ordinary people doing ordinary things for one another; it meant being practical and bringing God into the ordinary, everyday situations.

One new contact of the group is a girl from another village who came looking for help. After the group prayed for her little boy, who had trouble sleeping, her real problem came to light. She had marriage problems and the group is offering friendship and care.

Jeremy's perception of his ministry has been heightened, as he says, 'Every little thing we do has become important because of its seed-bearing potential, for nurturing and growth. Therefore this whole ministry, which I didn't think at first was all that important, has become something I now recognise as infinitely important.'

Jane recalls how a friend had given them a picture when the family arrived in Shipton Oliffe: stones were being gathered up one by one to make a well, a drinking place, with a pool of clear, fresh, good water, where all the people from round about could come and drink. As local people have taken responsibility for the ministry of this church, it has become more firmly rooted and is no longer subject to ministers coming and going. If the vicar should leave, the caring can continue. The church, as a whole, can and will affect the quality of life in the village; the church can offer the neighbourliness which Angus and Prue had seen disappearing. The grace expressed through the whole church, not just through the ordained ministry, will continue as it is founded on the committed discipleship of local people.

There has been a gradual growth in the church at Shipton Oliffe. The vision in the small core of leaders drew people into the worship. Those who were hurt received help. Those who came have taken responsibility and have turned to help others. On this is founded the caring ministry that belongs to the church, a ministry that cannot be sustained by any individual. The loving nature of God, the Trinity, in close, self-sacrificing relationships, is a unity that is expressed in the community of the Church.

8
A Local Community Where No-one Cared

Low Hill, Wolverhampton

A vicar in a rather pleasant part of Yorkshire put up a new poster outside his church: 'Only sinners welcome here'. His congregation was shocked; it was embarrassing to go into church on Sunday mornings; some passer-by might get the wrong impression about their morals. On the other hand, there are churches and parishes where the people would have laughed and said, 'Yes. That's us!'

Low Hill is a huge and dilapidated housing development on the North-East side of Wolverhampton. After World War I, local authorities were empowered to build such sprawling estates. Garden cities sprang up around the major population centres in Britain, presenting a new approach to urban development. However, Wolverhampton was short of money in creating what was to become its biggest housing estate; the streets and roads of Low Hill were laid out in the geometric patterns typical of the Garden City movement, but without regard to the lie of the land. Essential social and community facilities were not added until years later. Slum clearance in the city centre was Wolverhampton Council's most pressing concern, as well as housing for the influx of people looking for work in the area. Low Hill soon got a bad name.

Bushbury was the Anglican parish into which this new development fitted. In 1938, this was Wolverhampton's largest parish, with one-third of the city's population. In

Oxley, a similar estate but consisting of predominantly private dwellings, the Church built a vicarage, a hall and a church. In Low Hill, a mission hut was built under the pastoral umbrella of the parish church—St Mary's, Bushbury.

Mrs Summerfield, now the only remaining member of the congregation from the first days of the mission hut, remembers thirty people coming to the first Sunday evening services. In the morning, the Holy Communion was at quarter to nine, and the Sunday School met at eleven.

The mission building found additional use as a day school, and Mrs Jordan, who lived in Goodyear Avenue, was the caretaker.

In 1946 the mission church was burnt down and left derelict. The congregation made a Council Office in Fifth Avenue into a church to hold their Sunday services. With regret Mrs Summerfield recognised the attitudes of those outside Low Hill when the services at the Council Office were stopped. The congregation had to trail up to the parish church. But members were lost in the change—friends of Mrs Summerfield's whom she remembers with sadness: the Prices, Mrs Jordan, Mrs Lewis. They went to the Methodist church, and the children had to go to the community centre. Mrs Summerfield continues, 'The parish always looked down on us. We were not as good as them. Mind you, when we used to have the Mother's Union in the old mission hut, they used to come down every month.'

Local churchgoers looked forward to the rebuilding of the mission church, wanting a place of their own. They were told that on the site of the old hut they would have a church house as well as a little church. The Church authorities wanted to extend the facilities so that there could be a place for the children. But, as Mrs Summerfield notes wistfully, 'In the end we didn't have anything—just the one building.'

The new Church of the Good Shepherd was built economically, its shell the half cylinder of a Nissen hut and its floor of cement, more familiar as Army barracks than as church architecture. It was, and is, bleak, bare and noisy. Mrs Summerfield says sadly, 'I was hoping the floor would be covered.'

The Church of the Good Shepherd seemed hopeless. Located in an area in which institutional and personal hopelessness prevailed, it stood no chance of being different. The prognosis of closure was predictable and realistic. The Anglican Church could pull out the few resources that it had invested there for a constantly diminishing return. The local people would have to stay in Low Hill, but they found no relevant meaning in the Church. So who would care if the church pulled out?

The unexpected factor, that which was catalyst to the turnabout in the church's vision, was that someone in the church *did* care; the Reverend Robert Johnson and his wife cared and were committed to the church becoming meaningful for the ordinary people in Low Hill.

The church gathered its own group in 1984 to report to the Archbishop's Commission on Urban Priority Areas and drew up its own resumé of the more recent history.

> Once rebuilt on the old site, [the Church of the Good Shepherd] was served by a succession of curates who were expected to see as their primary responsibility the preservation of the Parish Church of St Mary's. A steady decline took place in the 1960's, arrested briefly in 1968 to 1970, with the promise of a new building, but accelerated when the promise was not fulfilled.
>
> When a team ministry was set up just after Robert Johnson [vicar] arrived in 1976 from Liverpool, it was assumed that it would be impossible to maintain a viable church in Low Hill beyond two years.
>
> Instead there was rapid and unsustainable growth. A new vision was conceived and the number of clergy was extended to two.[2]

Lin was a biker whose friend had started going to church; and Lin wanted to know more. 'I wanted a bit of what she'd got. She had such a lot in her life, so much happiness, peace, and joy. I thought—how can you have that when you live in this sort of place? So I said, "Dave, come on, let's go."'

Lin's husband Dave thought, 'The only way to get me in there will be in a box.' But Lin wanted to go, and she kept asking him to go with her. Eventually he agreed, meaning to make fun of the service when he got there. But the way he was welcomed showed love straight away. At first Dave took the love the wrong way, understanding it as a sexual love; and it took a while for him to realise that Christian love was different. The only love he had known was, as he said— 'Getting into bed, and that was the only love I wanted to know.'

Dave and Lin were among the remarkable influx of new members that changed the plans for the Good Shepherd. The change in their lives was profound, soon expressed in a longing to help others out of positions similar to the one they had been in themselves. The love they had received could be expressed in love and concern for others. Lin said, 'I want to give the bikers what we have found. I know what it's like—a biker's life—and it's not a happy time. Lots of things have happened that I'm not proud of or like to remember. I want to give them the faith I have found, which has changed my life.'

A Trapped Existence

Low Hill has seen developments over the years. Social amenities now include four schools, a library, a community centre, a doctor's surgery, and several pubs and shops. Under the surface, however, there were still problems, as the group reporting to the Archbishop's Commission continues in its description:

> There is an increase of social problems, and areas of difficulty are increasing; a decline in law and order, and an increase in juvenile delinquency, criminality and prostitution ... are obvious. This trend of the 'undesirables' and the 'problem families' being seen as an acceptable part of Low Hill has led to the following:
>
> People of Low Hill have low self-esteem, no sense of self-worth, a lack of purpose and no goals to aim

> at. The children receive no encouragement at home, and the teachers don't seem to give them any at school. This trapped existence can blow up as tension comes economically and parents have to choose between something for the kids and a bill. Then comes the decision to 'blow' it and that is what happens with the bill money from the fortnightly payment. You never make up the 'borrowing' and the involvement with debt agencies only makes it worse.
>
> Those outside Low Hill see it as 'not a nice area', and the people ... as not 'human'. Parents have been distraught at the thought of their children having to go and live there.[3]

These social problems are reflected in the daily experiences of the church members and stories are told with laughter; still, the commonplace nature of the social 'problems' decreases but does not remove the intensity of the stress created by them. The people of Low Hill feel trapped.

In areas around Low Hill where factories do operate, for example, a person has a good chance of getting a job when one comes vacant, if his or her father or uncle or aunt already works in one of these factories. This is a chance that other young people don't have. Thus it is not just a middle-class and working-class separation. The children of those of the working class who have work get opportunities that other children don't get. The local union representatives make sure that jobs are kept in the family. When factories have operated Youth Training Schemes, approval has been given on condition that first choice went to the workers' children. As fewer and fewer people in Low Hill work, the opportunities for their children get fewer and fewer, so the unemployment problems multiply. Since 1971 the unemployment figure here has gone up by a multiple of six.

The attitudes of the people outside Low Hill affect those who live here. Many of those who do get a job move to better areas. Robert Johnson notes that as local people are continually pushed by people in authority, after a while they begin to believe in the validity of the rejection. The church asked a number of young people on the Youth Training Scheme to write about themselves and found the responses were pathetic. Without exception the youngsters wrote, 'I am worth nothing. They tell me that at school. I know I am no good.' Not one wrote anything positive about himself. Yet some of their qualities were quite impressive, though they were never allowed to be seen. Pressure was put on them in schools, so that if they were not going to do a CSE or a GCE exam, the system had no time for them.

Lin observes that many of the parents wonder, 'What's the point?' and they then pass on that message of meaninglessness to their children. That circle has to be broken. Dave and Lin remember their own childhoods with warmth, when people were more friendly. Now Lin finds her family accused of snobbery for the way they care for their children, but sees her own son Matthew 'as much a little toad as any other little boy of five'. But Dave and Lin do things with their children, taking them on outings, so that the children learn about things in a way uncommon among their peers on the estate. On one occasion they were talking about tadpoles and sticklebacks with some other children—who didn't know what they were. Dave and Lin were surprised, having taken their children up to the pools and talked about the swans and the trees. But to some of the children the trees are there to be chopped down and put on a bonfire, not to be looked at or enjoyed. For a while, then, Dave and Lin's children wouldn't go to the park because they seemed to be picked on for being 'different'.

Does Anybody Care?

As I interviewed Robert, he was called to the door in the midst of our conversation; it was some minutes before he returned, with an explanation. A Mrs R. wanted him to do something about her husband, who had been hitting the family with a stick again. He had also struck the daughter's boyfriend. The husband had begun regularly sleeping in the park. So now she came round to see if Robert would help.

Robert told me that a couple of years before the man had sent his wife to the post office for the Giro payment. She wanted the money for food shopping. As she came out they had a big argument; he hit her and took the money from her. Robert added that sooner or later someone would be badly hurt; the man has a very heavy stick that he'll swing at someone's skull, or his wife may even be driven to stick a knife in him.

The tragedy is that there are whole groups of such people, and nobody cares.

Prostitution is one flourishing part of the depressed local economy; a few prostitutes are picked up at the traffic roundabout outside the vicarage at pre-arranged times. A local woman from the same street made the front page of the national daily papers. The church had helped her with what they thought was her first fine for prostitution, but it turned out she owed £180 for previous offences.

After a while the pressure becomes so great when a street is riddled with problems of violence and prostitution that families move away. Then the only families who will live next to each other are families that are equally disruptive.

Evangelism

In the report to the Archibishop's Commission the compiling group made the following appraisal of the role of the Anglican Church in Low Hill and similar places.

> What has the Church to offer? Not a lot, on the face of it. In fact, the Church is irrelevant. People here see the Church as a place for the middle class who don't care. Jesus is portrayed as the one who fits in with the nice place and the nice people who present him as one of them.[4]

In seeing the Gospel as the answer, and new life in Jesus Christ as what is needed, the Church of the Good

Shepherd has recognised that Jesus himself was a friend of prostitutes and sinners. He came bearing Good News for the poor. To bring life and hope to the poor and disadvantaged the church must—as Jesus himself did—break through many of the established protective attitudes and patterns with which the religious middle classes protect themselves.

Such a redefinition of the church's identity as the base for ministry has paved the way for reaching out to the neighbours. The Good Shepherd has set out some key words and phrases from their experience that apply to ministry in Low Hill. HOPE—there isn't much on Low Hill; ACCEPTANCE—of people as they are; MATTERING—you matter to God; you have worth and are important; PEACE OF MIND—helps you cope with pressures and problems; LIBERATION—from oppression; FREEDOM—from defensive attitudes; LOVE—that lifts you, doesn't make demands, and is free; SENSE OF BELONGING—in a fellowship that holds you together; NON-JUDGEMENTALISM—some people ask when they meet a member of the Church of the Good Shepherd, 'Can you really mix with someone like me?'

In a sermon, the previous curate, Alister, said, 'We are children of God. That places us in a tremendous position. We are heirs to the Kingdom, joint heirs with Christ. We are sons and daughters of the King.' The congregation—representative of the locality—is 50% unemployed, includes single parents and ethnic minority families, and is mainly young. Yet, struggling with its social heritage, church members seek to clothe themselves in the Gospel and take the message of Good News to the neighbours.

Clive, a lay reader, says, 'We see evangelism as a practical thing. You evangelise by what you do for individuals, so the Gospel comes alive.'

Maureen, another church member, adds, 'Around this area it is a case of the proof of the pudding being in the eating. The people round here want to see the proof of our faith in action, not in words.'

Such practical evangelism has carried the church into

projects to help the neighbourhood. A Youth Training Scheme, government funded, was set up at the church in 1981, with one of the church's trained lay readers co-ordinating the programme. Despite some surprise shown by passers-by at the use to which the building was being put, the link with local people was developed considerably. On the premises were a nursery group, a drop-in centre, and a catering service that provided very cheap meals. Painting, decorating, gardening, and building teams used the premises as a base, as well as those working with the elderly. Sadly, a change in policy designed to provide more training through local industry resulted in the funding for the scheme being withdrawn and the work stopped entirely.

A more recent and successful project has been the development of a church-sponsored scheme to provide housing for homeless young people. Vacant flats above a row of shops were acquired. Young people who were unable to look after themselves have been provided with a place to live, with some supervision, until they are able to move into other private or Council accommodation, or more permanent sheltered housing.

Milestones on a Road to Hope

The Church of the Good Shepherd sees the necessity of presenting the Gospel in experiential terms. There is a high personal and corporate cost to such discipleship; being salt and light in this neighbourhood is no easy task. In becoming not just Sunday Christians but everyday Christians, the church has recognised that it is its own life that is laid down.

There have been rows among church members, and sometimes they have felt that the whole place was being torn apart, yet there is a strong sense of togetherness in the church. Everybody has stayed, even at the times when the pressures were severe. Lin talks about the nature of the group, saying, 'We have quite a volatile group; there are so many different people all together. We know we are called to live together as one body in unity with each other.

We have a responsibility to each other, but it doesn't always work out, and we let each other down. But deep down we do see each other as important.'

Worship Means Seeing and Hearing

On Sunday morning the Good Shepherd's echoing shell rang with the music, 'Joy is the flag flown from the castle of my heart...', and moments later muscles were flexed in the actions to 'God is so big, so strong and so mighty'.

The music at the Good Shepherd is lively and enthusiastic. Why is the music such a significant element of this service, in its simple, heartfelt expression? Dave says, 'I can't really put my thoughts into words, but I can put them into songs.'

Music expresses elements of human experience in a manner where words have less significance. The logical side of a person uses words for the logical processes and communication. Music expresses joy, hope, feelings and moods, with or without words, reflecting the affective rather than the logical or reasoned. While words have their place in all cultures and societies, when a church is rooted in a sub-culture where the more verbal forms of the dominant middle-class language are inappropriate, the music reflecting the local culture can be a strong vehicle for worship.

The Church of the Good Shepherd is struggling to find a kind of worship that works both to sustain the life of the members and to include the nearby people whose lives are in disorder, and who bring that disorder in through the doors with them. Qualities of worship and nurture, of stillness in the presence of God, of moments of silence for reflection, of gentle music and quiet voices, are annihilated by a cacophony of sound, echoing back from the circular roof. Every step and movement causes a clatter on the bare cement floor. As Dave says, 'A lot of the kids run around, and I don't mind except when they carry a ball and chain with them. That makes it worse!'

Lin puts into words the principles that the church works with in planning each morning service, the service to which the whole church family comes, along with a number of neighbours. It is good for parents to be able to bring their children, and people feel free to do so. If, however, the church were to insist that all children must sit still, what welcome could they offer the parent who is in church with children she cannot control? When Lin and others try to help by picking up the children, they scream. 'What else can be done?' is the question they ask themselves.

In some churches it is necessary to fall in with the established pattern, no matter what. When Lin was small her grandmother used to take her to church and say, 'This is how it is done, and you have to do the same.' Not so at the Church of the Good Shepherd, where members know each other well. They may see that someone is going to have a problem—perhaps they know that another person doesn't read well, or somebody else is going to have difficulty with a child. It isn't so easy, then, to make hard and fast rules about how worship should be conducted, when the aim includes compassion and consideration for neighbours and people who are new to the services.

The people find God in the reality of what they are seeing and hearing, and in what they are learning in the Christian body. Worship is a very important part of finding that reality. The church endeavours to make worship real for its people, but that is not easy when there are so many different needs, so the Good Shepherd has tried using a variety of forms and liturgies.

The tension of rediscovering a reverent atmosphere in the busy worship service—a tension which appears in the polarity between inclusiveness for a disorderly neighbourhood, and a traditional quiet reverence—could have resulted in conflict between members. The two needs cannot be simultaneously met in this primitive and noisy building. In his book *The Power of the Powerless*, Jürgen Moltmann[5] speaks of the fact that oppressed people blame and fight each other and eventually become inwardly destructive. In the case of the Good Shepherd the source of the difficulty lies not so much in the people and the problems they struggle with, as in the church authority, which built very cheaply, and perhaps inexcusably, a building that by form and nature destroys worship. An atmosphere of reverence would be more possible in a building that was designed to absorb sound, not rattle it back.

Local Leadership

Maureen, a member of the church council, comments that church members have been given responsibility: having ideas and being allowed to see them through. Some ideas have failed, some haven't, but it's having that chance which has been important. She talks of overcoming a personal sense of vulnerability. As in other churches, those who carry responsibility have discovered the strength of the church being constructively critical, but never competitive. Also, the individual has no status to lose from ideas or actions that failed. At the Good Shepherd, where so many of the people have been endlessly condemned by the competitive systems in education and the job market, an accepting and supportive attitude to fledgeling leadership has been an essential foundation.

Another essential element is a priest or pastor who can hand over the real responsibility for the life of the church to the people who are the church. Where the leader cannot do this, for reasons of attachment to his own status or of insecurity, such a process does not happen, and any growth in numbers is based on the charisma of the leader and so shrivels away when he moves on.

Robert Johnson has found ways to give leadership responsibility to lay members of the church. Clive himself is a local man from Low Hill who has had opportunity to develop his leadership potential as a lay reader. He has grasped the difficulty of powerlessness in Low Hill, that of the people being pushed, manipulated and controlled with no means open for them to take charge of their own lives. This sense of powerlessness has to be overcome, for the next and probably most significant stage in the development of the church in Low Hill is finding out how to say 'No' to external pressures and controls.

When people come into the church from outside, they bring with them all the neighbourhood ill-feeling, and the church suffers. Clive sees that the church first needs stability. Over the last five years there has been considerable growth, and now it is time to look at the direction of future growth, examining the whole structure in order to build in a positive way, and looking at the harvest of the last few yars and sow seed from that for the ongoing church. He adds, 'Usually we reach a sticking point where we can't get any further. Then that triggers off new thinking. We should *plan* what can happen to the people of God in Low Hill from the inside and not be controlled by some superficial act of the government or people outside. Looking back shows the importance of our doing that ourselves.'

When Robert first came to Low Hill, the church building was going to be demolished because necessary repair and modification to the structure would have cost an estimated £35,000. It had not been thought a worthwhile investment unless the church grew in numbers over the next few years. A second crisis happened more recently when, in financial terms, the church's viability was so weak that the parish discussed whether it was at all worthwhile to continue the ministry at the Good Shepherd. The church council adopted a strategy which provided sufficient money to keep the church viable: the members committing themselves to finding the necessary fund even though many received only Supplementary Benefit. With this move came a new awareness among the council and the members that the future of the church was theirs and in their hands.

Faith in the City

There is regret and concern in Low Hill that the essential caring ministry in an area such as this is under such pressure from outside, from the Church at large.

The Church of the Good Shepherd asks itself, as many

other churches ask the same question, 'Have the powers of the Church the will and resolve to take chances and truly achieve something?' Is there fire under the smoke that people in Low Hill see as the impotence of the Church when real action is essential?

Robert comments on this weakness in Church structure. The Archbishop's Report was displayed to the world as a sign of caring about the poor, but in practice this care is not evident. The report was published; criticisms of the government were presented; ideas have been put forward expressing a desire to work within the local community in those areas of the country that have not been touched by the Gospel. But what now? For the people of the Good Shepherd it seems that the more people come into contact with the decision makers of the Church, the more disappointed they become. It seems that the structure itself is incapable of understanding people, and when individuals become part of that structure, they lose their ability to relate to the actual situation.

Clive adds another perspective. Because of its systems and structures across the whole country, the Church should have a handle on everything, and it ought to be really effective. But it has never moved into the modern age—a recurrent problem in history. Where there is life and growth and the local church *is* relevant to society, the Church, because of its total lack of understanding of that relevance, is in a position to destroy, not build.

Lin adds, 'God has given us confidence as we have grown. More people want to meet together and pray, to see what God wants of us. We used to expect things to happen because a speaker had come. But we have grown to know it is going to happen without having outside speakers. God and we can do it together.'

As the Church—in the light of the *Faith in the City* report—wants to develop relevance to urban priority areas, it must find a positive response to the questions and problems raised by the Church of the Good Shepherd.

The members of the church have matured to responsible discipleship, gradually being renewed in spite of the chaos of their setting. However, their love for their neighbours will continue to bring disturbed and disordered people into the church and into the services. Can the Church, both nationally and at the diocesan level, deal with the challenge of helping the Good Shepherd with a more appropriate building, one that is simple and fits into the neighbourhood but is, above all, supportive of their worship and fellowship?

The cultural gap between the churches in Urban Priority Areas and the rest of the Church could be narrowed through the development of new and more appropriate liturgies. Such churches can be encouraged by having a common liturgy with their brothers and sisters around the country. Such liturgy would not be a watered down or simplistic version of those currently in use, but would recognise that there is a valid and real culture of the poor that is at present unexpressed in Anglican liturgical language. The gap, perhaps regretted by the Church, between its current membership and the majority of the nation, will not be closed by asking the majority to aspire towards the present patterns and norms of the Church. Rather, the Church at large must discover ways to make a *collective caring response* to its neighbours. It will be necessary for the Church to lay down its life. In both liturgy and leadership the greatest headway can be made, but undoubtedly only with the greatest sacrifice.

9
Caring for the Handicapped

Christ Church, Bayston Hill, Shropshire

It was 1972, Sue Andrews was five and her family moved to Bayston Hill in Shropshire.

Sue couldn't walk, and her parents were still having problems feeding her. When she was very tiny it had been a matter almost of life and death trying to get food into her, because she had been so bad at swallowing. She could now sit and play on the floor much like a twelve-month old, but she was unable to talk. The family had been advised fairly early in her life that the only thing to do was to put her in a cot and leave her there, because she would be quite happy and would never do anything. Not long after their arrival in Bayston Hill Margaret, Sue's mother, took Sue to see a local specialist, suggesting that Sue might benefit from physiotherapy. He responded, 'That's a waste of time because she will never walk; she hasn't got the sort of brain power.' Sue's condition, often called *crie de chat* (from the cries that people with this handicap make as they try to communicate) is an extremely severe mental handicap.

John and Margaret Andrews had seen themselves as typical nominal Anglicans, going along to the major festivals and occasionally in between. Before their move, Sue was baptised at a service with just John and Margaret and their three children present. There was no-one in the church particularly supporting the family; the Andrews were not active members, but—as they said—'It wasn't an active sort of church.' One or two people in the village had helped occasionally.

Then the family moved to Bayston Hill and on the first Sunday they went down to Christ Church. Sue was in short-term care during the move. They were met by John Fieldsend, the vicar, with a very warm welcome. John Andrews says, 'So we started to talk about who we were and about Sue. John came up to see us at home in a very short time. Both he and others realised the problem immediately and began to talk about what might be done.'

The church realised that the Andrews family had special needs, and the concern they felt was expressed in prayer.

A group met to pray with Sue every Wednesday afternoon in the old vicarage; Margaret used to bring her on the way home from school. Margaret herself felt she needed the prayer for the support this gave her.

Elizabeth Fieldsend, herself a mother with three young children, saw the effects of their prayers. The Lord worked miracles, and very soon Sue showed distinct signs of being able to learn to walk. Her eating was still a battle but was transformed; she started recognising things and gave signs of talking. It wasn't only all those miracles, but also Sue's spiritual understanding and perception, which seemed far beyond her mental capacity, which really gave Christ Church a vision of what the Lord was doing in their midst, helping them to see his vision for the Church. Those who met together to pray shared news of Sue's progress with the rest of the church family. Sue's marvellous responsiveness was faith-building to everybody in the church. As Sue slowly improved in her walking, speaking and eating, they realised that the Lord had given the church something very special and important. They should never let that go, never lose sight of it.

However, medical opinion was still low. Sue began to do things the doctor said she wouldn't do, but in a sense the more she achieved the bigger the problem became. She was more difficult to care for than a mere 'cabbage' would have been. In her newfound mobility she could wreak havoc. Once she learned to stand she could reach things on shelves and mantelpieces that previously were safe.

Care Force

Sue was still very much on the floor, needing lifting and manoeuvring. Margaret had arthritis, which was worsening. The family began to be concerned about friendship for Sue as the other two children grew older. Then Care Force happened.

Michael and Jane Tupper, leaders in the church, had a friend who recommended the church get in touch with Care Force, an organisation that is under the umbrella of Scripture Union. Young adults, often having left school but going on to college or university, give a year to work in the church. They are paid very little above their keep, but offer themselves to caring ministry related to their own interest.

The first of a succession of Care Force workers arrived at Christ Church. Sarah was the same age as Sue and a real friend. Sue went to Sarah's home a couple of times, once even after Sarah had left Bayston Hill. Sue is still excited at the mention of Sarah's name.

Another Care Force worker took Sue to a disco. Mental handicaps require much patience, as the helper learns how to stretch the handicapped person. Each of the Care Force workers has been a tremendous help caring for Sue but has also spent part of her time with other handicapped members of Christ Church.

Many people have been willing to invite Sue round for a meal, accompanied by the Care Force worker, who got to know people, making a list of would-be hosts. The Andrews family also invited people in for meals so that they could see what Sue did and how she behaved; then it was much easier to ask if they would have Sue for a meal. People grew to realise there was nothing to fear, that they could cope and knew how to care.

At the church's fellowship meals and walks someone would push Sue in the wheelchair. The walks were chosen for where the wheelchair could be taken. At times teenagers would babysit, and families would take Sue when they went on a day's outing. Some, like the Fieldsends, would take Sue for a complete weekend. In all these ways, dozens of people have helped.

Sue is more difficult now in families with small children; she does not know her own strength when playing and, additionally, no longer enjoys children's games. She prefers company nearer her own age.

Sunday Morning

John and Margaret have brought Sue to church with them, and her involvement has grown as the church members have learned how to include her and care for her in the services. In church Sue listens like an eighteen-month-old toddler who can hardly speak. She has a knack of shouting at the appropriate moments. The bishop was very happy to confirm Sue, and the handicapped come forward and share in Communion.

Amanda, a deaf and blind member of the congregation and younger than Sue, is also confirmed. They both make their various noises in church, but people are used to it.

After the service, during coffee, Sue needs very little supervision by her parents. People look after her. She pulls on a person's shoulders to get their attention. She pokes people to find out their names if they are new. Margaret may go up and say, 'She's asking what your name is.'

Sue's Future

When Sue was very young, the family's other two children played with her, and she mixed in with their games. The family noticed how the years brought their own changes and made adjustments necessary in caring for Sue. The other two children were no longer downstairs playing on the floor with her; they had to go upstairs and get on with their homework. John and Margaret began to see Sue on her own and to realise what the new problems were. It became harder work to have Sue as the only child at home without the stimulation of friends and schoolmates. She still needed constant attention and constant watching.

Sue is the normal height for a nineteen-year-old girl, reaching anything that an adult can reach from standing. Parents who have coped with removing objects from the reach of an inquisitive toddler will appreciate the difficulty and the tension, as Sue has been at this stage for the majority of her life. Sue used to enjoy children's story books, but now that she is emotionally more developed these are no longer satisfying. Each aspect of discovering first her need, then a means of helping her, with very little established knowledge, is hard and relentless work, but many people love Sue and want to encourage whatever development is possible.

The church and the Andrews family looked at all sorts of possibilities for Sue's future care, at various hospitals and homes, to see what was available. There didn't seem to be anywhere that would offer long-term special care, other than a hospital.

A Task for the Church?

John Fieldsend felt strongly that this was a task for the church, but nothing they tried seemed to work out. With such a degree of handicap, in this country there is only one future: a mental hospital. He really could not face that, nor simply go on praying. None of the church had the faith to say that Sue would be totally healed and become normal. That was not within their range of faith for a child so brain-damaged. They accepted that despite whatever progress Sue was making, she would be severely handicapped for the rest of her life. They also realised that emotionally and socially it would be criminal to put her in a mental hospital, to be left locked up in a ward all day, as she was such a sociable child. John felt they had either to abandon the whole concern for Sue's future or do something practical.

Christ Church began to recognise that they were part of the Lord's solution for a long-term situation, not simply for the immediate future. The Lord began to make them part of the answer to their own prayers; they had a service to perform.

Eleven members, representing the church as leaders, went to a camp at Post Green Community in Dorset; they wanted to find out what the Lord was saying to them.

The theme of the week was God's bias towards the poor. God has a specially deep concern for social justice. They all found it easy to agree with what was being said about the inner city and the call of churches there to meet desperate needs. But they also found themselves saying, 'But what about us, where does that leave us?'

Was God saying, 'This is where the need is, you'd better move.'?

They could understand that they should pray for the inner cities and support the people working for the Lord there, but this left them on the outside, feeling a bit uneasy. Perhaps they were second-class Christians; perhaps that's how other people saw them; or, worse still, perhaps that was how God saw them, because they were living and working in a place where the needs are very different, not so obvious, nor so material.

During the teaching, the seminars, and time for just talking together, the Lord underlined that the poor are the unemployed, the homeless, the hungry, those who live in the concrete jungles of violence and fear. In the Old Testament Bible studies they read of God speaking about his love for the poor: those who were the aliens, the widows and the orphans, who in Israel were the powerless ones with no voice. So it was legitimate to see the poor in a slightly broader sense than just those who hadn't got many worldly possessions.

God was not saying to Christ Church, 'Move to Toxteth' or 'Move to Brixton', or 'Go and work abroad for Tear Fund'. He was saying that the religion he accepts as pure and faultless is to look after those who cannot look after themselves, who have no voice and not many rights in society. This is the message of James 1:27. That was the vision God gave to Christ Church.

Jane Tupper concludes, 'This is the burden God laid on our hearts. God is calling us to take hold of this vision and get on with it. He is ready to give us the strength, the love and the grace that we need to fulfil the vision he has given us.'

Thus Christ Church formed a small group to look into what they could do by way of life care. Could they provide a home for mentally handicapped people? Because they realised the enormity of the task, they looked around to see who else was doing similar work.

A meeting gathered at the church's request at the Community Health Council Offices in Shrewsbury, under the chairmanship of Sir John Holt, then the Member of Parliament for Shrewsbury, with a small group of medical and social specialists, including one doctor who is an international authority on mental handicap.

John Fieldsend saw this meeting as a significant milestone on the road to long-term care. Some of the social and medical experts were very doubtful and questioned whether a church was the right organisation to pioneer such specialist work, because it was and is pioneer work for this country. Shouldn't this be left to the medical and social experts? Why, they asked, would a church pioneer this? John remembers what Dr York Moore said to those who raised the questions: 'In general I agree with you, that this is not the job that churches need get involved in, or can specially do, but there is one church that can do it, and that is Christ Church, Bayston Hill.'

How much Dr Moore knew of the church, John didn't know. But it seemed to be a word from the Lord, a word of knowledge, and that was the Lord's commission.

The small group looked at one large international Christian organisation, the L'Arche Community, formed under the leadership of French Canadian Roman Catholic, Jean Vanier. L'Arche has homes all over the world for mentally handicapped people. Should Christ Church work with them? Could they offer advice? The chaplain of the English communities came to visit Bayston Hill. It became obvious that although the L'Arche community was doing a very good work in France among the severely mentally handicapped, their communities in Britain were only working among the less profoundly handicapped, and they didn't feel it was part of their vision for this country to go further at the moment. So although they got help and advice, love and encouragement from L'Arche, there was no way for Christ Church to fulfil their vision under L'Arche's umbrella.

Should they be independent? they wondered. Christ Church tried to form a Trust of its own. It is not difficult to form a charitable Trust, yet at every stage through simple and silly little things, the doors seemed to be closing.

The Andrews family themselves heard of a new possibility. With Sarah, the first Care Force worker, they took Sue away for a week's holiday. They were near Swanage and when looking for a church on Sunday morning, found there were three different churches near the middle of the town. To make the choice they decided, 'We'll park the car and walk back. We will look at the people arriving, and we'll go where we see people with smiles on their faces.' They drove up the road, and the first possible parking space was outside a Baptist Church.

The congregation were coming along with big smiles on their faces, so the family asked, 'Do you mind if we come in? Sue might be a little bit noisy.'

'No, don't worry. Do join us.'

They sat down, and a man sat in front of them with a Mongol child. He came and talked to them after the service and told them of a group that was working with the handicapped, Christian Concern for the Mentally Handicapped. On their return to Bayston Hill, they told John Fieldsend that they felt God had led them to this church and to this man to tell them something specific.

At the same time the church's new solicitor wrote to them, saying, 'I could give you some advice myself, but I think your organisation should get in touch with Christian Concern for the Mentally Handicapped.'

John Fieldsend contacted the director, David Potter, who visited Christ Church. As an organisation they were not working among the severely mentally handicapped but were still very interested that somebody was, and were very keen to work together with them in building a home.

Building a Home

The Sunday morning service at Christ Church was focused on re-stating the vision for life-long care for mentally handicapped people. Since the time when Sue first arrived among them, the people of Christ Church had built a new church, moving from a tiny building on the edge of the village to new premises that were more central, on a new and attractive housing estate, with spare land for expansion around their new building. The congregation grew dramatically, and not everyone knew the history of the call to care for handicapped people, nor quite why—having worked and sacrificed so much for the new church—they should now begin a new project to raise funds and build houses on part of the land. John Fieldsend led the service during which the vision was again spelt out, and the congregation offered themselves again to serve God in this way.

John began by saying that church people need a vision that gives them a common identity and a common purpose. Each church must have a vision that is unique to it, and yet any vision or direction that God gives to a church has at least four basic dimensions. All four are necessary for a balanced life. The first is worship, by which they relate to God. The second is fellowship, by which they relate to one another. The third is witness, by which they proclaim the Good News of Jesus to the world around them. And the fourth is service, by which they demonstrate God's love and compassion to a needy world.

One might say that the latter three—fellowship, witness and service, that which the church does amongst themselves and in the world—are encompassed in worship. Worship thus becomes the offering to God of the totality of the other three ingredients.

As God works through the life of a particular church, not every one of these four dimensions will be as prominent as the others. God may be speaking especially about one of those aspects at any one time. The Holy Spirit will cause a church to major on one or other from time to time as the church's vision is renewed, and as the vision is retold.

Worship had always been very much at the heart of Christ Church. The fellowship was strong. Witness went out with the Good News teams and missions. But the aspect that God wanted them to concentrate on that morning was their service, and especially on the Lord's call to them to build a home for mentally handicapped adults. The Lord wanted to renew that vision in them, and because so many new people had come into the church since it was first given, now was the time to renew and restate that vision.

The arrival of John and Margaret Andrews and their family was the beginning of that vision. It was Sue's arrival in Bayston Hill and in the church with her family that was God's prompt to lead them in this way. Now they were building a home for ten people.

A lesson was read from II Chronicles:

> 'Now, my God, may your eyes be open and your ears attentive to the prayers offered in this place. Now arise, O Lord God, and come to your resting place; you and the ark of your might. May your priests, O Lord God, be clothed with salvation, may your saints rejoice in your goodness. O Lord God, do not reject your anointed one, remember the kindnesses promised to David your servant.'
>
> When Solomon finished praying, fire came down from heaven and consumed the burnt offering and the sacrifices, and the glory of the Lord filled the temple. The priests could not enter the temple of the Lord because the glory of the Lord filled it. When all the Israelites saw the fire coming down and the glory of the Lord above the temple, they knelt on the pavement with their faces to the ground, and they worshipped and gave thanks to the Lord, saying 'He is good; his love endures for ever.' (II Chronicles 6:40—7:3)

After the reading, those present were recollecting the miracle of rebuilding and dedicating Christ Church, aware, too, that the vision was for two houses. The first they were already using for worship—they had built half the temple. John underlined the task ahead as he said, 'Let's look forward to that time when the Lord's glory fills this house, to the completed temple that we will have here, of the worship that we offer to him and the service that we are offering to the disadvantaged, to the underprivileged, to those who have no voice in our particular society. Let us establish the Lord as the giver of that vision and us as his obedient people.'

When the church had applied for planning permission, there was a vocal minority in Bayston Hill who thought the project could devalue their houses, and some local parents were afraid for their own chidlren. They were not fully aware of the distinction between mental handicap and mental illness. There was more than one public meeting allowing opportunity for local people to question and comment, but when the outline planning permission was given the opposition died down. A television documentary film showed the work of Christian Concern for the Mentally Handicapped; that reassured the local people. As one said, 'If only we had known. If we had seen something like this film earlier, we wouldn't have opposed it.'

Christ Church were determined not to have a building that looked like an institution. They looked at various plans. One building would just dominate the church. Then one architect came up with the brilliant suggestion of three linked bungalows. They hoped to start building in August 1986, finishing in the autumn of 1987. The home for handicapped people had reached the stage of having all the necessary pieces in place; the permission given, the plans drawn, and it was time to look for builders.

There are to be three bungalows on the land behind the church. The first bungalow will be for four more severely mentally handicapped people, like Sue, mainly containing their sleeping and living accommodation and a social area. A longer house will be for six less severely handicapped people, who might eventually go out and live in a sheltered house by themselves, such as those affected by

Down's Syndrome. Then the central building will have a joint day area, lounge and eating facilities. The house for the less handicapped is deliberately set slightly apart from the other two, to give independence. The houses will have a large garden of their own and share the access way to the church.

Each person will be sponsored by Social Services and selected by Christian Concern for the Mentally Handicapped, who also employ the care staff. Christ Church will be the day-to-day management committee. Having a central organisation with overall control is an asset: 'There will be such a demand that it will be good to have someone remote to carry the can. That way we can't be accused of favouritism,' adds John Fieldsend.

The cost of the home will be in the region of £200,000, a figure to be raised by the nation-wide charity, not by Christ Church alone. To raise that kind of sum immediately after building a new church would seem rather daunting, and though the church will certainly play their part, the building will be vested in trust of Christian Concern for the Mentally Handicapped, and that organisation will be overall responsible.

A Wider Concern

Looking forward to the building of the Home, John reminded the congregation that the Lord has brought other handicapped people among them to be nurtured and loved. The Home is not their only concern. For some years now they have had the Care Force workers to help develop the work and ministry, not just with the mentally handicapped but to the physically handicapped, in an increasingly wide field in the community. An obvious example is Amanda Armitage, who is not mentally handicapped. Her handicap is physical, in deafness and blindness. Her needs are great, but very different. The commitment to her and her long-term future is as great as it is to anyone else's. How the Lord is going to work that out the congregation hasn't seen yet. The need is not as great, as Beryl, her mother, is not asking for immediate help because she wants Amanda living at home. The church seeks to pray with her, support her, love her, in order to make that last as long as possible.

There are others in the community whom the church knows about. They are on the buses, and are seen in the streets. The church has an ongoing service to the handicapped of the local community as part of its God-given vision.

Christ Church follows God's call to care, with all the accompanying joys and sorrows, aptly summed up in the words of the offertory used in the liturgy each week, 'All things come from you, O Lord, and of your own do we give you.'

John Andrews shares the understanding he has of what his daughter Sue has brought to his life and to the church.

'The Lord is trying to teach us all something about ourselves, trying to say to people that a handicapped person is as real and as whole and as much of a person as anyone else. He says, "I see you all, and at first sight you may seem worse than she is, because you are handicapped by sin. But I see the person underneath, and I have washed away your sin and I love you." Then you see the real beauty of yourself and of the handicapped as well. That is how we should be looking at each other, too. The handicapped are like visual aids.

'Suffering is an essential part of our life. If there was a church without any suffering, then I would doubt if Christ was there.'

10
Building and Establishing a Ministry

Christ Church, Bayston Hill

An individual Christian, a church or fellowship may, in reading, relating to the Scriptures and looking at the world around, discover an almost endless list of ways in which compassion and caring can be expressed today.

What takes a church from a good idea or a worthy cause to the founding of a stable, long-term ministry? Are there criteria by which ministries develop that could be applied in other places? The St Luke's Community Project in Holbeck was the reflection of a biblically founded concern in the church, but it took several factors coming into perspective before the project could move from idea to drawing board. Physical resources—premises and money—were necessary, as well as the human skill to develop and manage the scheme. Then John Grieves came into the church as a catalyst, so the group could draw together the biblical concern, the reality of the neighbourhood needs, personnel and money, and all in the context of God's timing.

Christ Church, Bayston Hill, had in much the same way a worthy vision for a caring ministry. The experience of raising funds for its church rebuilding programme enabled the congregation to anticipate the feasibility of raising the money to build a specialised home for handicapped people. The specific need was present, and while John Fieldsend commented that it was a question of either doing something or abandoning the project altogether, the latter would have been emotionally hard because the handicapped people had already been adopted into the life of the church. There was no denying their presence and the sense, from all points of view, that they belonged. The families' commitment to their own members was, however, still not enough to make that happen: there needed to be an additional catalyst in the church. When the question of a Home came up, Christ Church was already significantly including the handicapped people in its life as a result of the giftedness of some members; the ministry was already there. When Jane talked of seeing the needs of their neighbourhood, the handicapped were already with them.

Individuals or churches are often oblivious to their own natural gifts; these are so obvious that they are counted as normal. At Christ Church both individual gifts and corporate gifts were obvious to an outsider, but the members had not remarked on them. There was little conscious change in worship or lifestyle for their members, yet the whole system of church life was affected and coloured by the presence of the handicapped members. Occasions of conscious adaptation to the handicapped were far fewer than those that reflected the total way the church lived, and they dealt mainly with points where there had been tension and discussion. When the new church was built, *any* member of the church would have looked at the plans and said, 'Where's the wheelchair ramp?' It would not have been, 'Should we include a wheelchair ramp in our plans?' The only question raised was about the addition of a *second* ramp at the back of the church.

Two particular individuals bring a natural gift to Christ Church in its life with handicapped people; one of them is handicapped, one is not. Elizabeth Fieldsend worked with blind babies and young children before her marriage, and has an innate sensitivity to the needs of handicapped people. She says, 'It is nothing I consciously developed, except I knew the Lord was saying something to me, and I wanted to be part of what he was saying.'

Beryl, Amanda Armitage's mother, is blind. Elizabeth

and Beryl have a friendship in which they have worked together to help Beryl fit into the life of the church, with the result that others have understood more about how to make friends with their handicapped brothers and sisters. Beryl's ability to talk about what is helpful to her and what is not, and her openness, mean that other handicapped adults and children are approached with more understanding.

We were having coffee one weekday morning in the church and I turned to walk with Beryl into the lounge. I took her arm, to help her find direction, so Beryl moved her arm to a different position on mine, and most helpfully explained why she did so; if she put her hand under my arm she could feel which way I was turning and could follow without me having to say very much.

Minutes before I had seen Elizabeth take Beryl to 'see' the flowers that were still displayed from Beryl's elder daughter's wedding on the previous Saturday. For Beryl the experience included touching and smelling the flowers. Not having eyesight is less limiting when people like Elizabeth think themselves into others' shoes and find ways to help them see. Beryl and Amanda have been in the church some years now, with Amanda attending a nearby special school.

Awareness and Sensitivity

Elizabeth thinks that many handicapped people don't realise how special they are. They have taught her, she says, that they have something special to offer in who they are, how they are, and the way in which they develop their other senses—such as memory and touch. Beryl has contributed to that learning. The church can make it as easy as possible for her to feel normal, to feel good about herself, to feel included as part of the church family.

A handicapped person hates to be related to in a manner that points out the ways in which he is obviously different, less able or 'odd'. The *Mission Praise* hymnbook in Braille is bulky and therefore prominent. The sensitivity in Beryl's fingers is not what it was, so it's not easy to read quickly during a service, so Elizabeth has encouraged people who are interested and want to spend time with Beryl, to make a note of the hymn numbers and tell Beryl in advance so she can read them at home and be ready and prepared to sing. One person goes every week to read aloud to her the green church notices leaflet.

Having a deaf-blind daughter brings an added dimension. Amanda participates in worship provided there is somebody who will stand and sing right into her ear. It has to be somebody who is familiar with the words and can sing in reasonable tune, then Amanda can join in.

Other considerations are made in the church's way of organising itself. Beryl explains that when she is at home, she can normally remember what food is in which bowl or container in the fridge, and if she is unsure she can touch or taste it. When she and Amanda join the church meals, this is not possible. Someone could just fetch her a plate of food, but the sense of belonging is important to Beryl, so Elizabeth has found another way. She now goes up to the table with Beryl to face the food, and then tells Beryl what is nearest to her and what is being served.

Enabling and Teaching Others

People have asked Elizabeth from time to time, 'How can you do this with Beryl?' Elizabeth talks with them so that they can really *think* themselves into Beryl's position.

Very often people without a handicap avoid relating to handicapped people, as they are unsure and awkward themselves. They treat the person in a wheelchair as if he is deaf or non-existent, as if he cannot see and has no thoughts of his own. The cause is not a premeditated malice, but an inability to see the world from someone else's position. So when people ask how they can help, Elizabeth also looks for ways to show them. She explains that it is a question of introducing people and giving them confidence, to help them know that they can be of value to the handicapped person; then of helping the handicapped person to feel confident with them. That can be hard with somebody who may be fairly nervous and apprehensive, or may not have had any previous experience with handicapped people.

As Christ Church has grown in numbers, so Elizabeth has urged people to go and introduce themselves to Beryl. Within a large congregation a lot of people never meet each other. That's as true of Beryl as anyone else, yet Beryl is particularly good in that she tells people her needs—she's an enabler.

A month or two before I spoke to Elizabeth, a group had gathered: those who had had more contact with Beryl, members of her housegroup, and others who had asked how to support her. Among the Christ Church congregation is a teacher from Condover Hall, a school for children with multiple handicaps, who joined the group.

Elizabeth had said to Beryl, 'We would like to spend an evening with you, for you to show us and teach us and tell us more about things you want or that would be helpful for you and Amanda.'

The group did activities and games. They split into pairs, one in each pair blindfolded. Elizabeth sent the blindfolded partners out of the room, and then explained to the others that they should first lead their partner by the hand to see how this felt. The pairs walked into the worship area in the church and into the rows of chairs, helping each other to experience what it is like for Beryl to be led incorrectly. They redid the activity, leading in the right way. Beryl was delighted and thrilled with an evening that taught everyone a great deal.

Beryl is quite competent with her white stick, in many situations. She laughs when she tells what happens when she takes her daughter with her. Amanda has a very little sight, enough to see large shapes or sunshine. If they are out together, Amanda holding onto Beryl's arm and Beryl using the stick, she will just about have got her sense of direction when Amanda wheels off to look at something, pulling Beryl with her. Beryl, with no sight at all, is disorientated and has to re-establish her sense of direction.

A Special Person

The word 'special' is often used in association with handicap, as in 'special education' and 'special care'. Amanda is special in another way too. She was born with her handicaps, and perhaps because of them she was put into a children's home. Beryl and her husband wanted to adopt a baby, particularly one with a handicap. Out of their own appreciation of life they wanted to offer love to someone else who particularly needed it. When Beryl saw Amanda (Beryl's blindness is more recent), she fell in love with her, rather than with the more healthy and less handicapped child who was being offered to her. So Amanda was chosen; her handicap was not a 'shock' to a parent looking for a *normal* child, for Beryl wanted to offer her love.

In her concern for Amanda, Beryl has found that people readily confuse Amanda's handicaps with mental subnormality. Her deafness is the reason for her making unexpected sounds and for her slowness to communicate. With the addition of blindness she learns slowly but well. She needs help to broaden her experience and find ways to join with others, as she is a very able and sociable child. She loves to dance; when the music is turned to its highest volume, Amanda can feel the vibration and has a great sense of rhythm.

There are lots of activities to which sighted people can introduce Amanda, where Beryl can't. Elizabeth takes Amanda after worship on Sunday mornings to go to ask for her own drink, helping her at the hatch to speak to those serving, saying whether she wants orange or coffee and then encouraging her to return her cup. In this way she is encouraged to do the same things as anyone else. Then they go to find one of the babies. The mother hands the baby to Amanda so she can have a close look. She has a lovely whimsical smile as she enjoys those few minutes. It is good for the children to get to know Amanda, too. They can really enter into a friendship with her, which is not possible with others like, for instance, Sue Andrews.

Feeling Their Value

Sue has big communication difficulties, but she has a delightful smile, which is always welcoming. Other members of the church can respond to that and give her a hug.

Amanda has to look at things really closely and adores books. She looks down her glasses and is very willing for others to spell words out on her hand, and she signals 'very good'. Communication is hard. Usually it is the other person who asks questions, and the more she communicates spontaneously, the better it is.

When Elizabeth is serving Communion and Amanda has received the cup, she signals, 'This is good'. It is exciting, and Elizabeth signals back because this is a shared experience, a special touch in the Communion service. Amanda feels very much part of the group. That feeling of being more than accepted, part of the whole, is so important to her.

Because of Amanda and Sue and Beryl, there are dimensions of worship that go far beyond ordinary expectations, and Elizabeth loves to participate with them. These are things she wants to point out to other people, as it is easy to think that, because of the handicap, people do not experience things on the same level as everyone else. But they are experiencing something on a deeper or higher level, rather than a lower level, in human terms.

Help That's Not Patronising

A recurrent theme in caring ministry that is life-giving and affirming, is that of giving to the recipients of help, the responsibility to say for themselves what help they would like. For those outside the particular circumstance to assume and do what is 'needed' is patronising and reduces the self-worth of the recipient. Of course there can be conversation and suggestions from others, but in the end the decision about what help is needed or accepted belongs to the recipient, if he or she is being respected as a responsible adult. For someone as handicapped as Sue, there are many ways in which she is unable to be responsible for herself, but at every level, whatever the handicap, friends and helpers *can* listen to the spoken need of the person.

As more handicapped members have joined Christ Church, members have learned this fact by experience. Both those handicapped and those not, have contributed to the learning process. Elizabeth has explained that every individual has different needs, and their families have different needs. The church members have had to be very careful not to trample on people in their eagerness to help, but encourage the handicapped to say what their needs are, and what they would appreciate most. Those needs may be different in two months' time, so those who help must be very flexible. Little is worse than being patronised.

A mother, whose son has an incurable and quite rare disease, had recently been converted. The church were only just beginning to skim the surface in giving her the nurture she needed as a new Christian, building up some sort of relationship with the whole family. Only later might she be able to ask them for help with the practical aspects of caring.

The way in which people look at what it means to be a person results in all kinds of attitudes to handicap. If they think of intelligence as a criterion for holding a superior position in human society, then they will look down at the less intelligent and be patronising. If good looks are high on their list of valuable attributes, they will shun people whose handicap results in deformity. In his book *Bringing up Children in the Christian Faith*, John Westerhof comments on such definition.

> The norm for human life should not be the physically attractive and capable adult, not the mentally bright, rational adult, not the emotionally stable adult. We would understand human life better if the norm were the exceptional physically, emotionally, mentally retarded child. When we begin our understanding of human life with the fully functioning adult we strive

> to manipulate the 'normal' child to be like us, and we depreciate and patronize the 'abnormal' child because he or she can never be like us. We need to a affirm that we are all exceptional children, and that they represent what it means to be human. In that important sense, true maturity is being what we are to the fullest. If we have been blessed with other physical, emotional, mental, or behavioral gifts, then more will be expected of us, but we will not be of greater value.[6]

Westerhof shows that a church which struggles with inclusiveness runs into its own negative values and misconceptions about humanity and in the struggle finds more of God's view. In that context the handicapped person is a gift to show us the sin in our lives that causes us to devalue what Christ values infinitely.

The Tasks

Parents of handicapped children feel the most burdened and responsible; whereas someone outside the family can approach things with a sense of humour. Elizabeth sometimes takes Sue into the supermarket, and she grabs tins from the shelves. Elizabeth doesn't mind as long as the tin is returned and no-one is too inconvenienced, and she doesn't feel embarrassed. Sometimes she can see what Sue is thinking, but at other times there is no forewarning when she grabs something. Elizabeth has only to let her know that she should not do it. Having other church members around can be helpful!

Elizabeth has been practically involved with her since Sue was five—on her arrival in Bayston Hill. It is much easier to cope with a young handicapped child than with an older one, but as Sue has got older it has become more and more evident that people can be really embarrassed about being out with her. Sue has learned to walk, but if it's a long way, the wheelchair is still necessary.

Elizabeth let Sue know that when she sat down on the pavement, that was all right. Sue may be mentally handicapped, but she can play up like any other child. Elizabeth knew she was safe and so said, 'I'll go,' and walked away from her. Sue was actually waiting for a reaction, and when it didn't come, she found it wasn't really very worthwhile sitting on the pavement.

Church members have learned the sort of things that can help them relax at home with Sue, like ensuring that there is a safe place where they don't have to keep grabbing things out of her hands. The mental and emotional insecurity of someone feeling anxious about having her there can cause Sue herself to feel apprehensive; she may start grabbing or pulling people's hair; it's not aggression but insecurity. Eizabeth has observed, however, that Sue has a lovely relationship with her older brother, and that they have a lot of rough and tumble together. He has helped a lot in her being relaxed. But there still seems to be some reason for her being slow to trust herself or other people. Her physical tension must reflect some mental tension as well.

As already mentioned, the Care Force volunteers took an interest in Sue from the moment they arrived. The Andrews family need practical help with Sue, as she has to have a bath several times a week. John and Margaret cannot manage that on their own, because Sue is too heavy for them, and neither of them is physically fit. Sue is also incontinent, though sometimes she can remain dry all day. She asks, saying 'loo,' and 'Go', and always uses the loo when taken to it, but she may still be wet a few minutes later. There are some particular days when she is difficult: during pre-menstrual times or if she is really anxious. These are some of the times when the Care Force workers have helped especially with her practical needs.

Learning to Care

Liz, a young mother with a little girl, moved into Bayston Hill. Her husband worked abroad, coming home only occasionally. Her neighbour, a church member, looked after the house if the mother also went away. On one visit home both husband and wife were converted through one of the evangelistic teams from Christ Church and became members of the church. They then had another child, a boy. Soon afterwards Liz became slightly lame. After many tests, the doctors diagnosed motor neuron disease, which is a terminal illness usually affecting the over sixties; Liz was thirty. No-one could tell how long she had to live, but the muscular disability would increase. Eventually she would be not only bed-bound but might have to finish her days in hospital. Everybody had grown very fond of her and thought and prayed about how best to support the family.

The church members made a commitment to the family: people who thought they would like to be involved offered themselves as helpers. They made sure that help was given in the way it was wanted. They learned a lot about respecting other people. Nurses would come along saying, 'I will give her a bath.' They might get the answer, 'Thank you, but maybe she wants her husband to go on bathing her.' That was right for both Liz and her husband, respecting them and their decisions.

While the church struggled with many questions—'Why did God allow this to happen?'—Liz deteriorated quite rapidly. It became evident to other church members that they had to talk about Liz's illness with their own children. Liz encouraged the children to ask and was glad to answer their questions about why she couldn't walk any more.

Another couple took Liz and her family away with them, making sure they got a ground floor flat that could accommodate a wheel chair. A group of men occasionally took the husband out for a drink at the pub. At home somebody would be with Liz, who was still teaching art.

When the new church was built it included a handicapped persons' toilet, and Elizabeth asked for a wheelchair ramp at the back as well as at the front door.

Somebody said to Liz, 'Do you know what Elizabeth Fieldsend said? She said we needed a ramp at the back door. That's a bit unnecessary, isn't it?'

Liz said, 'No, I want the privilege of putting things in the dustbin in the same way as you do.'

Liz helped with the planning of the church kitchen,

looking at the heights and widths to check that, as far as possible, members in wheelchairs could help with the chores.

Grief

The church members here wept together over some of the painful things that have happened.

Liz had helped with the last-minute cleaning up of the church, ready for the Consecration Service. In some ways it was unbelievable that she was dead the following morning when the whole church gathered. John Fieldsend had to break the news to the church in that service, with the bishops and local dignitaries there. Liz's husband said he wanted to come to the service with the children and knew his wife would have wanted him to. 'We ensured that he was sitting near to people whom the family knew. His coming helped the congregation to weep and grieve together.'

Inclusiveness

The church's active life includes social dimensions, and here, too, the consideration for the handicapped members is evident. In church activities it is ensured that the handicapped members can be involved in a fairly normal way; not everything is visual and not everything requires physical expertise. When the church has a social event they make sure they have games in which Amanda can join with other children.

When everyone joins into big teams for games together, Elizabeth often has Amanda with her. If they are throwing rings over sticks, Elizabeth gets Amanda to start off at the same place as everyone else. She is often as good as anyone. It is demeaning to make allowances for a handicapped person when it is not necessary.

At a bring-and-share meal the church has places where people can sit and eat, not just a buffet with everyone standing up. The older people need places to sit as well as the handicapped. Sue may need a little table on her own, near to others so she feels part of the group.

The Continuing Challenge

Elizabeth talks of her continuing concern. While handicapped people have an experiential sense of who Jesus is through the church to which they belong, they have the same need as everyone for basic teaching of biblical principles and concepts. It is not easy to communicate, and the challenge is how to deal with that. For example, what is death? For Amanda, pets have disappeared, and that has been an experience in itself. But how can the church teach about death with regard to Jesus, the significance of death on the Cross and the Resurrection, and the possibility of her having eternal life in him? That has not yet been explored. Amanda and Sue enjoy saying their prayers. For Sue, Elizabeth sings the chorus 'Two little eyes to look to God,...' every time she comes to stay with the Fieldsends. It is an important part of her being with them and it may be lovely, but it doesn't say who Jesus is.

God has not finished his work with Christ Church in building his temple, both the church building and the Home next door. He has not finished his work in making them a people who are themselves home and family for handicapped people. As the stresses of ministry have fallen upon them, they have been broken and remade, in that constant remoulding that God undertakes in the Church: the potter with the clay. As the church discovers its own weaknesses and limitations, God is ready to redeem and renew, that through the church he might give life to those who have come among them.

11
Someone by Your Side

Christ Church, Bayston Hill

Jane Tupper comes from Bayston Hill. Much of the village is new, and only a few years ago, Christ Church—built originally on a hill overlooking the village—had ceased to be at the focus of the village as new development had moved the village more to the west. The church left the old premises for new ones at the heart of an area of private housing nearer the centre of population (see Chapter 9).

The village is pretty, the housing pleasant, the surroundings attractive, but for many people these qualities are superficial. What goes on behind the closed front doors is just like anywhere else. Christ Church has for a number of years been helping people in the local community as they have struggled to reorder and re-establish their daily lives after crises and illness. Jane's work and ministry has involved helping a variety of people pick up the pieces of their broken lives to put them back together, or helping them make the most of difficult situations. Jane comments, 'The Lord was giving us many people who were in one way or another poor, either emotionally —totally unable to cope with life—or economically—as when a husband had just walked away from the family.'

Several people have been under regular psychiatric care and are unemployable, even in a full employment situation. One recently returned to full-time employment, which was exciting to Jane and to others, because his breakdown had resulted from his being a travelling salesman in highly stressed circumstances. (He was unemployed for ten years and is now the organist at the crematorium, a job he enjoys and does well.) If such people are moved directly from the shelter of hospital care into a normally stressed situation they will quickly be back in the institution; but at Christ Church they can find their feet again emotionally.

Three couples moved to Bayston Hill from the inner city, brought by their work, and all felt extremely guilty about being there, finding it such a restoring place. Could they justify the ease of life when so many friends in the inner city struggled on? For these people Bayston Hill has been a healing environment. Two have gone back to work in cities. The city is stressful even to those people who grew up there, because so many everyday events touch on old memories and take people back to the appalling situations they may have known as children. If the smell of poverty, despair and rubbish in a house reminds a woman of the despair and hurt of her own childhood, she has to be strong to be able to offer help. She is too easily overwhelmed by despair and discouragement. Jane comments, 'You have really got to know the Lord's victory to be able to do anything. When their pain and your pain get mixed up, you have had it. You must not only have received a lot of healing but go on receiving it to be able to face the situation at all.'

Keeping a Balance

Pastoral care is always protected by privacy, an agreement spoken or unspoken that problems discussed are private between counsellor and client, as in a confessional. Most often that is well appreciated by others, but less well understood is the discretion needed when the help is practical.

The PCC gives vicar John Fieldsend and Jane a discretionary fund, which they keep topped up, for which Jane and John do not have to account. It is extremely difficult to keep the balance between unconditional giving and teaching people how to be responsible for money. It is easier as John and Jane know the circumstances, know the people, and know the awful situations they have been through.

The church were trying to subsidise a parent who was really on the breadline with two children, and were doing things such as paying for the babysitter once a week and giving small amounts of money fairly constantly. She bought butter, while other church members only bought margarine, and it was quite heavy going trying to help others in the fellowship to give her the freedom to spend what she had got on what was important to her.

Many people who are helped are what some might call 'bad managers' anyway, but however well they manage, Social Security payments are insufficient to buy them new saucepans when the handles are falling off the old ones.

When church members come to Jane and grumble, she has to try to educate them. It is hard, since they don't know what those who are helped are going through, or what it feels like when the electricity bill pops through the door and there is no money. Even if Jane goes to the local electricity board to sort the problem out so the bill can be paid bit by bit, it still has to be paid.

Jane sometimes wishes she could tape some of her counselling sessions and play them back to a wider audience so that they, too, can have tears in their eyes, But she can't do that. Occasionally, when Christ Church was a smaller congregation, people would stand up and testify to what the Lord had been doing in helping them through such difficulties. Now, with a bigger church, conversion testimonies are shared, but the everyday needs are too personal to share in a larger group.

The Church has had to make increasing financial commitments. One member needed to move house as he was in a wheelchair. The church leaders had to raise—from among the congregation—the money to buy a bungalow while his house was sold. Giving was sacrificial, and people lent the money, taking the leaders' word that this was necessary. There was a similar request for a young couple, who were in considerable difficulties. No names were given and nobody knew who they were, but the leaders asked for £10,000 in interest-free loans, with no guarantee that lenders would ever get their money back. In two days the money was there. The money may come back, to those who lent it, but it may not.

Contending with the Help System

Jane has found that the sick don't get any of the ordinary things that the disabled need for survival, unless they fight, and when they are sick they can't fight. Allowances are a question of filling in forms and going to the appropriate department, often several times. But obtaining equipment is a different matter, as none of the departments or authorities explain what is possible, and the individual has to persist in asking.

Jane studied sociology, concentrating on social work; this means she has acquaintances in the Social Services to ring up and say, 'What should I do about this? Whom should I speak to? Where should I go?' These relationships and those with others who carry power or authority or know their way around—including doctors and solicitors—are strategic. Sadly, too few people in need of such help have such an advocate.

There is a fairly small group of people who really do co-operate, who see that Jane and the church have something valid to offer and treat her as a fellow professional, including several local doctors. She finds it rewarding to ring up the Child Health Clinic and talk about a family with a problem; the staff trust Jane enough to take somebody on her recommendation without needing to go through other channels. Jane spends time working on these relationships; there is a limit to what she can do by herself, so she needs these agencies. Help can also go both ways, to the benefit of local people. A local doctor may ring up and say, 'I know that you know this person. It is absolutely urgent she be in the Queen Elizabeth Hospital in Birmingham within the next twelve hours. Can you help?'

Jane once took a woman who had been through a very nasty divorce to a solicitor with whom the woman had been doing business before. It was the first time Jane was there, and she felt strongly that simply because she was there, the solicitor treated the woman with more respect than would otherwise have been the case. It is important to protect those who cannot protect themselves. If Jane has a choice, she uses solicitors who will care for clients, but she finds she needs to keep going with people to solicitors; if they are deeply distressed, they cannot always put the picture across nor retain what is said to them.

Callous Treatment

Once Jane got angry when a family was not allowed to rent a house. The housing agent would not on principle let a client's house to someone who was unemployed—regardless of how well the family had paid their rent where they last lived. He eventually allowed them to rent a house.

Jane is constantly appalled by the way people are treated. When she goes into the relevant department, she is not in tears. She holds up her head and says, 'This is who I am and where I come from, and I want to see someone about this.' Alone, on the other hand, the people are so knocked down already that even the first person they meet—the receptionist—can put them down so much more that they can't cope. Jane comments that the receptionist sees the brave face, but when the person turns round to go they don't see the tears; they just hear, 'Oh. That's all right.' Jane avers, 'It isn't all right at all!'

Jane does know how the system should work and so is inclined to be roused from the start. She has done some hair-raising things, she says, things that make her shake when she thinks of them. She once signed a piece of paper that stated that she would pay for a stair lift to be put into somebody's house. She hadn't got any money and hadn't asked anybody from the church, and the lift was going to be expensive. She had in fact been battling for the lift for someone who had a creeping paralysis, and because this person was unlikely to live for very long, Jane couldn't get anything for her without a fight. In the end Jane had thought 'This has got to be done; she can't go another day without it.' So she signed the paper and then got more calls from the Social Services in the next twenty-four hours than ever before. (Usually she had to ring them!) Ironically, they decided to pay the whole cost. The woman died only a few days later, but a good relationship with the Social Services resulted, because they saw that Jane was actually prepared to pick up the responsibility. Jane adds, 'I couldn't do it alone, not without the Lord's compassion and a sort of righteous indignation.'

Christian Concern

Jane is aware that the beginning of social concern in Britain was Christian, and it makes her not only sad but indignant that the very structure that was built on Christian principles is now run by people who have, almost without exception, lost that basis. The staff often work on the principle that everybody is trying to get something out of Social Services that they don't deserve and don't really need. Inevitably there are some scroungers, but one must not completely lose the sense of direction and compassion, the ability to assess the situation without starting from the assumption that everyone is trying to be deceptive; that they haven't got thousands of pounds stashed away while asking for a ramp to their door. Jane says, 'If only we could help the agencies start off with fairer assumptions! Things seem to have happened the wrong way round, because the assumption crept in—during the thirties—that if we improve our surroundings, our education, and our health enough, we should all be good and perfect; things will get better and better. But because that false idea has crept in, disillusionment has crept in with it. It is really, basically, a non-acceptance of sin. If you start without that recognition of sin, you get disillusioned so quickly by everyone and everything that you have a crooked attitude to life.'

Christians do work to hold together right standards and compassion, yet Jane discovers that many people in caring professions make sweeping assumptions that Christians will not help because those in need haven't come up to a certain mark. An individual is in difficulty because he or she has made a choice that violates Christian morality or ethical standards. Outsiders unfortunately assume that Christians will not help them out of the resultant difficulties.

Support in the Church

The presence of a corporate life within a church fellowship with deeper qualities than a casual friendliness is necessary for the ongoing support for such a ministry. To be constantly in the thick of the struggle of negotiation between authority and the individual is to be in the thick of a spiritual battle. Without a church that provides constant refreshment and renewal, the person who desires to care for others simply begins to do the work as everyone else does—along the lines of the very system she is struggling against. Kingdom principles of love and compassion, of going the extra mile, and of giving without measure 'pressed down to overflowing' can only be maintained when the carer has opportunity to drink deeply of the Word and the Spirit, and to be accepted with compassion during the times she herself is overcome by the pressures. She needs this expression of footwashing, cleansing away of the burdens that belong to others. A healthy balance is only possible in a healthy and deeply committed church.

The chief element that makes a difference to Jane, then, is having such a support base that is at one and the same time critical and disciplining, uncompetitive, truly supportive and understanding. She does have the chance to explain what she has done and also an opportunity to ask for help or advice. If Jane found herself emotionally unable to cope or out of her depth she would have that support beneath her and wouldn't lose face.

Jane adds, 'I also find that the worship itself, on Sunday and in housegroups, helps challenge me and keep me to the mark. On occasions I get pulled down by what I am doing, or somebody else's pain gets on top of me. But I only have to come in here on a Sunday and someone has the courage to say, "What's the matter with you?" That is very good discipline, as I then have to accept that there *is* something the matter with me, and perhaps I haven't got it quite right. I need help, too!'

12
Problems with Institutions

St Agnes, Burmantofts, Leeds

Attempts by the State—in whatever nation—to provide help and care for citizens are always a general provision. In institutionalised care, much of the personal element is lost, and many people fail to get the help they most need. The ability of the care system to cope with the problems of any individual is often only as strong as the receptionist or interviewer at the care agency desk. The Church often finds itself the defender of those people for whom the system has ceased to function helpfully, trying to offer love and compassion, as well as acting as a form of advice bureau to help people get the care they need—whether legal or health care. Inevitably, in urban areas, the Church has to concern itself with the pressures of inner-city redevelopment and the breaking up of community which has resulted from the demolition of old housing.

The parish of St Agnes, Burmantofts, presents the visitor with the contrasts of large, green expanses overshadowed by high-rise flats, new, neatly-packed streets of council and private dwellings, old and sometimes dilapidated Victorian terraces and streets of shops, derelict and decaying industrial premises, and abandoned rows of houses. The church itself is a small, blackened building, its spire now an incongruous landmark among the cleaner brick dwellings outside its graveyard walls. In the north of the parish, the old back-to-back houses are predominantly council owned, though there are a few privately rented houses occupied mostly by elderly people who have lived in them for years.

Redevelopment of urban areas and the large-scale clearing of poor quality housing have been going on in Burmantofts for the last two decades. The Victorian housing, often lacking bathroom or indoor toilet, is faulty in too many aspects to be worth renovating. The solution of complete clearance involves rehousing all the residents from a street or area in new properties, followed by the demolition of all the buildings; the churches and sometimes the pubs are left standing for the new community that will form around them. Unfortunately, the effect of such clearance is normally to destroy the existing, predominantly working-class communities whose common history, language, and culture are held in collective memory, maintained by conversation and social intercourse. The streets—the sites of the events that feature in those stories—disappear, and those who hold them dear find after their relocation that their new neighbours have come from another area and so do not remember or relate to the same recent past.

Around St Agnes church the area was also cleared, though just fifty yards away from the church one street of vacant and vandalised houses awaits renovation or rebuilding. Just around the church many of the Council houses are being bought by the tenants, who are staying. Chris Burch, the vicar, speaks quite hopefully, 'There's the making of quite a stable community here, but it's not old enough yet. A strong community could come into existence in the next ten years, both inside and outside the church.'

The charismatic renewal has brought new life to St Agnes Church. Brian Ellis, Chris's predecessor, came into a renewal experience in the 1960's—at a time when everything in the community except the church building was being pulled down. Brian Ellis moved to the new vicarage, the first house to be built, next to the church. He stayed for eighteen years, a focus of stability while everything round him was being cleared and demolished. As he had discovered a new depth of the love of God and began to share that, the church began to draw in outsiders, others who had read what Brian had written in the magazine *Christians in Industrial Areas*. Some came with established ideas about mission and politics, but in the pulpit Brian preached mostly on the theme of loving one another. He set out to build up a strong nucleus of committed Christians—committed to each other as well as to the Lord. In his teaching ministry he brought in as the next step, the mission of the church to the local area.

Much of the present impetus for mission has come through lay people, through political involvement, through Aslan Education Unit (which is a Leeds based group working for radical Christian discipleship) and through local issues as they have arisen. The changing neighbourhood has resulted in only a tiny residual congregation, and some of the newcomers are those who buy their first home in the parish but are upwardly mobile and move on before too long.

Chris talks about how the quality of caring that is present in St Agnes is affected by the movement away. There's a very well developed informal and unstructured network of caring relationships in the congregation. This has not grown fast because so many key people have moved on just when it seemed that friendships were getting established and people have had to make new relationships. One or two people have said, 'This seems to be the story of my life. I made friends with so-and-so and she moved. Then I made friends with so-and-so and he moved. You're not moving, are you?' Chris has to reassure people that he is not moving on.

The World into Worship

St Agnes Church has spent time developing its worship and beginning to articulate its everyday concerns in that worship, to bring the world into worship as well as bringing their experience of God into the world. It is very perplexing to Chris, who would prefer to see an orderly development, to discover that the caring ministry in the church is much like couch grass: it spreads underground. Couch grass doesn't blossom where it's planted, it blossoms about six feet away! Chris was originally quite suspicious of one of the most caring groups, the women's Bible study, when it started. He thought the women might be pietistic and inward-looking.

Chris was to be surprised. The group brought new dimensions into the church's worship and pioneered action on a number of issues. Its members started writing to Members of Parliament about issues about which they (and subsequently more church members) were concerned. The concerns adopted were not necessarily as parochial as campaigning for new pelican crossings but included concern for imprisoned Russian Christians.

The social concern expressed has informed and strengthened particular individuals. One woman had been a Liberal Party member for a long time, and after seeing that active involvement in politics was part of her Christian commitment, she stood as a candidate in Council elections.

The group invited Chris to lead a study on part of the Book of Nehemiah. They looked at the relationship between economics and the identity of the people of God. Nehemiah was angry that the Levites had no income and as a result had gone back to work on the land. The group argued out the issues involved and out of the discussion arose all sorts of questions about what the Bible said about certain members—or their husbands—who were unemployed. What does it mean, they wondered, for a person to have no fixed or regular income? What does relying on God mean, economically and not just 'spiritually'?

Monday Break, a lunch-time gathering akin to a parent-and-toddler group, has speakers on everything from cosmetics to baptisms. They have had somebody speaking about pacifists, another about cider, and particularly one about hyperactivity in children. Some children have been proved to be prone to hyperactivity as a result of the orange colouring used in foods, so two people have started a wholefoods group. One family has made a decision, on very little money, to eat an additive free diet. They say that initially it made a very significant and visible difference to the behaviour of two of their three boys. Chris had never thought of diet being particularly tied to the ministry of healing, but he has found that it is. The family receives support and affirmation from the group and from other church members in its decision.

The church has begun to make contact with the locality through the local schools. Chris and his curate have access to these in the ways common to clergy in this country, through helping to lead assemblies. For other church members there is an expressed concern for the quality of life in the area, and they expect to take active roles in the life of local schools. Four lay people are now school governors: one through the deanery, two as nominees through political parties, and one as a parent governor.

Flowing out of Sunday Morning

Worship is the centre, the focus, the climax, which is why it is so important that worship become relevant to the rest of the caring at St Agnes.

Worship is the focus of the healing and caring ministry. St Agnes has prayer with the laying-on of hands in the chapel during and after Communion, at every service. There are always one or two people who go for laying-on of hands, and sometimes there is a line of people waiting. There is a rota of members from the local ministry team, newer members being paired with more experienced folk, to pray with those who ask for such ministry.

Arising from that ministry and out of some recent teaching in the city on healing, with John Wimber and with the Anglican Renewal Committee conference, a group has begun prayer counselling and healing. There is one woman whom the group meets regularly; members are seeing how the Lord might be working with others as well.

People are praying with one another and asking for prayer, outside Sunday mornings. Prayer is a key element in Sunday morning services, but it also flows out of it.

Prayer has also led church members into helping in other ways. A couple of people from the congregation were in court and, for different reasons, weren't represented by Probation or Social Services, or even by a solicitor, so Chris and others put together a sort of social inquiry report. This was a shared caring ministry, as one of the team knew the people in question very well and had a pastoral relationship with them. Roz (Chris's wife) had been a social worker and knew all the jargon. Chris then wrote up the report. One of the three who compiled the report then went to court with the person charged.

Each time, rather to their surprise, the magistrates did what the church suggested. The magistrates were quite impressed that the church was supporting these people. One, who was labelled a recidivist, totally beyond correction, has re-offended far less frequently and far less seriously since he came to St Agnes. The magistrates felt able to give him non-custodial and fairly mild sentences. Over a long period real growth can be seen to have happened.

Sometimes people come to the church presenting nothing but needs, and members try to minister to those needs and are thrilled to see the steady growth. Initially they offer hospitality, which is emotionally costly when people are socially inept. Their worth is recognised by involving them in housegroups, by affirming their enthusiasm for football, or by asking them to do the things they can do; by trusting them, but not trusting them with what they cannot really be trusted with. People with a history of being 'light-fingered' may not trust themselves when purses are left around. Chris has found that helping does not mean being soft. When people fail, commitment involves correcting without dropping or rejecting them. Those who have trouble managing money have been helped to manage and save if they want to. This involves spending time, listening and counselling.

Every now and then Chris realises the Lord is doing something deeper and more inward, and finds he can help. He adds, 'Worship is so important in this way, though not always exciting; sustaining is not always the same as exciting. We are quieter than most charismatic churches, I suspect.'

Chris found considerable tension between the charismatic renewal with its emphasis on victory, glory and power, and concern for the inner city and the dimension of suffering. It is interesting to him that those dimensions are being carried on by the same people but not always at the same time in Leeds.

Chris concludes, 'But we haven't got our theology integrated on these issues. I go through some pain because the renewal songs are not saying the kind of things I want to say to God. On Sunday we sang "When the Spirit is in my heart I will sing as David sang, I will dance as David danced, and I will clap as David clapped, and I will shout as David shouted,..." and I wanted to add: I will weep as David wept.'

There is a poignant quality in the church of St Agnes, of a church with a tiny flame alight in the midst, looking up at the giant tower blocks of the neighbourhood. In a community without much heart and soul the church stands for a different life, for values that seem all too obvious in their absence from local life. But the church is like a flower in the desert, a sign of life and a taste of hope for those who come in through the door.

Oftentimes in finding healing for their own pain and discouragmeent, those involved in the caring ministry discover a source of strength for their work with others. The realisation of the strong link between discipleship and political involvement will find its healthiest expression in churches like St Agnes, for whom the issues at stake are not theoretical but spring from the struggles of the people with whom they live and work. The next stages of any study of the meaning of Christian discipleship in the inner city must grow from the roots of reality in the inner-city churches.

Efforts may be made to support these churches, not by changing them through giving too much money or drawing in too many professional helpers from outside, but by recognising that they represent a pioneering spirit, a cutting edge in the Church's quest for understanding and developing an appropriate and realistic ministry today. The gift that the Church receives from the inner-city congregations should be recognised in a change of mind and attitudes. There must be listening on the part of those in authority in the Church today, an acceptance of the truth that the real leadership lies with those who live and work with the harsh realities of city problems. The problems the Church faces today may not be solved in ivory tower theology but on the streets of parishes like Burmantofts, Leeds, where Christianity faces practical challenges and problems of an order similar to those faced by the Early Church. Out of such a melting pot comes the real progress in theology, in understanding and in knowing the meaning of the parable of the Good Samaritan in our age.

13
You Can't Legislate Caring
The Church of the Redeemer, Edgbaston, Birmingham

Angie Anfield and her husband Dave were looking for a church to belong to. They had visited the Church of the Redeemer, and Angie overhead a conversation in which one of the pastoral leaders was talking to the minister's wife. She talked about someone she had been to visit that day; she had been two or three times. Angie thought that was the sort of caring Christianity that she had never actually met. She had seen how the Mormons cared and the Christian Church hadn't, in her estimation, measured up to the Mormon standards, in their care for one another. So Dave and Angie moved to live across the street from the church.

The Church of the Redeemer, a Baptist Church in Edgbaston, Birmingham, had moved some years earlier from its old, traditional building into new premises on Monument Road, just a few streets away from the extensive Ladywood Council Estate. A light and attractive entrance hall now opens into the worship area, a spacious room, the floor of which slopes down and inwards to focus on the table. There are extra rooms; those upstairs are occupied daily by a playgroup that brings in parents and children from the multi-racial estate around the church. Above the church premises, which are on the lower two floors, are flats for old-age pensioners.

The church has changed its emphasis over the years, struggling both to understand and integrate Christian teaching in their daily lives. A group named Riverbank meets regularly for fellowship, and prayer for the various tasks undertaken by the members.

The older members who moved with the church from its old location have seen change and growth. Yet some things change little. A small group of women meets to pray regularly, as it has for many years, with several older women from the Catholic church around the corner. Many of the newer members who were attracted to the liveliness of the church while they were students at the University, have married and bought houses locally in the first streets of private dwellings beyond the Council estate of Ladywood.

There's a high level of burglary and theft. Jan, who with others runs the youth work, finds that offering open house to a stream of young adults means, 'If you have nothing of value, then no-one will steal it; anything of value goes very quickly. It helps you live a simple lifestyle!'

The Church's Dilemmas

Facing the issues that their neighbours have to accept as a *fait accompli* can be difficult. Olwen, a church member and playgroup leader, talks about the future for her two small daughters: should she try to take them to a school other than the nearest local one (which has a bad reputation) when none of her neighbours has the opportunity to make such choices? It is a painful dilemma for parents who value education; Olwen's children have been to playgroup with the children from along the street. Is the beginning of school the time to struggle with issues of educational values? The choice to be disciples in an area of deprivation calls many such values into question; many are cultural values, and the members of the Church of the Redeemer struggle to discover a relevant basis for decision-making, in the Scriptures.

Angie recognised that her Christian discipleship had been oriented around a very private form of religious expression, one that had to change in her new setting. She realised that her personal salvation didn't explain the whole truth of the resurrection, that Christ was what mattered and the coming of his Kingdom.

It is relatively easy to be trapped into seeing the church as an arena for conversion and a panacea for one's personal aches and pains. Some people use their Sunday worship only as an uplifting experience to carry them through a week that is seen as entirely separate from worship and from laying down one's life for God and for one's neighbours. A church can be inward-looking, never getting beyond concern for its own comfort. But by being located in this particular neighbourhood, the Church of the Redeemer has moved to another kind of spirituality. To be the church in a difficult neighbourhood requires a clearly defined identity as the people of God, standing together—a corporateness. Angie believes that living here has done what nothing else could—in terms of community and learning to care for one another—because it has brought members closer together.

In the quest for a biblical lifestyle, radical discipleship that is prepared to stand against the tide of contemporary cultural norms not only raises questions that challenge the myths and norms of the church's own prejudices, but also causes a renewal in the quality of life. How has this happened? The Church of the Redeemer, through daily contact with the problems of both members and neighbours, has worked to lessen the stereotypes and prejudices of class, sex and race. Several women are discovering their giftedness in leadership, in worship and in teaching, and this church gives enough space for them to learn by experience.

In what used to be a traditional church structure, the minister has also found presuppositions about his role challenged. In talking about servanthood, Chris Walton, the then minister, tells a story about himself that indicates not just the servanthood as a Gospel principle, but the extent to which his own role involves escaping from the conventional trappings.

He received a letter after a recent Evangelical Peacemakers' conference from a woman who wanted to thank him for looking after everyone at the conference. Not until she was going home in the car did she realise Chris was a minister, mainly because of the unassuming tasks he had undertaken in doing his work. On another occasion, Chris wandered across to the church to check the supply of loo-rolls and other details when someone strode in asking, 'You! Are you the caretaker?' and Chris found himself saying 'Yes'.

Advice Centre

The members of the Church of the Redeemer have been making their faith present in practical ways alongside their own struggles to understand the relevance of theology and tradition to the society in which they live. The Advice Centre is a ministry to the local people that is not under the direct control or support of the church, although people in the church send clients along.

This Centre uses the church foyer on Tuesday mornings, officially from 9.30 to 11, though it usually lasts much longer. It is staffed by Raj Patel, who works for Evangelical Christians for Racial Justice, and by Angie Busta. Raj previously worked for an advice centre in Small Heath, so he has had considerable experience.

People from the neighbourhood as well as the church drop in to the Advice Centre. Every problem is different. There are people who come week after week with continuing problems, and some who come once or twice—having problems with the Department of Health and Social Security, or housing, or immigration. Coming from Ladywood—a very bad inner-city housing estate—most are Council tenants, with never-ending problems with the Council, over repairs and related issues. Usually they want to move and the Council won't move them. Most have already spoken repeatedly with the Council about moving but haven't got anywhere. So they come to ask advice on what to do next. Often it's a case of writing letters for people, or making phone calls on their behalf. Those who come in are mainly Asians, and most of them don't speak very much English, but Raj speaks Gujerati; others who come speak very good English and can help one another. The Advice Centre gets more attention from the authorities than individuals do, but it is usually a long battle, and they come back week after week.

Very often past clients bring in their friends, and new people come as they hear about the Advice Centre from neighbours. Some mornings there are two or three, others nine or ten, and sometimes there is a queue patiently waiting.

The coming together of local cultures and the willingness of the Church of the Redeemer to be open to its neighbours of other backgrounds was apparent in a recent wedding, when the traditional service was rewritten to include traditions of Raj's own background. This wedding between Merry and Raj Patel was a celebration that brought together the traditions of two races and transformed the service with ceremonial presentation of flower garlands as well as rings. Relatives and friends of the two sets of in-laws were able to celebrate in ways to which they were accustomed, in a service that was as intricate as it was unconventional. Raj and Merry's house is now close to the Ladywood Estate, and many clients, who have now become friends, drop in on them at home.

Raj's own background is of prime importance for the Centre. As Angie says, 'Most of the people come to see Raj; without him there wouldn't be an Advice Centre. Because of who he is, they trust him to help.'

The Advice Centre is one of the several areas of community involvement which is run independently, but those who do the work are members of the Church of the Redeemer. The Hostel is another project, run by David Brennand, together with several members of the church who live in the Hostel—a residence for homeless young people, many of whom move on to more permanent accommodation in houses and flats in the area.

Looking for Meaning

'You should go and meet Phil Shiner,' several people insisted. 'He's doing something to help council tenants.'

Phil and his wife Jean live just round the corner from the church, quite near the hostel.

Phil Shiner was brought up a Catholic. He says now, 'There is something very attractive and down to earth about Catholics and Catholicism. In my experience, the people are from the working class.' His attraction to the Catholic Church has grown out of a further realisation: 'The middle classes and churches that are predominantly middle-class have got far to go before they realise how privileged they are, and how little other people have got. You could put someone like me on the dole and I would still be five times better off than most people, because I have so many other resources. I would work things out, and I wouldn't sink.' Phil's own spiritual journey has resulted in this linking together of his political consciousness and his Christian faith. For Phil and his wife Jean these are integrally related.

Phil qualified as a solicitor in November 1981 and at the time was employed with a firm that worked for trades unions. He had become increasingly aware of political issues since starting his Articles several years before. 'When I walked through the door of the solicitor's office where I did my Articles, I was hit by the fact that here was a different world that I didn't want to be part of.'

For a while he worked at a Law Centre at Small Heath. He started doing housing work, and found this was what he was happiest with, for he was working with people. Phil left Small Heath to begin further study in law at Warwick University, in a department dominated by Marxists. He appreciated the opportunity to understand what socialism and Marxism were all about. He enthusiastically embraced Marxism as an intellectual discipline, and went along with it more and more until he reached a block and found himself asking, 'What about man's spirit?'

Socialism, he thought, could change people's material conditions but couldn't bring in any worthwhile change, because it hadn't changed man; it hadn't created a system in which each person cares about others. In a socialist state the authorities could not say, 'We are going to have an Act against loneliness.' You can't legislate caring!

Phil and Jean had begun to go to church occasionally and slowly they realised what was staring them in the face. For Phil, becoming a Christian was a rational and logical decision growing out of his understanding of society and humanity. He reached a realisation that he now had something to offer the people he worked with, something that would last. This was a turn-around from concentrating on politics and action. From busy activism he had come full circle: to that quiet, personal relationship with God. Phil and Jean had started attending the Church of the Redeemer in March 1985. They became more involved and were baptised in October.

People have said that Phil and Jean really had nothing to offer the oppressed until they had experienced a personal conversion. This is not true. Phil realised that he could be working for the poor for his own reasons and could be banging his own drum far more. But if in banging his own drum he also worked with poor people, it could not be said that he had nothing to offer the oppressed. Such attitudes, Phil argues, deny that there are some superb people who are not Christians, working for others in a totally committed way. Such people may be socialists, or they may put no label on themselves. There are many of whom it might be said they are working for the Kingdom, but are not Christians.

The Council Estates Project

Phil worked towards a Master's degree on system-built housing, relevant to the law, and found himself thinking, 'I don't want to be in private practice or be an academic. I want to work with tenants—but not in a law centre.' He was talking about a form of legal operation that did not exist. Then the possibility came to mind that he could set up a project that could be self-financing through the Legal Aid scheme.

There were some obstacles before this dream could become reality. He had to win Law Society approval in London for such a project. (In Britain the Law Society has to give formal permission for solicitors to work outside private practice.) He needed the approval of the Birmingham Law Society and initial funding from somewhere. However, as Phil says, 'About the beginning of June I started doing a lot of work on it. By the end of July we were having our first management committee meeting. We had funding more or less as we needed. Things fell into place.'

Phil had worked on schemes in the past, but hadn't followed them up. This idea was working. He did not feel he could attribute what was happening entirely to his own dynamism. The enormity of what he was attempting to do began to dawn on Phil, and he repeatedly said to God, 'Look, if this is just an ego trip which I have dressed up as something else, then make it clear. I don't want to go that way.'

The Birmingham Council Estates' Project aims to work with tenants' groups. Birmingham has a massive housing problem: there are 429 tower blocks and 130,000 council dwellings, many of which are in disrepair. Clearly, then, one person, ten or even twenty can't do much. The only way to achieve change is by working collectively in tenants' groups. Phil does no individual case work. Instead, if an individual problem arises, he explains what the project is about and refers the person elsewhere.

Phil works with the tenants' groups to build their self-esteem, confidence, and ability—through working *with* them. A major test case recently involved the tenants' rights to have essential repair work done to their dwellings by the Council. If successful, the case would have implications for other tenants in Britain. Phil describes the problems he encounters. If there is a tower block with eighty people in it, for example, ten people could get together and take out a summons against the Council for the whole block. The particular Act that Phil is using has always been applied to the individual dwelling, but he has established in the preliminary stages that it can also be used against the whole block. There are 156 dwellings in 3 blocks, and 42 people have signed a summons. But those tenants, if they win, will get an order requiring all three blocks to be repaired.

From the first day the situation was full of conflict. Having worked in a law centre, Phil already had a low opinion of the Council, whether Labour or Conservative. Phil had to start off writing a letter that would give the Council no room for manoeuvre. There was heavy pressure from individuals within the Council to stop the project, but the Council didn't actually deal with the issues Phil was raising. At last, however, the Council did begin to take the Project seriously.

Some organisations that work for or with tenants have been drawn into the state system and so cease to be very effective. They are made 'safe' by the way the system embraces them and says, 'You can be represented on this committee' or 'Do this and we'll give you that information'. Sadly, it's often a process of selling out. Not surprisingly, Phil is very keen for the Project to remain completely independent of the State.

Some Sort of Hero?

One evening, Phil was walking through the Ladywood estate where much of his work is done. With virtually 100% council ownership, both the property and the people are very poor. Phil found himself reflecting that he could easily convince himself he has a *calling* to work in Ladywood. He says, 'In the end it's as if you are trying to make some sort of hero out of yourself: "I'm working for God and I have this wonderful vision about what I am going to do and of what God wants me to do." But then I concluded that if God has given me a calling to work in Ladywood, I shall just continue to work here, it's no more than that.'

Does taking up the Cross make a Christian into some sort of hero? Phil continues, saying that really no-one knows about it. 'You may just go under, and still no-one will exclaim "What a wonderful person!"' Taking up the Cross is not about having fun, nor does it bring fame or acclaim. Phil does this particular work both because he is a socialist and because he is trying to do what he can for God.

The Cross is both a symbol and a means of experiencing reconciliation and peace. In Colossians 1:22 and 24 Paul writes, 'But now he has reconciled you by Christ's physical body through death to present you holy in his sight, without blemish and free from accusation, ... Now I rejoice in what was suffered for you, and I fill up in my flesh what is still lacking in regard to Christ's afflictions, for the sake of his body, which is the church.' Paul writes personally but here reflects on a truth that is relevant to all who look for the meaning of ministry in the Church and who are concerned to take up the Cross and follow Christ.

Discipleship means to take part in the suffering of Christ. The Cross is the link between the despair and the hope of all Creation. On the Cross Christ was afflicted with all the weight and pain of sin. It was a perfect once-for-all act, yet it is (paradoxically) ongoing, for Paul talks of completing that which was lacking in Christ's affliction. Paul was called to serve the Church that had been redeemed but which is also still in the process of being redeemed. Others have a calling from God to particular and different ministries, and this is always inclusive of the affliction of taking up the Cross where evil dominates lives and fights against the peace and wholeness of Redemption. Christ paid for that redemption in his death, and Christians still share in the affliction of the redemptive process.

The hope which enables Christ's disciples to continue is not one in which they can anticipate a reward. The parable of the servant in Luke 17:7–10, makes that clear. Resurrection hope is present, or it would be impossible for anyone to be a disciple. That hope is present, yet is still to come.

The presence of the risen Christ is in the Church. In the Eucharist, he is present in the elements, not only to commemorate what is accomplished but as a sign of the future coming of the Kingdom when all things will be reconciled in him. Grace is given to the Church for costly ministry, since Christ has also taken redeemed humanity into the presence of God, by his own ascension. As the Church meets together in his presence, it is given a present hope, a present experiential knowledge of the salvation it has received and which is to come.

Discipleship, which is by definition a sharing in the cross of Christ, is not for reward or acclaim. In discipleship, both individuals and churches are a sign of who they are and what they are becoming: Christ in the world. They are a fulfilment of the loving nature of God, who because of that nature chose the Cross.

Just as Jesus was true to the nature of who he was created to be, he who follows a calling to a particular work or ministry is fulfilling the intended nature of the individual Christian or of the church as a whole. The empowering of the Spirit is not superimposed upon the person, as something alien or essentially different. A calling is much like a seed, which when it is warmed and watered begins to grow. There is that seed of life in all of creation. Because of their God-given tasks of stewardship and responsibility, as people begin to live in the fullness of the nature God gave them, redemption is reflected in society. To be a disciple is to choose to be faithful to that God-given nature.

When people seek to control others, for good or ill, they use punishments and rewards. This process is necessary for the safety of children, for example, or is negatively used by despotic leaders to control the majority of the people. Mature people, however, are self-disciplined, choosing for themselves to be controlled in a particular way: they are self-controlled. The same is true (if not more so) of mature Christians. They *choose* to live as the fulfilment of what God created them to be. God does not command them as one would a robot, automaton or slave, he speaks and has spoken, and of their own free will his people respond. They do not follow because they have no choice, nor because they will be punished or rewarded, but because they have decided to.

14
Mission, a Changing Image
Cambridge University Mission to Bermondsey

Many Christian missions were founded in the cities of Britain when the terrible deprivation of people who lived in the decaying slum areas became apparent. In Victorian times, when state help was negligent or grudging, many philanthropists and concerned Christians set up projects to relieve the suffering of the poor and destitute. Often such projects provided food, clothing and medical care as well as preaching the gospel.

Against the backdrop of our contemporary society, where increasing unemployment has resulted in increasing numbers of people living in poverty and despair, such missions are grappling with the need for changing identity. Many missions had veered towards a concentration on the spiritual needs of the people but are now once more responding to the broader needs and pressures of the communities in which they are located.

The Cambridge University Mission to Bermondsey, London, was founded as a medical mission before Britain had a National Health Service. It was the vision of a man called Pa Salmon, who had been a Cambridge student, and it was to Cambridge that Salmon went when he needed resources for the Mission. As a result, there is considerable goodwill from Cambridge in the shape of both financial and practical assistance. One old booklet, entitled 'Miracles of Grace in Bermondsey', refers to a list of people waiting to join Bible classes there. Pa Salmon personally found two hundred jobs for people in one year.

The Cambridge University Mission evolved, eventually providing Youth Clubs for young men, and later in the 1960's offering clubs for girls. Its present building also dates from the 1960s.

Bermondsey today is still a clearly identifiable community within the London conurbation. On the northern side of Bermondsey is the Thames, and there is a clear view west from the Embankment, about half a mile to Tower Bridge. Much of what has been, for a couple of decades, decaying dockland along the river is now being redeveloped by the London Dockland Development Corporation, a massive enterprise that affects not only Bermondsey but many nearby communities north and south of the river. For the majority of the traditional, conservative working-class community, the effect of the development has been to shoot the price of private housing to unreachable heights. New luxury dwellings are beginning to flank the river, creating for most of Bermondsey's population (living in Council flats) an irritating sign of the great gulf between rich and poor in the city. Issues that stir local reaction now have not only to do with the struggle to obtain refurbishment grants for deteriorating dwellings, but to stop heliports being built on areas of grassland between the Council flats and the river.

From Country to City

Snowy Johnson came to the Mission in 1967, when the emphasis and patterns of communication were changing. He came as a Boys' Club leader, was from a strong church background, and was a licensed lay reader in the Anglican Church.

The family's last home had been in a small village. For them, living in Bermondsey was initially like living in an alien culture. Snowy had been used to saying, 'I'm going home for the weekend', meaning he was going to his parents. Some three years after they came to Bermondsey, while away, Sybil, Snowy's wife, said, 'Oh, it'll be nice to get home!' To Snowy, that confirmed that they were at last established in Bermondsey.

It took just as long for local people to realise they were going to stay. Before this they had had curates who each ran the Mission for a year or two. David Sheppard had once said that if you went to an area like Bermondsey, it meant staying at least ten years to get to know the locality and what it was about. Snowy therefore knew his family had come for at least that long.

Having accepted the job at Cambridge University Mission, Snowy found out the size of the task. There were nearly thirty voluntary helpers, and about ten residents in the Centre who join in and support the work. He was running ten football teams on a Saturday, six in the morning, four in the afternoon, and running Sunday schools on Sunday afternoon. 'We were very busy,' he comments drily.

Bermondsey Ways

There were significant differences in ways of life to which Snowy needed time to adapt. There were aspects of neighbourhood, culture and church to understand. Snowy and Sybil once went to Stan's house for a nice three-course meal. Stan said to his wife, 'You're a bit of a silly old cow, but you're all right.'

Sybil nudged Snowy, 'If you ever spoke to me like that, it would be the end!'

For Snowy, who was always polite and well-mannered and had been brought up 'properly'—as his mother would have said—to hear these people talk to one another was shocking.

Then John, one of the local helpers, took Snowy aside one night and said 'Snow, I've got something to say to you. You won't last long here.'

'Why's that?'

'I've seen you flinch, I've seen you get highly embarrassed whenever we say anything. What you've got to come to terms with is the way we work and the way we talk. Either you accept that or you don't, and if you don't, you'll leave.'

Snowy answered, 'That's fair enough. But I'll tell you one thing, too. I'm not going to join you, I'm not going to be like you. I'm me. You'll have to accept me and my politeness. It'll have to work both ways.'

'That's fair and straight. We wouldn't expect you to be like us.'

Years later Snowy realised that he, too, had always called his wife an animal, calling her a 'duck'. He realised he was not as different from the Bermondsey people as he had first thought.

In the 1960s, 75% of the young people in the Cambridge University Mission were Roman Catholics. The Irish had come to London a century before to build London's railways and docks, and Bermondsey became predominantly Roman Catholic, with a number of churches and a big comprehensive school.

Snowy and his team of workers went to see the Canon of the Roman Catholic Church because children would say in school they had been to CUM, and he had told them not to go again, saying, 'You only hear the Gospel from us, not from anybody else.' That attitude has changed radically.

Most of the Mission's Christians were Roman Catholics, and some still are. Over the years there has been a cooperation with the Church that was not there nineteen years ago. The Mission is now on friendly terms with the Canon.

The Boys

When Snowy came to the Mission, Tom was introduced to him as a Christian, along with a group of other eleven-year-olds. Snowy could not understand why among these boys there was no thirst for God. There seemed to be no way for Snowy to get through to Tom at all.

Trust grows slowly, taking years, and it was a long time before the boys felt they could tell Snowy their story. The group had been away with the Mission on a camp in North Wales. They had heard Gospel talks using climbing as an illustration, with footsteps all beautifully drawn; Christ gave the tools and the map and the compass and the climbing rope, and as long as they were tied on they couldn't lose their grip. Later, when Snowy was running their football team, the boys began laughing about what had happened as they prepared to break camp. Each helper had taken one boy for a walk alone. As Snowy wryly says, 'These boys are green, but they aren't idiots. They realised they were going to get *converted*. So it was just a matter of how long they would make the helper wait for the decision, whether they walked all the way down the valley to Bangor, or whether they took only twenty yards. So the boys became "Christians" and made professions. No wonder that for two years I'd battered against these *Christians*!'

Tom continued going on Easter Weekends and camps until he was seventeen. That was where he started going out with Kate, who is now his wife. They became Christians through the Mission, and now have three children.

The Bermondsey housing is 90% Council houses, so families have to go on a waiting list. When a family has two children and is still living with parents, the family may be offered one of the hard-to-let flats some distance away. So most young people try to buy a house, to get a mortgage, and move out. Tom and Kate moved to Welling. They had a comfortable house. Then in 1985 Tom heard God say he should move back to Bermondsey.

Redesigning and Rebuilding

Cambridge University Mission, by its founding Deed, is for the boys of Bermondsey, with a strong emphasis on the evangelical Church of England faith. The girls were in a separate building, six feet away from the boys' building.

Snowy went through the stages of linking the clubs together to work as co-equals, rather than the girls' leader and the boys' leader working separately. Whereas such change had created adverse reaction in many missions and centres at CUM, there were fewer ructions here, because change took place over a long period and happened naturally with rebuilding and redesigning. Change also came through the grace of the CUM chairman at that time, who had said at a crucial planning group meeting that for the next hour nobody over the age of thirty-four would speak. Nearly every person on the committee was older, so Snowy and the other leader had an hour to put their cases. Snowy adds, 'Touches of grace like that were beautiful. That man had a lot of experience and wisdom.'

The central hub of the club needed to be a social area, with music and a relaxed atmosphere. Any other facilities had to spread out from that centre. There had been an 'epilogue room', with 'Christ our Hope' on the wall, a lectern and pews. This was reorganised during the rebuilding, with a view to 'chatting' rather than preaching the Gospel, so the epilogue room moved into the café. For the helpers who had been with the club from the age of seven until now when they were twenty-one and had gained considerable confidence, this was a drastic change in the familiar structure.

New Ways

Snowy's discipline was different too; a hard issue in a club in this type of area. There seemed to be an established pattern that worked tolerably well. When leaders laid down hard and fast rules, which were unflinchingly upheld, the system held together, though it was authoritarian. When the rules were relaxed or only loosely applied, the boys brought in with them the chaos and noise of the streets. For a while, when Snowy was new, the helpers thought their hard-won standards were slipping. 'But,' Snowy adds, 'I had nineteen-year-olds on the football teams. They were married men, and there was no way I was going to say, "Spit on the floor and you're out for a week."'

Probably the most dramatic innovation of the 1960s was the recognition of the needs of girls as well as boys. The change of attitude to women in society generally has progressed steadily in the last twenty years, affecting places such as the Mission. In this area there were no clubs for girls and very few mixed ones. Boys were allowed out on the streets to play, and as teenagers hung around or ran wild with their friends, but girls were kept at home. So clubs and missions looked for ways to meet their needs. As patterns changed, organisations such as the Mission had to come to terms with the challenge: If boys and girls were mixed together socially, would this increase the danger of sexual misdemeanour? After all, the mores of Bermondsey society were already significantly different from the conservative evangelical standards represented by the club. For many it seemed better to slow down the process of change than to risk the problems that might result. Snowy again set a challenging lead.

The Mission began to take mixed groups away to camp. Snowy went away with a female leader to check out the campsite and stayed overnight in a boarding house; worried prayers went up that nothing untoward would happen. It was a shock to traditional attitudes and a challenge to Snowy.

For the first mixed camp Snowy took the seniors, and there were many questions about how he was going to control the lads.

'What rules are you going to impose on them?' asked club supporters.

Snowy stopped them. 'All right, I'll make a rule. No male will be able to touch a female except between the elbow and hand on the outside of the arm.'

One person said, 'There's no need to be sarcastic.'

In the end Snowy got so frustrated with them that he retorted, 'The way you are talking, anyone would think I was taking a gang of rapists! I'll have an electric fence and barbed wire, a sentry and searchlights, if that's what you want!'

Such reactions have changed. There are open discussions about such issues today. Snowy adds, 'Sexism is still around, but it isn't as prevalent as it was then. I thank God for how far we have moved, even if we don't explain ourselves as we should, yet.'

Most of the young people who came to the club had police records, but even so, Snowy feels they were always friendly. He reflects that he didn't then face the pressure of violence that youth workers face today. Any violence in the 1960s was very much a gesture; if a mission resident was too pushy, a kid might hit him—boomph!

Snowy would go across and say, 'You don't hit anyone in this club.'

And the kid would say, 'Look, Snow, if I had really hit him he wouldn't have got up; that was just to tell him he'd gone too far.'

So it was often the resident's responsibility to cope. Snowy would say 'Now look here, buster, you push too hard; lay off.' Nowadays there are knives. Drugs came in five or seven years ago and went out again. But now the drug problem is increasing yet again and affects a younger age group, a change Snowy greatly regrets.

Being in Touch

Restructuring management was important to Snowy, who was aware that the interviewing Cambridge University Mission committee consisted of businessmen in the City of London, in black pin-striped suits in a solicitor's office in Queen Street. 'I kept thinking, "I know you are kind people, but I don't know if you know anything about Bermondsey, and what it's like to rub shoulders with a dustbin man." So it came to me that I wanted local people in the management area.' Snowy got more local people onto the House Committee, a day-to-day management group, and eventually onto the Council. 'We also decided to meet at CUM instead of at Queen Street.'

Stan, a London Transport mechanic, became a member of the Council. It then changed from a Council of Management to the Cambridge University Mission Trust Company Ltd, so Stan became a director. As soon as he realised he would have to put on his Tax Return form that he was a director of a company, he rang up Snowy and said, 'I'm packing it in. I'm jacking the lot in. If word got out to my mates that I'm a director—we sit all day slagging directors off. Here, I'm finished, I'm packing in.'

'The name doesn't change anything.'

'It does! It's on my Tax Return. If any of my mates see that, I've had it!'

'Look at it this way, Stan. If CUM Trust Ltd goes bankrupt, you pay a pound. If CUM management committee goes bankrupt, you could be in debt for £75,000.'

Bermondsey people don't necessarily aspire to middle-class badges of status!

Meeting God in Ordinary Ways

The Mission has always had a struggle encouraging people to go to church; it is strange and foreign,—'They sing and do things with books'—and not normal to local people. Snowy says, 'Seven or more years ago we started our own fellowship at CUM to meet with the Christians.' Snowy took the opportunity to ask questions that would help him know what would support people in their discipleship and what kind of bridge might be built to the church. For these people the most important aspect of their meeting—the most helpful to their faith—was meeting one another.

Receiving Grace

Snowy had come from a very strict evangelical background: no Sunday newspaper, no TV or icecream on Sundays. It enriched his family, he says. But one of the glorious things was to learn new approaches in Bermondsey.

One of the local girls came into the Mission one Sunday night, and Snowy asked, 'Where've you been?'

She said, 'One of the residents took me to All Souls.'

Snowy immediately assumed it would have been terrible for her, and thought, 'I'll have to have a word with that resident, taking one of our lot there.' He said to the girl, 'What did you make of it?'

'Oh, it was fantastic! The singing—about five hundred, all singing—it was gorgeous!'

Maybe it hadn't been such a bad idea after all, so Snowy said, 'Tell me more.'

'It was good. Mind you, they rabbit on with the prayers, and then this bloke got in the pulpit and rabbited away. He went on so long I got the Bible and read it instead.'

Snowy was shocked that even John Stott couldn't get the Gospel message across to this girl.

Later Snowy asked Sybil, 'What do you make of that? What struck me was how she said that he "rabbited on" in the sermon. How can we preach to these people, then? What do we need to do?'

On Sundays his family usually came back from church and talked about the sermon; if it was good they thought the service was good, or if bad, the service was bad. But this girl had not even heard the sermon, yet she had thought it was worthwhile being in church.

Snowy said, 'Next week, before we go to church, we'll sit down and say, "God, show me this morning what is important in this service."'

The family compared notes afterwards. For Snowy, the most important thing had been talking to Vi and to another old lady, over a cup of tea afterwards. For Sybil, it was the prayers.

Now Snowy says each week, 'God, show me what is important this morning.' Very rarely is it the sermon. Once, for example, a little child came in, and one of the oldest members of the congregation said, 'You come in here, my love,' and gave her a book. Snowy said, 'God, it's been worth being here this morning, to see one of the oldest people and one of the youngest share in fellowship. That is beautiful. I don't care what the vicar preaches about now.'

Willie was a drinker who, when drunk, could be quite wild, but then he became a Christian. He got a job he had always wanted, as an undertaker's assistant. He was to be paid by cheque.

He came to Snowy and said, 'Give me a reference for a cheque book, will you?'

Snowy laughed and wrote something like, 'Willie has always paid his subs in club, and I'm sure during your interview you'll assess whether he is really reliable.'

Willie came rushing in one Saturday, saying, 'I've done wrong! I wrote a cheque out yesterday, and I don't have any money in the bank.'

Snowy responded, 'I hoped this wouldn't happen. The bank manager took a risk. What did you do?'

'I had to buy something, so I wrote a cheque out for ten quid.'

Snowy advised him to see the bank manager and to pray over the weekend as well.

On Monday afternoon Willie came running in. 'Praise the Lord! Praise the Lord! I got the money.' At funerals people would give a few pounds for the attendants, and this was put in a tin and shared out once a month between them. It had been shared out that Monday morning. Willie rushed down and put thirty-five pounds in the bank. That evening at club he told most of the Christian people the story.

Tuesday night was the Christian get-together evening, when they would meet and have a time of prayer. That Tuesday, Willie prayed, 'Dear Lord, I want to thank you for how good ... You see, what happened was...'

He stopped the prayer meeting to tell Billy the story, as he was the only one who didn't know.

Billy said, 'That was great.'

'Yes, it was, Bill. So Lord, I really want ...' And the meeting continued.

At another prayer meeting, when everyone simply couldn't stop laughing, Snowy said, 'Look, we've got the giggles. We'd better stop. We aren't going to pray. I just hope that God laughs with us.' Snowy added, 'They released me from an awful lot that bound me up.'

Joy Shared

Stan once booked a London Transport bus to take local families round the Christmas lights in the West End. Seventy-five people came to the Mission to join the outing. Stan had decorated the inside of the bus with little Christmas trees and streamers.

They went down Oxford Street five times—they'd get to

Marble Arch and then—'Everybody on the top deck downstairs, and all you downstairs go up.'

Stan gave a commentary, and then he came to Snowy and said 'How much are we charging them, 50p a head?' The cost was £8 for the bus and £20 for the driver as a tip.

Snowy said, 'We're not making a charge. I put a bucket in the porch. They can sling in what they want to when they come in for tea.'

'You can't do that, look at the cost.'

As people said, 'How much, Stan?' he responded, 'There's a bucket by the door; put in what you can.'

This seemed fine to Stan till, on the return journey, the bus was going up Tower Bridge Road towards Bermondsey and one family said, 'We'll get off here.'

Then in Tooley Street some others said, 'Stop here, Driver.'

Snowy later counted the money. In the bucket was £28.04.

Stan came over, 'How did you make out?'

Snowy said, 'I've got a problem, Stan.'

'I knew you would have.'

'I've got 4p too much, and I don't know who to give it to.'

Snowy comments that Christians can make up their own minds about how they are going to do things!

His perception of the Christian faith has changed. It is not only in church that the reality of God's presence is experienced, not only in the ways he had traditionally expected.

Very often in testimonies and teaching Christians speak only of God answering in times of troubles and forget that God *enjoys living*. That's a danger: 'Oh dear, have you got a problem? Well, our God...'. Why not, 'You're excited? Our God is in it.' In Bermondsey, Snowy has discovered more about God who enjoys his people's fun and laughter. The local people are giving to him as much as they receive from him.

Recent Developments

Bob and Brenda Sleeman came to London's East End to work at the Mayflower Centre. Bob took a social work post in up-market Greenwich, and was wondering, 'Why am I working in Greenwich when we are living in the East End in the Mayflower?' Bob resigned and was unemployed for nine months. When he reached the point of really giving everything to God, saying, 'I put everything on the altar,' someone rang him up and said, 'There's a job going here at CUM. Are you interested?

There were similarities to the Mayflower, yet he found the Cambridge University Mission significantly different. CUM is a pragmatic place. The Mayflower is a place that has a clearly expressed theology behind its action, set out by people like Pip Wilson and Roger Sainsbury. Here at the Mission, Bob has found a pragmatic sense of getting on with the work, and although things seem to work more by accident than by design, they do work out.

There are inherent contradictions such as the strong links with Cambridge, with all the privilege that implies. Students come from Cambridge and get involved. At first sight Bob thought, '*What* is going on here?' But after a while he could sense the acceptance. People tend to be suspicious of anyone from outside, as there's a close community here, but the atmosphere of CUM breaks through that. The Mission has a strange assortment of people with funny accents and funny ways of dress, yet it seems to work.

Bob recognises an essential task of the Mission is to identify with the local population. But how can anyone identify with the local racism and the sexual bigotry? Many people who come to CUM are trying to understand the racists; others are feeling like kicking the racists out of the club. To identify with the community means beginning to pick up the attitudes. There is a tension in developing a radical faith while at the same time dealing with conservative mores and the norms of the area.

One man was openly racist in his attitudes. Bob took

him onto the Headstart Community Programme, and said, 'Look, you have got to do something about your attitudes to women and black people, and that's all I am going to say to you about it.'

After three weeks the man went off to a Frontier Youth Trust weekend; he mixed socially with black people, and this was a revolution for him. He got a taste of the presence of the Spirit because of the way young people are working with each other, and Christians were talking his sort of language. At that time the supervisor from the Community Work Scheme was also black. The man concluded, 'I think God is trying to tell me something here.'

He then went on a CUM weekend on anti-racism training, travelling in the Mission's bus. The others were white, predominantly middle-class people, and some started saying, 'You're a Bermondsey person; you're the racist.' Of course the man got more and more angry. Those people didn't know the struggle that he had been through during those few weeks and the rapid progress he had made from derogatory statements about 'spades'.

Speaking the Local Language

Meeting local people, Bob recognised the same linguistic and cultural differences as Snowy had; words and language were used differently. A local man wanted help in studying the Bible, so Bob worked with him, following a course setting out God as 'the Boss'.

The man's first comment was, 'Well, where I work most people think the boss is a ——.' So already Bob knew the study was going to be almost impossible to use.

Then they came to a section called 'Your Own Story' which said, 'God is a Father. What did your father say to you?'

The man answered, 'My father said I was an ugly so-and-so, and he didn't want anything to do with me.'

The basis of the study was the assumption that people had stable, good family relationships.

Headstart Unemployment Project

Bob Sleeman and Margaret Ramsey, his co-worker, have been able to work with unemployed young people, seeing the present unemployment crisis as an opportunity. Unemployment is less of a crisis for young people than is often portrayed, certainly less of a crisis than for a forty-five year old man made redundant. Because of the tradition of freedom and developing initiatives at CUM, Bob and Margaret have been able to discover ways to support people and give them a lot of encouragement, listening and understanding.

The Cambridge University Mission's Unemployment Project, Headstart, began with Bob's appointment, and was funded by the London Docklands Development Corporation. Headstart has worked with individuals and small groups of young adults in their early twenties, all unemployed. They have developed new skills and interests, and some have gone on to be employed by the Manpower Services Commission Community Programme, or to assist in running the Headstart Project. Headstart wants the young people to develop as adults and understands that individual development is part of the foundation. Also if a person is to respect himself as an adult, he has to experience working for his living.

Headstart has defined for itself two closely linked aims: to reach unemployed young people, and to explore with them ways in which they may find fulfilment through work. An additional aim is to share the resultant understanding of this biblical challenge with others in the Church and in society as a whole, in order to encourage change in the harsh way the unemployed are perceived and treated.

Unemployment deprives people of adult status, so Headstart encourages adult status through participation and responsibility. Many 'dead-end' and soulless jobs in the area do not offer a sense of worth in adult status, offering only token participation. Bob says he tries 'to pay people when I can. To work for nothing is very demeaning. It's a fine balance between using people to get things done at a place like CUM and actually giving them work.'

Giving people adult status by giving them work is an acknowledgement of their worth. When Headstart's hall was built, it so happened that there was a man who had some building experience, whom Bob trusted. The only time he could come in to do the necessary work was during the time Bob would be away for a week.

Bob gave him the keys, the materials and tools, and said, 'There'll be a group of young men on the Community Work Programme who will help you. See you in a week.'

Bob came back and went round to see the man and asked, 'How did it go?'

'Great to start off with, but it's terrible. I've just been down to the Hall and they've taken everything down and put it up the wrong way, it looks awful!'

Over the week the Community Project Workers had increased in confidence and realised they could do it themselves, and they had made a good job of it. Bob realised he had not trusted them.

One man, Charlie, came to the Headstart Project and said to Bob on the first day: 'I hate work. You'll never get me working.'

Bob assumed that he meant that he hated dead-end jobs. So the trick was to get him interested. The man liked music, so they set up a music project. Instruments and tutors were scrounged from the National Jazz Centre. They ran a music workshop for the Greater London Council the following summer.

Later Bob was out driving with Charlie to pick up equipment. After a day of work Charlie said, 'I'm totally knackered. We've been working all day.'

Bob asked, 'Did you hear what you just said? You've been working all day.'

Charlie spent a year with the Community Programme, and was talking about going back even to a dead-end job like warehousing. That made Bob wonder whether it was right to encourage people to accept soulless jobs, even if that did divert them away from crime.

Bob asked Charlie, 'What are you going to do now the Community Programme is finished?'

He said 'Well, I'll come in and help, but you'd better pay me. I think I'm worth ten quid a day.'

A couple of sixteen-year-olds had painted the toilets at the Hall. They painted the walls, the floor, the toilet seats; there was paint everywhere. But because they hadn't painted the ceiling first, it looked a real mess.

Bob asked Charlie to redo the job, saying, 'I'll give you twenty-five quid to paint the toilets again.'

Charlie came back and said, 'That isn't enough.'

Bob later reflected, 'That bloke has learned the principle of self-worth!'

The Work with Women

Margaret Ramsey works on the Headstart Project making contact with young women. She came to Bermondsey through Care Force, working for a year after studying in Edinburgh. When she came here, the three previous Care Force workers were still living in the area; now she, too, has stayed. 'I came from a farm outside Belfast and did quite a bit of work with the North Belfast Mission.' It has taken great effort and determination to get the local young women to visit the Centre, to get them to come out of their doors at all. Margaret has picked up on what they are interested in, and over coffee they talk to one another and make friends.

The women's project is closely related to the brief Bob had been developing, but Headstart was always aware that young women had particular and different needs. They are an elusive group, not readily apparent when considering unemployment because of their home demands, sexist expectations of them as women, and the traditional domination of men. The initial work has shown that women are interested in taking advantage of what is offered, and the task of meeting them in their homes and discovering their needs is under way.

The women's work has brought some additional aims to Headstart's first targets, including developing self-help initiatives, helping women choose appropriate changes in their own lives, looking at work values within the community, including parenting. The Project wants to encourage enterprise and the acquisition of skills for a variety of work, much of it related to the women's own needs.

A Last Resort

The Cambridge University Mission is seen locally as a last resort. Bob and others find people knock on the door asking for help. They can offer what other agencies may not, in that they work with people who do not readily come under other helping agencies' headings. There is a big, new community centre down the road, with enormous resources, and the people of the Mission were thinking, 'They've got everything; we'll lose people.' But the Mission is dealing with people even before they arrive at the point of going through those other doors. They are too isolated and too scared to go to such a place.

The people Bob and Margaret work with don't have the confidence to make a phone call. Bob came into his office one day, and a man was on the phone. It was tempting to say, 'Can I have the office, please? You shouldn't really be here.' The remarkable fact was that the man was using the phone, whereas two years ago he wouldn't touch it. That's the level of the work where lives are transformed as people are developing and achieving the ability to cope with everyday life.

Detached Work

Every mission or organisation that seeks to reach into a local community has members who find ways and means to become enmeshed in the life and structures of the community for the sake of contacts. The actual work of the mission will be reflected in the way that those outside members work. If the sole task of the mission were evangelism, for example, then the outside worker would be primarily an evangelist at the grassroots level, able to invite and encourage people to rallies and meetings at the Centre.

The Cambridge University Mission has always been concerned with the whole person, not just with conversions, though many people are converted here. Thus its outreach into the community has reflected these broader perspectives. For the last ten years detached workers have gone into the community, supporting projects on local estates, often working with local organisations and tenants' associations on site. The Mission is more concerned with developing links in the community than simply attracting people to the Centre. Community development has been going on, and the unemployment project went out to be where unemployed people were.

Dave is a detached worker funded by the Inner London Education Authority through a grant to the Mission. The Mission made the appointment, but ILEA plays an advisory role. The project was initiated by the Youth Office, not starting as a specifically Christian concern. Cambridge University Mission was asked because of its reputation and stability rather than its specifically Christian nature.

The principal work was to contact clubs and individuals, and these contacts in turn led into many kinds of community help. Dave doesn't know which comes first: being a Christian or being a youth worker—but the former is partly explicit as the Mission is a Christian organisation, and young people ask him about it. Adults have indicated interest in hesitant ways. Several have said they have become interested specifically because the Christian facet wasn't too obvious.

Dave has become involved in day-to-day life that has opened up the specific needs of adults. Sometimes these are problems around the estates. A sum of money allocated for refurbishment of dwellings was subsequently reallocated elsewhere by the Council. Dave found it was a question of helping the local tenants revive interest in fighting back; encouraging people that they could do things; chairing the occasional meeting when there was no-one else to do so. Listening to people, he says, helps them relieve the pressure of their problems.

All people can express something of God's life-giving

drive or motivation in all sorts of ways which don't have Christian labels and wouldn't necessarily be described in Christian words. Dave has helped people discover that as they have taken new risks; having a student stay with them during the summer projects at CUM, or going for a job that they think is a bit beyond them. It means finding opportunities to be a bit more open, to give something that they can give. All those things are part of the life of the Gospel. Dave says, 'People are valuable, and I hope that the way things are done carries that message.'

Dave serves the situation rather than dominating it, giving the people an opportunity to make their own successes, and so giving them confidence. He says, 'Whatever needs to be done to help people take new steps for themselves, that's the work. More often it is not up-front, like making sure that someone gets up in the morning to go for a job.' In this work, Dave is a channel for a grace that is so like yeast in a loaf of bread, a quiet and effective catalyst for change.

One boy who came to the Centre occasionally had considerable family problems, which resulted in his being sent to a boarding school. He had to go back to school each Sunday night and came home Friday nights. Dave went to take him to the station on Sunday nights to make sure the boy got there. Dave said, 'He needed someone to be an authority. His father couldn't do it. He needed boundaries. I acted as policeman or social protector for a while. I had to learn that, but it was hard to realise it would help someone to be the big stick, rather than be understanding.'

Dave had been given £30 for clothes for the boy, who was determined to get a second pair of trainers and equally determined they be expensive ones. Dave entrusted the money to him, but the boy went straight out and got the trainers. To help him despite what he had done, Dave went shopping with him to see if they could get some jeans that were acceptable but still within the amount of money that was left. This meant renegotiating and not rejecting the boy for his action.

When Dave first met him the boy was nine and on the street. He had been expelled from a secure school and had fallen through all the welfare safety nets that should protect children.

Dave organises and oversees the Mission's play-schemes, which happen on local estates. He enjoys the programme, with its link between the Cambridge students coming down to assist and the local people. Eight or nine students come to live with local families. They mix very well. Dave gives them opportunities to talk about what is going on and how the day has gone. If people are genuine and don't pretend to be what they are not, the work goes well.

Dave's contacts include groups of young people who meet casually, in the stair well of a block of flats, or for the occasional outing in the mini-bus. One of the members of the older group said to Dave that he was going to have to leave home. Dave gave him the name of the person he knew in the Council department. Just weeks later he saw the lad, who said, 'I have got the flat.'

One group of youngsters was in court for stealing some lead from a roof. They told Dave that they hadn't done it. Dave did quite a lot of work on the case, and, in fact, they got off. So others now come to him asking for help. Dave comments that it would be easy in this way to become politically active with the problems he sees locally, especially when young people are victimised. But he finds it is not straightforward, since it is equally true that some young people do some incredibly horrible things to adults in their communities. There is a political balance to find. Dave has thought a lot about Jesus, who had a similar fence to straddle. What did 'political' mean to Him? He faces the dilemma of trying to be true to the situation and communicating the differences of a Christian viewpoint, without sounding like someone from Mars.

Three local women set up a girls' club when they found there was nothing for their own teenage daughters to join. Dave supported and gave them contacts like the Surrey Docks Sports Centre. At first they needed a lot of support and ideas. One of the women visited the Mission and spoke of her appreciation of the link, as she sees herself doing Christian work, giving for other people.

A family on one estate wanted a playscheme and one woman was particularly gifted; very bouncy, full of life, but lacking self-confidence. She has over a period of time developed sufficient confidence to lead and organise a local group that compaigned against a heliport right next to the estate. She was also in the fight against the loss of a refurbishment grant, despite traumatic family problems throughout that time. Dave adds, 'Often my inclination is to do something, but that should be a last resort. I need to listen, be aware, communicate a sense of understanding, but not do what needs to be done myself.' His gift to these local people is that he believes in them.

Cambridge University Mission, like many other churches and missions, has been grappling for relevance to people in the local setting. In becoming relevant they have had to be careful not to abandon their own faith, and to avoid being overwhelmed by despair. The Mission's support groups, in regular contact with the workers, help keep the balance. Such a setting, however, with its stark contrasts, is a melting pot in which to examine principles of Christian lifestyle. In this area, the middle-class qualities of the Church become more apparent, and effective mission requires a refining before the real Gospel values shine forth strongly. Above all, workers have to keep in mind the understanding: compassion has to have perspective—one foot in the situation and one outside—so that those who seek to help do not themselves become helpless and powerless.

15
Mission Overseas
Kenya and Australia

In recent years Western nations have become more aware of the Third World. Television and other media have brought news and documentaries that give a glimpse into the lives of distant countries. Ease of travel, with increased wealth and technology to encourage it, has taken far more travellers to see and experience the life of others. Such experience has resulted in increased sense of outrage, compassion, and initiative in caring. Oxfam, Tear Fund, World Vision, Christian Aid, Traidcraft, and Band Aid are all expressions of this. Their caring has affected the outcome of the famine in Ethiopia and the Sudan, saving thousands of lives, and they represent the compassionate giving of thousands of individuals all over the Western world.

Some multi-national companies and their governments have constructed exploitive systems that effectively abuse the human rights of the citizens of poorer nations. They set up monopolies over locally produced commodities, food and minerals, which enable them to control the lives of the local people. This is not a new phenomenon; human greed and self-interest has been expressed this way for hundreds of years, most particularly in the great trading companies that were a driving force in the empire building of the nineteenth century. Too often there is an oppressive structure and a complete absence of human love and compassion. Oxfam and Traidcraft are both seeking to find an alternative foundation to these trading injustices.

Unfortunately, the empire builders often carried with them the Christian missionaries. The Missionary Societies were often unintentional exporters of Western culture and values as well as genuine apostles in the church-building ministry. This history has resulted, in recent decades, in the eviction of Christian missionaries from many territories, and has precipitated re-evaluation of the true nature of mission overseas. To recognise the rights of developing nations, the sense of superiority has had to be set aside, in favour of a knowledge that the people whose land it is must decide for themselves what help they want, and how they will receive it.

As the African Church has come of age, so the presence of helpers from the West is at their invitation, with responsibility resting with the African Church. More often a missionary is now a person who lives and works in the Third World, and the sharing of the Gospel is done through what would be recognised simply as good neighbourliness, offering one's resources and concern, hope and faith reciprocally in the community. The work is often to find ways to enable the local people to develop their own skills, using their own resources. Alongside this development approach is a newer realisation among Western churches that there is a unique gift that the Third World nations bring in their perspective on the Gospel; Western theology is not the whole truth.

With such renewal in understanding has come renewed understanding of worship. The music and the liturgies that we use are good only because they help us in our encounter with God. When Christianity is earthed in another culture, there are different but equally valid forms and expressions.

Appropriate Technology

Steve Burgess studied for a degree in agricultural engineering, during which time he was a member of a student society that was sponsored through British industry and charities to go overseas: one year to Malawi, and one year to Tanzania. He says, 'We did voluntary work in Africa. That was my first experience of working there. I enjoyed it very much.'

When his degree was completed, Steve felt that his qualifications were suited to work overseas and that this was what he wanted to do. He went to Kenya with Voluntary Service Overseas, where he worked with the Institute of Agriculture and the United Nations Children's Fund, introducing appropriate technology into the Institute curriculum as well as doing some outreach work.

If the people want to get clean water, Steve told me, they can either use the technology which they have, which is crude and doesn't always work, or they can look for ways to improve that technology by using some of the ideas and benefits of technology in the West. But introduction of new technology is done in an appropriate way, using the resources and skills of the community into which the technology is introduced, the skills they have and materials they can afford.

The technology used at the moment for collecting rainwater is an iron tank, which is very expensive, is made from imported materials, and only lasts two years. But the Institute has introduced a tank made from a local woven basket, which the people have made for many hundreds of years, cemented by local labour, as the local people know how. This forms a rainwater tank that is much more appropriate to them, yet still trapping water for later use.

Steve worked at the Institute for two years and was due to return to Britain but really wanted to carry on doing this work. Yet he was rather frustrated working at the Institute because he wasn't able to extend the technology to the rural population. Instead he was teaching those who would later become the front-line teachers and work with the rural people. Their motivation wasn't necessarily the good of the people, it was more a job which they would have once they finished their training.

While Steve was with VSO part of the outreach, he worked alongside some church organisations. He observes, 'It seemed that they cared; it was as simple as that.' They were very effective in reaching the rural communities with their development work. So Steve tried looking around for a job with the church. He wasn't a Christian, but it seemed the most appropriate place to do that kind of work. He thought he would earn more than with VSO, and had a desire to see something which could help people put new knowledge into practice.

Finding God

Steve first approached an Anglican diocese in Kenya for a job. He got funding through their main funding agent.

It was a place where the people were very poor. Steve's work involved going out to the local artisans in the churches—they have development groups within the church—so he was teaching them how to make water tanks, and how to protect springs. Though they hadn't much materially, they seemed to have something much more; they were very happy people, caring people. What they had was Christ. Steve became a Christian through the witness of the rural people in the churches where he was working. He was confirmed by a black bishop.

After about two-and-a-half years Steve came back to England, not knowing what he wanted to do, feeling that he needed a new experience in his Christian life. His whole Christian experience had been in Africa, but he felt he needed to earth it in his own culture. He wanted some further training, either in rural development or irrigaton, and eventually he chose irrigation.

There were times in Kenya when he said he would never be a missionary, but the Lord kept saying to him, 'Go back overseas again.' Steve wasn't sure with whom, or when, or how. He knew of the Church Missionary Society, having met their missionaries in Africa, so he talked to them and some other organisations about the possibilities of working with them. Finally God did call Steve back to Africa through CMS.

After his marriage to Cathy, an Australian, and after they had spent time in Australia, Steve returned to England with his new wife, and applied to the Church Missionary Society.

Missionaries

Steve and Cathy were selected to be mission partners in training and have been looking at five different countries: Kenya, Uganda, Zaïre, Sierra Leone and Southern Sudan. They chose those countries because of Steve's previous work in Africa, and waited for requests to come in from the dioceses in those countries for a person to do irrigation work.

They observe that today's emphasis in the sending out of a missionary is a little different from what it used to be when a society sent missionaries out 'for the good of the people' who received them. Today it is a sharing process, where Steve will share his skills with the church overseas because it has asked for someone with those skills. The responsibility lies much more with the overseas church to say what they want and how their development should be carried on.

The Church Missionary Society is putting emphasis on missionaries going to work under the church in Africa, and the African Church is responsible for them pastorally. Although CMS looks after them, the diocese will be directly responsible for Steve and Cathy. Steve adds, 'CMS will be more administrator than parent. This affects your attitude to the people you work with. You are more involved and much more committed.'

Cathy and Steve hope to become links between the Church here and the Church there—a bridge. They look to being a sign of reconciliation and comment, 'With all the things that polarise people, at least if there are some people who try to live and work together, then there is more hope of understanding.'

At first Steve wanted simply to help people, but as he reflects on what he has done before, he sees development in a Christian context as an integrated one, where he is ministering to people's physical, spiritual *and* social needs. The verses from Isaiah 61 'The Spirit of the

Sovereign Lord is on me, because the Lord has anointed me to preach good news to the poor. He has sent me to bind up the broken-hearted, to proclaim freedom for the captives and release for the prisoners...' have spoken to Steve many times in the past, and he can see that a holistic approach is important. The African people don't separate and compartmentalise their spiritual Christian life from their daily physical life. Their approach is much more unified, particularly with people living in the rural areas.

The Church Missionary Society has said the same: 'We need all parts of the body working together rather than just going out as evangelists.' Through the development work it is possible to minister to people's needs and care for them, but Steve feels that they have already given much more to him than he can ever give to them.

An Australian Experience

Cathy Burgess has spent ten years at an Anglican Church, St Marks in Malabar, a suburb of Sydney. It is located on a peninsula which is the northern headland of Botany Bay, famous from the days when Australia served as a penal colony.

British society was transferred to Australia in a manner that contrasts with the religious interests that were part of the colonisation of the United States. Australia had no Pilgrim Fathers, only convicts. Prisoners included Irish Catholics, often at odds with English authority. Since the Irish contingent included political prisoners, there were rebellions and fights between the English and Irish. The clergymen who went there were part of the establishment, so their role included keeping discipline, with the result that from the early days the Church, too, was associated with the establishment and repressive authority. This wasn't a good start.

Cathy observes that in Australia there are not the same extremes of wealth and poverty as she has seen in Britain. There are very poor people, but no equivalent to the huge numbers of unemployed and desperate people in Britain's cities. In Australia, many have moved up the social ladder through education in the last generation; social levels aren't as fixed, and money has much more to do with social standing than birth does. There are a few who consider themselves aristocratic, but they are seen by everyone else as an irrelevant minority.

The Churches

Australia is only two hundred years old in terms of modern civilisation so is without the long history of culture and background of the Engish Church. There has been a concern among Christians to develop an Australian theology; it's a serious search for understanding of what is distinctive in its Christianity. Cathy sees a growing understanding that Australia is a pagan society, a fact that is rooted in its origins. The Anglican church in Britain is the state religion and is part of the fabric of society. 'There's a link with the Queen,' says Cathy, 'and it's strange to see a coat of arms on kneelers, and to know that the government has a say—even if it's only a formality—in the choice of bishops.' The Australian Church is, however, not tied that way; it is neither established nor linked with government. People in a country town wouldn't see the church as the focal institution it has been considered in Britain.

The recent joining of the Congregational, Methodist and Presbyterian churches has given the resultant Uniting Church a strength similar to that of the Anglicans and Catholics. Australia is very close to the Philippines, expressing the kind of concern for the Church there that British churches express towards South Africa. The clergy, mostly Catholics but some Anglicans, were key in the opposition to the Marcos regime.

Becoming a Church for the Neighbourhood

Malabar is an area with wide open space, having been the site of the infectious diseases hospital, the jail, the Aboriginal settlement, the sewage works and the oil refinery. People are just discovering that it is a very pleasant place to live, and within reach of the city.

St Mark's parish consists of a mixture of people, with some council-type housing, but more and more young families are building private houses. The Aboriginal community is quite unusual; in Australia most people have never seen an Aborigine except in the inner city, where they are living in slums, or on the edge of country towns.

The church was concerned to be part of its neighbourhood in a relevant way. They leased a shop in the shopping centre so that church people could actually be working in the local community, and be concerned with people around. Whereas most people go off to work every day into Sydney and only sleep in Malabar, are only seen on Sundays and are not involved, the church's community households saw one another in a day-to-day way that they wanted to extend and see in the neighbourhood. In the beginning the church set up a craft, gifts, and toy shop, which Cathy ran for three years. Later the shop changed and sold second-hand clothes. Still later the shop took on the Post Office's former premises. The shop was always seen as an outpost of the church, but not a 'churchy' shop.

Cathy reports that the church was quite unusual; it grew from a very small congregation. Many of the people who joined it came from other areas, attracted by the life of the church. The congregation put great emphasis on building their community life and on the church being a family. This involved some drastic changes to the structure, stopping all meetings—ladies' groups, mens' groups, Sunday School—and then working on doing things as a family, only setting up meetings if there was a need for them, rather than because they had always happened.

When the Reverend David Crawford first came to Malabar there were three small churches with tiny congregations. He took the initiative of pulling down the three churches and buying land in the shopping centre to build a new, multi-purpose centre. It was a very painful process for people, but those who stuck with it learned to be a family together with the other congregations, as they decided together what kind of church building they wanted.

The result was a non-traditional building; the altar is

along one wall and the congregation surround the altar on three sides. It's a very open, light church with many windows. Cathy says, 'Everybody is able to see and be part of the Communion, and see all the people around them. You feel very much part of the body. The whole body of the church and the Eucharistic table are all one.'

Growing Unity

St Mark's has a particular gift in bringing together a wide variety of influences. Sydney is basically an evangelical diocese. David brought that background with him, and he also brought a concern to develop liturgy in a modern way. The charismatic movement was powerful; people could come in and not realise they were in a charismatic church, yet at the same time renewal affected the life of the church.

St Mark's looked more widely at Christians in the community and formed strong links with the Catholic church round the corner, developing the concept of being the Christian community together in this neighbourhood.

The little Aboriginal church is much harder to include, for its members do not necessarily want to be included. The Aborigines tend to be fundamentalist; often their churches resist change the most.

This pattern is familiar in USA and Britain, where ethnic minorities choose distinct churches, a reflection of their wish to maintain some area of their life that is not dominated by the majority culture. Those who have experienced considerable oppression are perhaps touched by the more fundamentalist traditions, for the hope these offer. Often the dominant cultural norms and values are kept more distant.

Cathy comments that local people from working-class backgrounds have struggled in the church because many of the congregation are university educated. While they are trying to live simply, they have strong values. Often that very effort to live simply means they have a style of dress and approach to life that cuts them off from local people as much as if they were typically middle-class.

Peninsula Community Services

St Mark's was developing a strong social concern in relation to the neighbourhood, starting with the setting up of playgroups. Eventually Peninsula Community Services developed out of a search for ways to help unemployed young people, operating alongside the church and working with secular groups in the community.

The church was able to initiate putting a community worker onto the Housing Commission; it also set up a development association. This was handed over to the local people for operation, but a body like the church had been needed to get it started. Fortunately, nobody sees the organisation as a 'churchy thing', and few even know it was the church that started it.

The Aborigine children and others were at a fairly loose end in the school holidays and tended to get themselves into trouble, if parents were working. Daycare Centres were set up for local kids. The leaders were able to get grants from the government to run them, but in the early days they were mostly staffed by volunteers. Everybody in the congregation got involved, different ages coming together to work in teams. They set up adventure playgrounds and one year built a village with a colonial theme, complete with a horse and cart. Gradually the work has become more specialised, and a few people are employed full-time to do it. But it still is a concern for the church, with a group meeting regularly to pray about it.

The Aborigines

Part of the church's aim with Peninsula Community Services was to make more contact with the Aboriginal community. The community is centred on a reserve which was its original land. The housing was built by the government, so they are a fairly tightly-knit community.

In their area the Aborigines are much like anybody else: struggling financially, often unemployed. There are many incentives for young children to stay on at school, but this is hard for aboriginal children, who tend to flout the educational system. If they don't feel like going to school, they don't go. Or if there is a relative's funeral down the coast, they go to that instead. They have few models to help them aspire to anything different. In 1984 there were only two Aborigine lawyers in the whole of Australia, and only a few university graduates.

For the Aborigines there has been a very strong history of dependence on welfare, which was imposed a couple of generations back.

Children in particular suffered in this system. That is still part of people's memory. They have to try and escape from that dependence on welfare, and are only just starting to become conscious of their own pride as people, not seeing themselves automatically as the inferior ones.

Holiday Centres were started by the Peninsula Community Services through the church, staffed by church people. The Aboriginal community now runs its own holiday centre. Some of the administration is still done by the church, but responsibility and control lie with the Aborigines. That control is reflected in the way the holiday centre operates: very differently from that which is mainly white—different cultural values operate within the programmes.

Positive Discrimination

A necessary gift of the Spirit in multi-cultural areas, especially where a minority group has been violated by the majority, is the grace and ability to recognise and affirm the expression of God's creativity in a culture entirely different from the mainstream. Where history has taught that an ethnic minority is inferior and untouchable, grace is needed on both sides to bring about a change in the basis of power, control and responsibility. The situation is not helped by the fact that power in most societies is dependent on wealth and education, which in this situation still rests with the white middle classes. God, in his grace, leads such a church towards a greater giving, which is not an attempt to compensate for history but a necessary stage in the development.

The process of working alongside the Aboriginal group when it set up a community organisation, running—in conjunction with them—projects that had formerly been run by the church, had—for St Mark's—its tensions in management. The Aboriginal community is struggling to keep projects going; they are people without experience of running organisations. It takes more giving on the side of the church organisations and more acceptance of different ways, in a kind of positive discrimination. Cathy says, 'It is no good saying we've got two organisations that do things in different ways, but equally. The fact is that we have to give more because of what has happened in the past.'

Cathy was book-keeping, either doing the accounts or helping to do the accounts for different community groups. Among all those groups, honorary treasurers often had no experience or insufficient time, so through her the church provided the service as people asked for it. She adds, 'It is very easy for people to be suspicious of you and feel you are trying to tell them what they should do, or trying to control them. That happened not just with the Aborigines but with other groups. The knack is in helping people see a better way of doing something without their feeling put down; they are not going to accept help till they recognise the need.'

For Stephen, coming from Kenya to England and then temporarily to this church, it was a tremendous experience to see a church actually involved in social and community work and effectively using that as a witness in the neighbourhood. From one or two people wanting to be involved in community work, the Peninsula Community Services evolved, setting up different innovative ministries in various parts of the local community, some of which have now become autonomous.

16
Hispanic Migration to the United States

Church of the Redeemer, Houston, Texas

When a household from the Church of the Redeemer, including Graham and Betty Pulkingham, moved across the city to the vicinity of the University of Houston, theirs were the only white children in an otherwise all black high school. Carl was being beaten up every day.

The household was praying together, and Betty heard God say, 'Now, if you were God, which children would you send into that situation: children who didn't have any knowledge of me and no support at home, or children who knew who God was and had support?'

And God didn't leave Carl to suffer; a black angel appeared on the scene. An enormous black man was on his porch nearby when Carl was beaten up yet again, right outside the school gates. Next morning, on Carl's arrival, this black man was standing close by and walked Carl to the gate in the fence. Again after school he was there and walked him to the car, though he never said a word.

There were many signs of God's presence in the life and ministry of the Church of the Redeemer, a church that was renewed in an area of extreme urban deprivation. In the late 60s and early 70s members were realising that the Church had to be relevant to its location. There were race problems and other problems attendant on a decaying neighbourhood, including poor whites who were outcast in the white society; there were drugs and teenage prostitution. As the area changed, what it meant to relate to the area changed as well, moving from material problems to those of psychological oppression exacerbated by middle-class morality.

At the height of its growth the church had a core group of some 350 people and a wider congregation of at least 1,000 people. A strong group supported and encouraged the people working in that area, and they certainly needed it.

During the next ten years the Church of the Redeemer changed drastically, having sent out Graham and Betty Pulkingham and several Fisherfolk teams with an international ministry in worship leadership and church renewal. Other leaders of the church joined those missionaries to become the founding members of three Communities of Celebration. (See Chapter 5.) At times the church itself was shaken by the changes, but it held on, and in the last five years has begun to see both new stability and new vision for ministry. This is not least because the neighbourhood has been overwhelmed by what has been described as the United States' most pressing social dilemma: the immigration of Hispanic people from Central and Southern America.

New Direction

Nan Cradle was a leader in the church through the time of transition when the church sought stability and direction. Now the church's director of Christian education, she says that the way the church heard the Lord was in being attentive to what he was doing among them and adjusting the balance of life in line with that. The Church of the Redeemer is again in the process of reforming, reshaping its life. Much of what was common life during the height of the renewal was lost along the way, and the Church has, in recent years, wanted to regain that sense of corporate life which was such a significant part of its spiritual renewal.

Housegroups are being developed to recover that sense of closeness. The Sunday morning service still follows the tradition established through what the Lord has done in the church over a couple of decades, building on the ground-work that was laid in the late 60s and early 70s. Nancy Newman now leads the music. She says, 'Everyone looks forward to coming together to share the Eucharist. It is a place where people really do feel cared for, uplifted, encouraged and exhorted; all the different things we hope will be accomplished in worship.'

In the context of drawing the church together into closer relationships with one another, the Lord began to speak to the people, at first quietly. But then it became more apparent that there was a recurrent theme in the prophecies and Scriptures that were offered by both members and visitors during the services. Two Scriptures came up many times, through a variety of people, over a lengthy period of time.

> Is not this the fast that I have chosen? to loose the bonds of wickedness, to undo the heavy burdens, and to let the oppressed go free, and that ye break every yoke? Is it not to deal thy bread to the hungry, and that thou bring the poor that are cast out to thy house? when thou seest the naked, that thou cover him; and that thou hide not thyself from thine own flesh?
>
> Then shall thy light break forth as the morning, and thine health shall spring forth speedily: and thy righteousness shall go before thee; the glory of the Lord shall be thy reward. Then shalt thou call, and the Lord shall answer; thou shalt cry, and he shall say, Here I am. If thou take away from the midst of thee the yoke, the putting forth of the finger, and speaking vanity, and if thou draw out thy soul to the hungry, and satisfy the afflicted soul; then shall thy light rise in obscurity, and your darkness be as the noonday: and the Lord shall guide thee continually, and satisfy thy soul in drought, and make fat thy bones: and thou shalt be like a watered garden, and like a spring of water whose waters fail not. And they that shall be of thee shall build the old waste places: thou shall raise up the foundations of many generations; and thou shalt be called, The repairer of the breach, The restorer of paths to dwell in (Isaiah 58:6ff, AV).

The Lord seemed to be saying he would do something in the congregation with regard to the neighbourhood, because of the extent of poverty and oppression found here.

Then the Lord began to bring back from around the world many who had been sent out years before to form communities elsewhere, but whose giftedness and calling were to be essential elements of the church's ministry once again. Ladd Fields, now Rector; Paul Felton, Assistant Rector; Grover and Nancy Newman and others—all gradually returned to find the family of the church still supporting and caring for the members, and around them an ever swelling need for active ministry to fulfil the church's calling within its neighbourhood. Paul discovered the change on his return and says, 'The Spanish-speaking people coming across our Southern border are the largest mass migration in the history of humankind. It continues to increase. El Salvador is a very small country, but in Houston there are at least 100,000 Salvadoreans; there are also 200,000 living in Los Angeles. A further 80,000 of them are even as far away as Washington DC. We are pretty much in the first wave of that onslaught.'

In Britain, little is heard of this American problem, though Terry Coleman, in a series of articles for *The Guardian* in August 1986 reported on the problems.

> The border of the United States with Mexico is over-run. The rushing-in of illegal immigrants amounts to an invasion. The US Federal Border Patrol, though it arrested 1.2 million last year and reckons it will catch half as many again this year, really stops next to no-one, because the Mexicans just go back and try again and again until they succeed.
>
> These are not my judgements. I am merely reporting what I was told over and over again in the two weeks I spent crossing the 1,800 miles of that land border that stretches from the Gulf of Mexico to the Pacific. I did, however, have abundant opportunity to see for myself that what I was told was true. I saw hundreds of Mexicans caught, 250 in one swoop off

a freight train north of Laredo. No one doubted they would try again the next day.[7]

In Texas, the Rio Grande marks the border, and Mexicans swim or paddle across the small but fast-flowing river, undeterred by the numbers caught out and drowned by the fierce currents. Others catch a ride on freight trains, lying on the top of the wagons, entombing themselves in the double decker tankers, or just perching on the linkage between the wagons. The twenty-year-old fence between the two nations near El Paso is holed in many places and the immigrants continue to flood in, attracted by the promise of wealth and prosperity.

Some US citizens welcome the new arrivals, but others fear the eventual outcome of the high proportion of illegal aliens in many major cities, reputedly now 40% in New York and 60% in Los Angeles.[8]

The problems become most apparent in areas like Eastwood, an area of Houston, the neighbourhood of the Church of the Redeemer, where the newer immigrants have crowded in with other Spanish-speaking people already resident there. Paul Felton, who lived in Britain for several years, observes that whereas in Britain everyone can get financial help and health care through Social Security, Supplementary Benefit and the National Health Service, 'Most of our people here, being undocumented or illegal immigrants from Central America and Mexico, are not eligible for any public help at all.'

Just a block away from the Church of the Redeemer is the Hope Building, and many years ago the church opened a resale shop. The customers were mostly Hispanics. About seven years ago Abdias Abalos and Sarah, who served in the shop, began to ask them if they knew about the Lord and if they wanted to learn about the Lord in the Bible. Some showed interest, so Abdias and Sarah began a Bible study on Saturday nights. Interest developed until in November of 1981, the group started celebrating a Eucharist in the church itself. The Bible study on Saturday night, and the resale shop continued, and during the week, in different homes, the church trained new leaders. Finally in 1983, the people asked if they could start having the Bible studies in church on Saturday nights. That transition has progressed, the people eventually *by their own resolve* becoming involved more fully in the church.

Paul found that this transition was not accomplished without pressure for both groups. Many Anglos (the non-black, non-Hispanic population) had a difficult time with the two cultures coming together. A natural fear arises when one person doesn't understand another's language. There is no substitute for providing occasions when more established members get to know the newcomers as individuals, and as persons, but that doesn't happen automatically. The church went through a period of trying to do a bilingual service, which was always extremely difficult. The Spanish-speaking people, especially the old ones, were not that comfortable in English; and certainly for the Anglos—if they didn't know Spanish at all—it was difficult.

The problem was also cultural. For instance, what does an Hispanic woman feel like, who comes here never having used a fork or spoon, but, being used to eating with a tortilla in her hands? And how does that impress an Anglo? Probably the most successful type of intermingling of the two parts of the congregation have been church picnics, where social and cerebral skills are not at a premium.

Among the youth more co-operative ventures are possible as, by virtue of their schooling, they do not have the language barrier that the adults have.

The church recently sent several people, including the church secretary, to Spanish courses. Paul has worked on his Spanish for years. But he sees that the American culture relates differently to the Hispanic culture than it does to other immigration waves, partly because the speed of immigration has meant that Hispanics have not fully picked up the English language as well as other groups might.

The result of such a massive influx of Spanish-speaking

people has been that many find no pressing need to learn English. Where a city has a major housing area that is completely Spanish-speaking, education, shopping, work and transport can all be in Spanish. It is not unusual in some cities to find street signs in Spanish. 'The English as a Second Language Programme may become a more crucial thing than at the moment,' observes Nan Cradle.

Susan Abbott was instrumental in founding this English as a Second Language Programme fifteen years ago, and lessons have continued since, on two or three nights a week. Now Nan sees the need to re-evaluate and redevelop this ministry.

The programme teaches English, but there is no specific ministry involved in it. The church is therefore trying to re-order its facilities so there can be a feeling of belonging to the church when people come to the classes. They want opportunities for fellowship, so that people can get to know each other and enjoy pot-luck suppers, or other occasions where they practice their English and become more integrated with other people in the church.

But language is not all. Ladd reflects that communication is the vital and important ingredient, and language *is* significant in that regard. Yet beyond the language barrier there are cultural differences to be overcome. That is why the church decided to separate its congregations.

Thus problems related to culture, customs and language in changing neighbourhoods like Eastwood shape and determine the life and ministry of the church to a considerable extent. The neighbourhood is now predominantly Hispanic. The Hispanic congregation needs an identity of its own so is now set up as an autonomous parish mission.

Employment

The Houston economy is particularly depressed. There is high unemployment and such competition for the jobs the poor would be able to do—the unskilled labour—that few have ways of earning much.

Paul Felton describes as the foundational principle of

the developing ministry 'One way we give worth and dignity to the people is by allowing them to earn what we give them.'

Grover Newman returned to the Church of the Redeemer in 1980 and found work. He went into business with another man, who furnished the investment money. They bought low-income housing in an Hispanic neighbourhood, and that was his introduction to the people and their culture. Much of it he came to admire, particularly their hospitality and their sense of celebration. The business went gloriously broke, because of the same depression that inflicted so much suffering on so many of the people of Houston, especially Hispanics and blacks. In that context Grover learned to have appreciation for the problems and difficulties they face.

From his caretaking, Grover learned about people's culture and their needs—often in basic areas like simple economics and sanitation. Many of the people who came to his housing had no experience of running water. So in any apartment he visited he naturally asked to see the kitchen.

One day on the way to the kitchen the tenant began to try to tell Grover, 'Oh, by the way, the sink is stopped up.'

Grover asked him how long it had been that way.

'Oh, *dos ... tres semanas.*' Three weeks—never mentioned it! These 'little' inconveniences the people have learned to live with, but Grover observed that they are really not such small inconveniences, especially those that have to do with hygiene and health.

Finding Resources to Help

In a Sunday sermon Grover, who is a lay church leader, pointed out, 'We are surrounded by a sea of human need for which our personal assets as a church are not even a drop in the bucket. It depends utterly on a faithful Lord.'

The church had run a food pantry for a long time. They distributed food to needy people who were referred to them. It was a rather perfunctory activity. Grover found himself much more in the position of a social worker than a minister of God. He became distressed by his experience. In conversation with others, he came upon some Scriptures.

Acts 4:34–35 said that in the church in Jerusalem those who had houses and land sold them, and that they shared everything in common; there was not a needy person among them. The church was finding itself in the midst of need that constantly confronted them.

As the Houston church began to grapple with the issues, members latched onto another Scripture verse in which St Paul said, 'If a man will not work, he shall not eat' (II Thessalonians 3:10). Grover and the others decided to get themselves out of the business of trying to determine who was 'deserving', who ought to be helped. They opened the doors and said that those who worked would eat; that was the only requirement. They also followed another overriding principle—again the words of St Paul: 'Whatever you do, whether in word or deed, do it all in the name of the Lord Jesus...' (Colossians 3:17). So Grover and the others offered their services in Jesus' name.

These procedures have simplified the work, except that it has now expanded so greatly that it almost consumes Grover's entire time just trying to keep things going—finding the means of supervising 45 to 90 people on any given day. Since the problem is unemployment, and the team invited people to work in exchange for food, they try to recycle that labour back into the neighbourhood. They have done everything from cleaning streets and cemeteries to painting houses, removing rubbish and tearing down houses. Grover is constantly involved, trying to find the means to give people even a little money as income, so that in addition to food they can have a little spending money, but that only happens with a few.

Grover says that the church's hope and vision is to do more, and extend into vocational training. Grover sees the potential for a Wesleyan kind of revival where people are elevated through the understanding of a strong moral Gospel of honesty and integrity and the payment of debts, for many of these people are driven to pretty devious means of survival. He longs for them to discover both the spiritual and temporal promises of Christ's Gospel, both in faithfulness to God and in feeding and sheltering his people.

Grover adds, 'I fully expect the Lord to fulfil this, though perhaps not in the way I see it or in the way I stated, but on his terms—which are better than anything I could plan.' Grover grapples with questions of how the Lord will feed, care for and elevate his people in a deeply depressed economy, among people who are always the last hired and the first to be fired when hard times come.

When the church began food distribution in return for work, Abdias discussed the project with the Bishop of Houston, who immediately responded with $1,000 from the diocese. The Church of the Redeemer always contributed to the food programme, which has now been replaced by the new 'food for work' project, and there is a food bank in Houston where members can buy food of many varieties at a cost of 10¢ per pound, or often at no charge.

The Bishop, in his excitement about this effort, spoke with someone in one of the wealthier parishes of Houston, and the project were given an anonymous $5,000 gift. Then they received notice that they were to be recipients of a $7,000 grant, from an organisation which is part of the national church in New York City. These things are very encouraging and provide the flow of food.

A daily pre-school operates in the church and is open to neighbourhood chldren as well as to children from the congregation. The cost is extremely low, and if there are applicant families who cannot afford even that, the same principle has been applied as in the food for work programe, so that the parents come and help out in the running of the pre-school in return for the education of their children.

Esperanza del Barrio

In 1981, the church organised and received a charter for a non-profit, tax-exempt corporation which is called

Esperanza del Barrio, which means 'Hope of the Neighbourhood', to meet particular needs. The most critical was for medical care, which particularly affects the people without official papers and the old, as neither group is entitled to medical care through the normal channels of local government. A medical clinic now occupies space in the Hope building. The clinic is open one day a week, Sunday afternoon, and the staff see 40 to 60 patients during that time.

Grover explains that a group had begun to gather and talk seriously about building a house and having the prospective owner participate in the building. Then the house would be made available to a family who would not otherwise be able to obtain a mortgage or loan to buy a house, but who were stable, economically and spiritually, and of good reputation. The house would be available to them as an interest-free loan and would be built largely with volunteer labour.

They were far from ready when two things happened. Joy and Giles came into the church. Part of Joy's gift has been writing grant proposals, and now they were being urged to apply for a grant to the amount of $20,000. Subsequently the Vestry of Church of the Redeemer gave *Esperanza* $10,000 toward the house, and they are now building a two-unit town house.

All this reminds Grover of those Scriptures which stirred the church's vision, speaking of building houses and being called repairers of broken walls, restorers of streets with dwellings (Isaiah 58).

Civic Association

The Eastwood Civic Association was started by people in the church, named for the area of the city two miles directly east of the centre. It meets once a month in the Church of the Redeemer and is an organisation that is run by the people of the neighbourhood, not by the church, even though the leadership is very often from the church. The Association puts out a monthly newspaper. There's a citizen band radio contact as members patrol the streets, making the neighbourhood very much more secure, especially for the older Anglos. Many have raised families here and still live in their homes but have not felt safe to go anywhere at night. The Association has been instrumental in getting street lighting, and in cleaning up the neighbourhood, themselves taking part in getting the work done.

Before the Civic Association was really going and there was an election for Mayor and other officers in the city, only one person showed up to talk to local people. With the Civic Association there was no candidate who dared not come and talk to them. The Association keeps people informed of what's going on in the neighbourhood; it keeps them in touch with the police, the constable's office and with other officers. It is a means of accomplishing many things and is changing the neighbourhood in ways not otherwise possible.

The clinic, *Esperanza del Barrio*, and the Eastwood Civic Association are not direct ministries of the church. A broader range of people take the responsibility and carry the vision. However, the people of the church have been instrumental both in getting them going and in their continuing operation, making a significant contribution to the direction taken.

The Cost of Caring

To be located in the midst of a 'sea of needs' with too few human resources has brought its lessons, tensions and costs for the Church of the Redeemer.

God's timing is really important. To be a caring church means to let the Lord arouse the church to the needs that exist. It means carrying the weight of responsibilty and the task of choosing together when to help. The leaders have felt this weight in the church and have learned from the way the congregation carry it.

Nan says, 'People have come here to visit in the past and thought our "household" was a wonderful, caring place. They went back and tried it, but fell flat on their faces. We've done that ourselves when we have tried to keep something going that wasn't there. It is really crucial, we've discovered, to be in time with the Lord. There are so many needs that we really must know what in particular we are being led into, what the Lord wants us to give ourselves to.'

Grover continues by saying that the strength to maintain a ministry and to hold up the source of hope in hard times lies in approaching the tasks as a church, not as a set of fragmented groups acting independently. The needs of the neighbourhood could be overwhelming. Even though there are different ministries, the burden of those neighbourhood needs and the support for the people who minister to them is carried by the church. The understanding of what it means to be the church is crucial. In addition to the personal, sometimes agonising prayers of many individuals, a service hardly goes by—and several happen each week—where there is not very serious intercession before the Lord for the needs of the church and the neighbourhood.

All the people in this church are working extremely hard and are under considerable stress, the likelihood of burnout being only too real. A part of their quest at this moment is to find the Lord's answer to that, to find both his rest and his wholeness and to watch him fill in the vacant places.

Paul adds further perspective that is crucial to the foundation of the caring ministry of the Church of the Redeemer. He says, 'It's not a human or personal place you are drawing people into, otherwise you are doing things *at* them or *to* them; so somehow our common life together is our priority. It all boils down to the fact that if the Church is not in some way a family, a loving, caring representation of the Body of Christ, we don't have much to say to other people and can't really do much for them.'

Notes

[1] *Faith in the City* (Church House Publishing: London, 1985).
[2] The Church of the Good Shepherd's reports for the Archbishop's Commission on Urban Priority Areas.
[3] *ibid.*
[4] *ibid.*
[5] Jürgen Moltmann, *The Power and the Powerless* (SCM Press: London, 1983).
[6] John H Westerhof, *Bringing up Children in the Christian Faith* (Winston Press: Minneapolis, 1980).
[7] *The Guardian*, August 26th, 1986.
[8] *The Guardian*, August 28th, 1986.

The Urban Christian

by Raymond Bakke with Jim Hart

Foreword by Bishop David Sheppard

How do we go about caring for people in the desperate and deprived areas of today's inner cities? Ray Bakke provides fresh answers – answers that are based on practical experience, notably free from academic and ecclesiastical jargon. He sets inner-city Christian work firmly into its global context and shows how the Church can rise above its urban malaise to discover God's rich resources.

> 'It should be required reading for all Christians in Britain.... The book is an essential supplement to *Faith in the City,* for it clothes the bones of theory with the flesh of theology, practicality and a global perspective.' *Third Way*

Dr Ray Bakke has lived and worked in inner-city Chicago for more than twenty years. He is now Professor of Ministry at Northern Baptist Theological Seminary in Illinois.

Co-published with ECUM

216pp £4.95

Ten Worshipping Churches

Edited by Graham Kendrick

'Worship'—the word calls forth images of people flocking to pay honour to God, to show their love and reverence in services as varied as the buildings that enclose them. But what is worship? How can we enliven and enjoy our worship and make it pleasing to God?

The ten contributors to this book show an understanding for and sensitivity to the feelings of some members of their congregations who wish to maintain tradition, while at the same time an open attitude towards new forms. They write with warmth about what is happening in their churches, charting both the joys and difficulties of worship within a climate of change and sometimes even conflict. What emerges is a dynamic picture of people of varied backgrounds learning to worship together.

Graham Kendrick, well known songwriter and worship leader, draws together ten churches of different affiliations across Britain to discover some surprising and exciting answers to these questions. Gone is the notion of staid, stuffy services. Instead, old frameworks are built upon and polished to a new lustre with experiments in drama, unstructured or free-flowing worship, music, liturgy, and full orchestral accompaniments!

A book to encourage and enlighten you!

Published jointly with the British Church Growth Association
192pp £2.25

Ten New Churches

Edited by Roger Forster

In a nation of redundant churches, what prompts the birth of a new church? An urgent need? An overflowing front room? Enthusiasm for mission and evangelism? Disillusionment with another church?

Ministers and leaders from six denominations across the UK describe the excitement and the setbacks, the people and the growth of their new churches.

Roger Forster, the editor, is pastor of the Ichthus Christian Fellowship in London. Previously he served in the Royal Air Force. The author of *That's a Good Question* and *God's Strategy in Human History*, he brings to this book first-hand experience of planting a new church.

Published jointly with the British Church Growth Association
176pp £1.95

Ten Growing Churches

Edited by Eddie Gibbs

Here are ten churches, from different areas and denominations, which are seeing their congregations grow and mature.

Eddie Gibbs, who has conducted many Church Growth courses for Bible Society, has chosen ministers from the Anglican, Church of Scotland, Methodist, Baptist, United Reformed, Elim, Free Evangelical and the House Churches. They come from the inner city, suburbia, industrial and rural areas. Together they offer a range of encouraging models, illustrating how God is at work in *ordinary* churches today.

With honesty and courage each has described both successes and failures. There are no check lists or patterns to be slavishly followed—but here is evidence, often dramatic, of God present in power.

Eddie Gibbs is author of several books including *I Believe in Church Growth*. He has recently moved to Pasadena, California, to become Assistant Professor of Church Growth at Fuller Theological Seminary.

Published jointly with the British Church Growth Association
196pp £1.95

SIX MOIS, SIX JOURS

Karine Tuil est l'auteure de neuf romans, parmi lesquels *Tout sur mon frère, Quand j'étais drôle* ou encore *Douce France.* Quatre d'entre eux ont déjà fait partie de la sélection du prix Goncourt *(Interdit, La Domination, Six mois, six jours* et *L'Invention de nos vies).* Plusieurs de ses livres sont traduits à l'étranger.

Paru au Livre de Poche :

KARINE TUIL

Six mois, six jours

ROMAN

GRASSET

ISBN : 978-2-253-15972-8 – 1re publication LGF

Pour Ariel

« Le sexe n'est pas seulement une chose divine et splendide ; c'est une activité meurtrière. Au lit, les gens se massacrent. »

Norman Mailer

Le corps avait été retrouvé dans la neige à quelques kilomètres de l'usine. Au sol, on discernait des traces profondes comme les abattures d'un animal. La nature semblait figée dans la glace ; le temps, objet d'un effacement temporaire. Quand reprendrait-il son cours criminel ? Au loin se dressaient les montagnes azurescentes, témoins silencieux du drame qui se déroulait là, au cœur d'un paysage lissé par le froid et la barbarie humaine. Mais restait-il encore des hommes ? Combien de mois s'étaient écoulés ? Six mois, six jours – le temps qu'exigeait la destruction d'un monde.

... les faits, rien que les faits, vous me demandez, et de façon méthodique, sans oubli de ma part, vous avez été très officielle là-dessus, je vous ai dit je me souviens je me souviens, je n'ai rien eu d'autre à faire pendant toutes ces années passées à les seconder/servir/protéger, bonjour madame, bonjour monsieur, à s'en rendre malade, mais je ne suis pas ici pour parler de moi, j'ai œuvré pour la famille Kant pendant plus de quarante ans, j'ai été fidèle, un homme de l'ombre; si je n'avais pas été aux relations particulières en qualité de conseiller, je serais assassin peut-être ou diplomate, j'ai le goût du secret, je suis discret, effacé, incolore disent certains, et cela m'est bien égal, à mon âge, on ne quête plus l'approbation sociale et il y a longtemps qu'on est brouillé avec soi-même.

Qui êtes-vous ? Que faites-vous ici ? Qui vous envoie ? Approchez… De l'iris, de l'ambre, de légères notes de tubercule et… non, pas trop près, l'intimité me répugne, un acte brutal, à la rigueur, quelque chose de violent et de rapide comme une décharge de chevrotine mais pas de baisers, de caresses, toutes ces niaiseries affectueuses que la psychologie occidentale nous a imposées comme condition préalable au bonheur – le bonheur, je m'en tape… Pardonnez-moi, je ne suis plus l'animal social que j'ai été autrefois. Depuis quelques mois, je manque d'exercice… Enfin… nous sommes en France, dans la suite d'un petit hôtel parisien au charme discret… je peux y mettre les formes. Asseyez-vous, ne restez pas comme ça, debout, les bras en croix. Que voulez-vous savoir ? Je m'appelle Karl Fritz, je suis allemand, j'ai soixante-dix-huit ans mais j'en ai moins sans prétention au premier coup d'œil, je n'ai ni femme ni chien ni enfants, ma mère s'est éteinte du côté de Berlin, mon père s'est supprimé en 45 aux fins de justification, je ne suis pas possessif et je le dis avec terreur : je n'ai jamais aimé personne. Ah, si, j'ai aimé les mots ! Plus que les hommes… les langues surtout, que je parle par quatre ou cinq selon l'humeur… C'est une passion que je tiens de mon père. L'alcool aussi – il fallait bien qu'il me léguât quelque chose…

Quoi d'autre… J'ai fait mes études de droit à l'Université de Bâle avant de pratiquer des fonctions alimentaires comme vendeur de parapluies sur Alexanderplatz, guide au Kunstgewerbemuseum, j'ai même traduit Giono il y a des années mais c'était une erreur de jeunesse, puis j'ai rencontré Philipp Kant, dans les années 60, à Marrakech, et c'en était fini de ma carrière littéraire. Kant dirigeait alors la société BATKA, une entreprise spécialisée dans la fabrication de piles et d'accumulateurs électriques, et venait de sauver de la faillite l'entreprise K&S, premier constructeur automobile allemand, dont la famille était actionnaire depuis les années 20. J'étais sur place pour conseiller un industriel français qui aimait beaucoup les enfants. Il avait échangé sa présence contre la somme de 4 000 deutsche Marks et un garçon de moins de quinze ans. Cela vous choque ? Oh, j'en ai vu d'autres pendant toutes ces années au service des Kant ! Croyez-moi, les Allemands aussi ont du savoir-faire…

Kant, à Marrakech, je l'ai détesté sans préliminaires. Je l'ai haï parce qu'il était la première puissance d'Allemagne, entouré de femmes poudrées qui laissaient dans leur sillon des parfums de musc blanc à vous brûler la tête. Je l'ai haï de ne pas être lui. L'argent, les femmes, le pouvoir, la renommée – il les avait, et dans l'ordre, un chauffe-la-couche, comme son père, Günther qui, dans les années 20, n'avait pas su refuser une deuxième offre de corruption conjugale avec celle qui le quitterait pour l'exécuteur des basses œuvres, Notre Docteur... cela ne vous dit rien ? Vous êtes trop jeune ! Quel âge avez-vous ? Vous n'avez pas connu la guerre – tant pis pour vous !

A notre retour en Allemagne, Kant m'avait contacté. Il recherchait un homme de confiance qui défendrait les intérêts de la famille, oh les affaires, bien sûr, mais ils étaient nombreux ces avocats, conseillers – les meilleurs d'Allemagne –, qui constituaient sa garde rapprochée ; qui protégerait sa sphère intime surtout... Que je fusse diplômé, polyglotte, âgé d'une trentaine d'années, était sans importance. Mon profil l'avait séduit pour une seule raison : j'étais célibataire et veillais à le rester – quitte à rater sa vie, autant le faire seul. Mes fonctions : professionnelles, uniquement. Reproductives, j'y avais renoncé, sciemment, d'un coup d'un seul, dès l'âge bête. Vous me trouvez cynique ? Je le suis. Et infréquentable aussi, mais personne ne vous demande de vivre avec moi. D'ailleurs, vous ne le supporteriez pas : je suis insomniaque, j'ai l'obsession de l'ordre et de la propreté, je ne peux pas me réveiller au côté de quelqu'un – ou alors d'un mort, cela m'est arrivé une fois pendant la guerre, c'était une sensation étrange, comme de pénétrer dans un abattoir. Une vie au service des Kant, faites ceci, faites cela, j'avais mes appartements privés dans la grande demeure familiale, trois pièces spacieuses avec un papier peint en tissu beige, du beau, pas comme chez moi, à Berlin… mon propriétaire attend qu'je crève pour libérer l'appartement, il le veut pour sa fille, c'est ce qu'il a dit ; en ruines, je le lui rendrai, vitres éclatées, papiers peints arrachés, parquet défoncé et j'y mettrai le feu pour conclure. J'CRÈVERAI PAS ! Je l'ai dit à sa femme, à mes voisines, je l'ai répété au gardien et à mon psychiatre, J'CRÈVERAI PAS ! Je ne suis pas un libérateur, je n'ai pas d'exploits à mon actif, pas de croix de guerre à épingler sur le revers de ma veste… Oh, je n'ai pas été un nazi non plus – j'étais trop petit. On recrutait dans mon village pour intégrer la *Verfügungstruppe*, une armée de réserve, on faisait quatre ans au lieu de deux au service militaire classique mais on avait l'assurance d'obtenir un poste de fonctionnaire – ça faisait rêver mon père qui m'avait contraint à me présenter. J'avais passé les tests de sélection et été recalé : « trop petit » avait dit l'instructeur, 1,65 m, le menton relevé, je tenais ça de mon père et c'était bien fait pour moi – j'ai la haine des uniformes, les vareuses en drap vert à deux poches de poitrine à plis Watteau, fermant par six boutons avec passepoil blanc sur le devant, pattes d'épaule cousues à l'emmanchure, manches à parements, doublure intérieure en tissu vert ; ça ne séduit que les cons. Et vous ? Vous avez l'âge des broches à têtes de mort portées sur des blousons en jean déchiré, vous avez deux étoiles au ski que vous arborez fièrement à votre anorak rose fuchsia… Quels risques avez-vous pris ? Quels choix avez-vous faits ? Votre C.V. précise que vous préparez une thèse sur Martin Heidegger et Hannah Arendt. La corruption érotique, ça vous excite ? Ah, vous avez écrit deux romans ? Vous prétendez être écrivain mais je n'ai rien lu de vous… Où sont vos livres ? Malaparte, Joyce, Céline… Des pans entiers dans la tête. Mais vous… Vous avez accepté de rédiger mes mémoires parce que vous ne gagnez rien – vos livres se vendent mal. Vous votez à gauche, votre compte est débiteur, vous crachez sur la mondialisation, le capitalisme, le patronat, le libéralisme, vous prônez l'ouverture des frontières, vous militez au sein d'une association humanitaire pour vous endormir la conscience blanchie par vos crachats. Vous appartenez au camp des juges, des défenseurs de la morale – vous n'épargnez personne. Le code pénal, la Bible, sont vos livres de chevet, vous défendez la veuve et l'orphelin, vous aimez l'étranger et le faites bruyamment savoir. Le nationalisme vous fait horreur – vous êtes une démocrate, une libertaire. Vous défendez la démocratie, cherchez à l'imposer, fût-ce par la force. Précisons : vous êtes une pacifiste, une humaniste, la détresse des autres vous console de la vôtre. Parlons-en, vous êtes incollable sur la chronologie de la Deuxième Guerre mondiale, vous connaissez les dates, les faits, quelle élève ! Ah Staline ! Répétez après moi : « *Je sais combien la nation allemande aime son Führer ; en conséquence, je voudrais boire à sa santé.* » Buvons ensemble ! Incollable, oui, vous avez tout lu dans votre chambre miteuse, vous avez lu avec effroi mais vous poussez un cri quand une guêpe bourdonne au-dessus de votre tête – vous appartenez à la communauté des héritiers aux mains propres. Vous me détestez ? Tant mieux, vous écrirez enfin quelque chose de valable.

Où en étais-je ? Les Kant… ce sont eux qui vous intéressent… ce sont eux qui font vendre… Leur fortune… leur puissance… leur légendaire discrétion… pas un scandale, pas une photo… On n'exhibe rien. Ni son argent. Ni son cul. La saga Kant… ça fait rêver dans les loges de concierge et au-delà, ça sent le soufre, l'argent frais, le sang coagulé, les cendres, ça sent le sexe, les chemises amidonnées, les chambres closes, les parfums capiteux, ça sent la mort… et moi, moi, moi au milieu d'eux dans la grande demeure familiale de Bad Homburg, près de Francfort, une belle bâtisse de vingt pièces plantée au milieu d'un parc de vingt hectares. Vous voulez voir des photos ? Aidez-moi à me lever. Où sont-elles ? Dans le premier tiroir de la commode, là, oui derrière mes pilules, donnez-les-moi. Quoi, encore ? Ne me regardez pas comme ça, avec cette distance respectueuse, je ne suis pas votre professeur, je ne veux pas être votre père, votre compassion me dégoûte, vous êtes austère, récalcitrante… je vous le dis d'emblée, vous n'avez aucune chance avec moi : la seule qualité que je recherche chez une femme, c'est sa disponibilité sexuelle. Soyez adulte, nous sommes ici pour écrire un livre, un livre et rien d'autre, une association de malfaiteurs, en somme, orchestrée par un éditeur français – quel professionnel allemand oserait prendre une initiative aussi risquée ? On survit comme on peut… Combien y aura-t-il de rendez-vous ?

Cinq, six… Nous avons moins d'une semaine… Puis nous ne nous reverrons plus, c'est peu et c'est bien assez. Nous avons cette chambre confortable à notre disposition, je parle, vous enregistrez, notez, nous aurons éventuellement une aventure qui durera quelques heures, rien de plus, et nous laissera aussi insatisfaits que nous l'étions avant. Et maintenant, donnez-moi ça, les Kant, vous les avez déjà vus ? Je n'ai apporté que quelques photos, j'en possède tellement, chez moi… je pourrai les intégrer à mon livre, à la demande de l'éditeur, mais je veux qu'il y ait des photos de moi, une dizaine, à tous âges, vous ne le croiriez pas, enfant j'étais très beau, un bébé rond et rose comme une poupée russe, vous voulez voir ? Là, c'est moi, à dix ans, rachitique, obsédé par mon poids, la tentation de la disparition, une inclination à l'effacement, oui j'avais les cheveux bruns, coupés très court, mon père me les rasait à la lame, ah ! la peur d'être égorgé ! il buvait trop… et là, approchez, la petite trentaine, droit comme un i, engoncé dans mon costume étriqué, on dirait un capitaine d'infanterie, l'année où j'ai rencontré Philipp Kant, maigre à faire peur, je mange rarement et de petites quantités, oh le visage creusé, le nez un peu trop long, la bouche lippue, et mes yeux, verts ou bleus selon l'humeur, gris en phase mélancolique, oui, les cheveux, j'en avais encore beaucoup à l'époque, ça n'a pas duré, à vivre avec les Kant, je me suis rendu malade et voilà où j'en suis, à près de quatre-vingts ans, encore plus frêle, une tige, un souffle et pff...

Oui, les Kant, j'ai compris, restons groupés... les voilà... A l'extrême gauche de la photo, vous le reconnaissez ? C'est l'arrière-grand-père, Anton. A la fin du XIXe siècle, il épouse une riche héritière et se retrouve à la tête d'une entreprise textile dans le Brandebourg – drapier drapant, tisserand de langes, tondeur de draps, armés de croix de chardons. A sa mort, il laisse trois sociétés à son fils Günther, le voilà, juste à côté, le blond avec sa longue mèche qu'il enroule autour de son crâne comme une couronne mortuaire – on l'appelle « l'Anchois ». Approchez-vous. Un physique de bon père de famille, n'est-ce pas ? Tout en rondeurs. Propre sur lui. Comme son fils, Philipp... Le voilà, plus fin que son père, plus aristocratique. Cette photo a été prise à l'époque de son premier mariage. Ah, là, c'est lui, sur le site industriel de K&S près de Berlin dans les années 70.

L'entreprise, vous la connaissez un peu ? Il y a le pôle automobile, bien sûr – qui n'a jamais rêvé de rouler à bord d'une K&S ? –, mais il y avait aussi d'autres sociétés dont la puissante BATKA. Avec l'aide de son père, Günther, puis seul à partir des années 50, Philipp a bâti un empire, aujourd'hui dirigé par sa famille : les enfants issus de son deuxième mariage ainsi que sa troisième femme, Katrin, et leurs deux enfants : Juliana et Axel. Les premiers, je ne les ai vus que trois ou quatre fois dans ma vie... A la mort de Philipp Kant, en 1982, j'ai été chargé de veiller sur les seconds, Juliana surtout, à peine vingt ans au moment des faits et des milliards accolés aux lettres de son nom... Regardez-la sur cette photo, grande, athlétique, une chevelure d'un blond platine... Un pur produit de la bourgeoisie protestante allemande, une fille droite, loyale, à l'esprit clanique. Vous avez vu son regard ? Une lame. Tranchante, acérée, à vous sectionner les nerfs d'un coup d'un seul, clac. Et Axel, ici, son frère cadet, le plus beau parti d'Allemagne, quarante-quatre ans hier, toujours célibataire, calme et réservé – et quelle simplicité mon œil « vous le croiseriez dans la rue vous n'imagineriez pas une seconde qu'il est l'un des hommes les plus riches du monde » – les journalistes sont payés pour écrire ce genre de choses... C'est lui qui, après des études d'économie, a repris les affaires familiales. Il habite seul dans un grand appartement, à Cologne, il a quitté sa mère l'année dernière, la veuve noire, chevelure blanche, mousseuse, collier de perles à trois rangs glissé autour d'un cou de cane... Y a qu'à serrer, serrer fort... Madame, la troisième femme de monsieur, c'est peut-être celle que je connais le moins et encore, toujours avec le sourire. Le père, le fils, la fille – ils ont longtemps été ma seule famille, vous comprenez ? J'ai trahi mes parents, mes idéaux politiques... J'ai trahi mes amis, ma patrie... Mais je n'ai jamais trahi les Kant. D'où je viens, on méprise la bourgeoisie de ne pas en être. Et puis, un jour, par la grâce des choses, on est admis dans le cénacle, on devient ce qu'on déteste, on en est plus heureux... J'aimais rester au côté de Juliana dans l'immense parc boisé de la propriété familiale. J'aimais entendre les cris que sa petite bouche lâchait quand son père rentrait de la chasse, les mains poisseuses du sang des bêtes trouées, lièvres, biches, renards aux yeux crevés dont il caressait les fourrures humides avec une excitation criminelle. Mais c'est fini, c'est fini...

A-partir-d'aujourd'hui-Karl-nous-nous-passerons-de-vos-services-vous-avez-failli-à-vos-devoirs-je-compte-sur-votre-discrétion-vous-trouverez-là-votre-dernier-salaire-et-vos-indemnités-pour-solde-de-tout-compte.

Clac. La décapitation sociale. Et pourquoi ? Vous n'avez plus toute votre tête, Karl, elle a dit Juliana, plus toute ma tête alors que je me souvenais de tous les détails, vous parlez trop, et à la presse, il faut vous taire, Karl, sinon nous vous y contraindrons, contraignez-moi, j'ai dit, contraignez, ma tête est une arme chargée, une épée baïonnette, prête à tirer – et pas à blanc.

Pendant des années, j'avais été l'un des hommes les plus influents, le dépositaire des secrets de la famille, j'inspirais crainte et respect, haine et envie, ça m'excitait d'être jalousé ainsi, détesté peu importe, j'existais. Le personnage incontournable affublé de surnoms ridicules qui trahissaient ma puissance et mon flegme : « le Pape », « le Sphinx », « le Parrain », c'était moi. Oui, pendant des années, avec les chiens autour, j'avais été là à les blanchir et avec quels résultats, ouvrez les archives, montrez les photos, toujours là à rôder, à remuer la boue – les loups ! j'avais dit à voir le beau cliché représentant la famille en première page des plus grands quotidiens internationaux avec ce titre en caractères gras : **SCANDALE CHEZ K&S**, à voir Juliana tenir son journal en pleurant de colère et de honte, et moi, derrière, toujours là à nettoyer, gratter, effacer. Et pourquoi ? Pourquoi ?

Alors, je raconterai tout, j'ai pensé – Oh pas pour l'argent ! Depuis l'affaire, on m'a bien proposé des sommes à triple zéro. J'ai tout refusé. Pas par scrupule, non, je n'en ai plus, mais je n'ai pas besoin d'argent : je n'ai aucun goût pour le luxe, j'aime les films d'auteur, les grands classiques, les œuvres d'art – tout cela est accessible gratuitement. Quant à mon goût pour les putes, je l'assouvis de moins en moins et toujours en promotion. Non, j'ai décidé de raconter cette histoire par ambition personnelle, je rêve de voir mon nom imprimé sur la couverture d'un livre. De l'orgueil, bien sûr, mais chacun a droit à son heure de gloire, non ?

Car je savais tout : les secrets de famille, les numéros de comptes bancaires, les trahisons, les jouets sexuels, les infamies, je savais quels cachets et à quelle heure, codes et habitudes, rendez-vous officiels ou non, je savais la dissimulation, la ruse, la ronde des chattemites, les questions pour plus tard, Mademoiselle rentrera à 15 heures, jamais de fruits de mer ni de noix de cajou, je savais la peur du noir, les chats-huants, les parkings, les hommes cagoulés et les mots pleins d'épouvante, je savais les objets de désir et de haine, les anniversaires aux rythmes militaires et les goûts – quels goûts ! –, les invités de la chambre 23 et les œuvres caritatives, sur le bout des doigts. A l'échelle humaine. Au cœur du système Kant – ah ce mélange de rigorisme moral et de cruauté érotique ! Alors j'ai pensé je raconterai tout en quittant l'hôtel particulier où j'avais passé tant d'années de ma vie – tout –, en écrasant les parterres de fleurs structurés comme des plans de guerre, ô espèces menacées, thélyptères simulatrices, chardons écailleux, arrachant les plants taillés, ce qui glissait sous ma main, propriété terrienne, foncière, sentimentale, piétinant, piétinant – tout –, en vomissant ma bile sur la carrosserie rutilante de Monsieur, le plus beau modèle K&S, intérieur cuir, toutes options, peinture grise métallisée – tout –, en rayant les portes irisées, brisant le pare-brise d'un coup bref, qui volera en éclats comme mon cœur prêt à rompre, débris de verre plantés là, détruisant leur réussite, l'argent ! l'argent ! la bouche poisseuse de mépris et de rage – tout, puisque je n'avais plus rien.

« Nous ne sommes responsables ni juridiquement ni moralement. »

Axel Kant,
au cours d'un déjeuner familial.

« Chaque famille a sa part d'ombre, ses secrets, mais dans la nôtre, il n'y a pas de linge sale à laver. »

Axel Kant à son porte-parole,
pendant une partie de tennis.

… les faits… j'y viens… laissez la porte ouverte, s'il vous plaît, je suis claustrophobe depuis que j'ai arrêté de fumer, quelques semaines avant que Juliana Kant ne fît la connaissance d'un homme avec lequel elle allait avoir une liaison qui bouleverserait – saccagerait, pulvériserait, serait plus juste – sa vie. Une aventure sexuelle, la tentation du désordre. Une escapade érotique sans aspiration conjugale – Juliana était déjà mariée à Chris Brenner, un ingénieur de quarante-cinq ans issu de la grande bourgeoisie allemande : pas de tendresse, pas de sexualité ou alors le minimum conjugal – un associé procréateur, en somme. Elle l'avait rencontré au cours d'un stage qu'elle effectuait dans l'entreprise paternelle pour valider ses trois années d'études économiques, un stage auquel elle s'était présentée sous un faux nom, Wittgenstein – ne pas être aimée, jugée, appréciée, dépréciée en fonction de son nom et de la puissance qu'il évoquait : la grande affaire de sa vie. Brenner, son futur mari, n'avait découvert la vérité qu'au bout de six mois d'une sage liaison. La fille du patron ! Le gros lot ! Vingt ans plus tard, il s'en félicitait encore.

Cette vie réglée, ce mariage organisé comme une entreprise, cette inclination naturelle au retrait, à la contrition, à l'effacement de soi jusqu'à l'annihilation définitive de ses désirs, de ses instincts primaires tels que manger, faire l'amour, pleurer ; cette construction intérieure que rien, ni les plaisirs qu'on lui proposait, ni les fantasmes qu'elle nourrissait, oh malgré elle, images romantiques conformes en tous points aux rêveries des petites filles, que rien ne pouvait fissurer ; cette maîtrise d'elle-même, c'était le fruit de son éducation protestante ou le prix de sa tranquillité ? Une vie ennuyeuse mais calme, sans tourments, sans passion mortifère, une façon adroite et placide de glisser sur les eaux sans être éclaboussée, sans risque de noyade. Et voilà qu'il avait surgi dans sa vie, cet homme à l'élégance racée, la personnification d'un mythe chevaleresque dont on percevait instantanément la charge érotique. Herb Braun, vous avez vu sa photo dans la presse, n'est-ce pas ? La rencontre, je m'en souviens : j'étais extrêmement nerveux.

Mais à mon âge… Obstruction des artères, a dit mon cardiologue… Arrêtez de fumer ou vous crèverez ! Oh ! Les faits… Vous êtes venue pour cela… Il m'arrive de confondre les couleurs, les visages – les faits, jamais. Des journaux de guerre, j'en ai tenu – et bien. Chaque lieu, chaque date, et le nombre de morts en bout de ligne. Les noms, oui, ils restent – à vie –, mais les visages… un jet d'acide dans la gueule et…

… donnez-moi à boire, oui, du vin, un jus de fruits, ça me tuerait. Que voulez-vous savoir ? Ah, vous aimez ces histoires de perte, c'est humain… ces histoires d'amour… un homme, une femme, une passion obsessive… j'ai tout vu, tout entendu, car j'étais là quand Juliana a fait la connaissance de Herb Braun pour la première fois, dans cet hôtel de luxe situé au cœur des Alpes tyroliennes. Un hôtel pour riches stressés qui promettait lumière, détente, repos dans une langue mystique. Des Allemands, pour la plupart, venus pour se purifier. On leur décape le côlon, ça les rend moins méchants. Nous sommes arrivés un lundi, chacun dans sa petite chambre intérieur sable. Un paysage à s'en brûler les yeux : des montagnes chenues et au milieu, cet établissement tout en baies vitrées pour voir et être vu. Juliana m'avait demandé de l'accompagner, je voyageais toujours avec les Kant en dépit de mon âge. Qu'est-ce qui les liait encore à moi ? L'affection réciproque, une certaine connivence intellectuelle ? J'avais été si proche du père, si loyal, lui sacrifiant tout, cherchant à lui plaire. Au fil des ans, je m'étais rendu indispensable. Ce que trahissait mon dévouement, je le savais sans oser l'exprimer : je voulais faire partie du clan. J'y étais parvenu au-delà de mes espérances…

Durant les deux premiers jours de vacances, Juliana passa ses matinées et ses après-midi à boire des tisanes dépuratives. Le soir, elle dînait légèrement d'une soupe, et se couchait tôt, à vingt et une heures. Moi, dans ma chambre à siroter un scotch en lisant les mémoires de Günter Grass – ses *Pelures d'oignon* me faisaient pleurer. Enfin, le troisième jour, elle décida de se reposer au bord de la piscine, pas pour nager, l'air vous cinglait la peau à s'en écorcher les paupières… La vue de l'eau l'apaise – oui, sous lunettes noires. Coup d'œil à gauche, à droite, personne en vue, elle s'allongea sur une chaise longue, un livre à la main. Je m'en souviens parce qu'elle avait acheté ce texte à l'aéroport, en format poche. C'était *L'Alchimiste* de Paulo Coelho. J'avais emporté avec moi quelques livres, je lui avais proposé de lui en prêter un – Cervantès, Shakespeare, Goethe – mais elle avait préféré cet achat ridicule – du prêt-à-lire, à penser, à vivre, ça me tuait. Elle se donnait en spectacle avec sa quête spirituelle de dispensaire, aimez-vous les uns les autres alors que les hommes se haïssent quoi qu'ils fassent. Pourquoi me regardez-vous comme ça ? Je choisis mes amis en fonction du contenu de leur bibliothèque, c'est ainsi depuis soixante ans et je n'ai jamais eu à m'en plaindre. Quand serai-je invité chez vous ? Un écrivain, mon œil, une espionne sûrement, envoyée par un concurrent pour connaître le fonctionnement de l'entreprise, l'espionnage industriel, on a vu ça. Montrez-moi vos papiers ! Oh, pardonnez-moi… je perds un peu la tête quand… La piscine, oui, reprenons, vos digressions me tuent, vous parlez trop et pour ne rien dire…

Juliana était allongée quand Herb Braun apparut, simplement vêtu d'un peignoir de bain blanc, un dossier sous le bras, l'air absent, évanescent. Braun est beau, il faut le dire car tout est là, concentré dans cet adjectif, la gloire et la tragédie, l'attirance et la dépendance sexuelle, tout est annoncé par sa seule présence, cette sensualité que rien n'entrave, ni le port de petites lunettes en écaille ni ces espadrilles taillées dans une toile blanche un peu passée qui lui donnaient une allure sportive, simple, sans apprêt. Il marchait lentement, d'une façon légère, athlétique. Il y avait de la douceur dans son regard de héros biblique mais une douceur corruptrice où l'on devinait l'instinct de possession et la possibilité de la violence. Grand, brun, mince avec des yeux pers, une peau laiteuse, quarante-cinq ans peut-être, un âge abordable. Il s'assit, oh pas très loin d'elle, commanda une bouteille d'eau minérale et ouvrit son dossier. Il en sortit des photos, de grands clichés en couleurs ; de là où je me trouvais, je ne distinguais que du rouge, le sang, ça crevait les yeux. Des images de guerre prises pour ébranler les civils qui pousseront des cris d'orfraie et iront se coucher le ventre plein. La terrasse était presque déserte. Juliana l'observait, Braun sentait son regard, il prenait un air concentré alors qu'il ne pensait qu'à la façon de l'aborder sans la brusquer. Au bout de quelques minutes, il leva les yeux vers elle, absorbé, la scrutant comme s'il s'agissait d'un objet d'étude, un sourire accroché à la commissure des lèvres. Vous avez vu ses dents ? Droites, blanches, courtes et parfaitement alignées – un sourire carnassier. Ils étaient là, face à face, intimes avant d'avoir échangé un mot. L'attirance, le désir, la passion à venir – on voyait tout, dès le début... il n'y avait pas où se cacher... Vous avez déjà connu ça? Vous n'êtes pas le genre à tout quitter par amour, ça se devine tout de suite... vous avez la trouille... vous êtes lâche, en somme. Comme moi. Embrassons-nous.

Juliana détourna les yeux comme ces voyeurs qui contournent un gisant en se retournant de temps à autre pour voir s'il bouge encore... A quoi pensait cette femme dans la force de l'âge au contact de cet homme qui lui souriait – et dans quel but? Pressentait-elle la dévastation?

Le téléphone portable de Herb Braun se mit à sonner, il se leva et commença à parler assez fort, de bombardements, de l'horreur, c'est ce qu'il disait, des victimes, des immeubles éventrés, je n'écoutais que d'une oreille, ça ne m'intéressait pas, la guerre, les morts, etc. Mais Juliana... Fallait voir... Les balancements de son corps, ses mains qui sautaient comme des félins... au combat, contre qui? « J'ai les photos! », il gueulait, pour qu'elle l'entende, à s'en crever les tympans. Puis, soudain, il raccrocha brutalement. « Pardon d'avoir parlé si fort, pardon de vous avoir importunée, je sais qu'il est recommandé d'éteindre son portable ici – *il rit* –, je reviens de Géorgie et... »

Elle demanda : vous êtes journaliste ? « Pas vraiment. » Et vite, comme s'il craignait d'être entendu au-delà, il ajouta : « Je m'appelle Herb, Herb Braun, je suis photographe de guerre. »

— Et vous avez couvert quels conflits ?

— Rwanda, Bosnie, Géorgie entre autres... et vous ?

— Des conflits familiaux, uniquement...

— Ce sont les pires ! Laissez-moi deviner : vous êtes psychologue, médiatrice familiale, non, vous ne seriez pas à la piscine de cet hôtel au milieu de l'après-midi, vous êtes écrivain, dramaturge, peut-être, une tragédienne ?

Elle hochait la tête à chaque réponse – à quoi jouait-elle ?

— Psychanalyste ? Conseillère d'éducation ? Avocate spécialisée dans les affaires familiales ?

Elle rit. Allez, avoue ! Qu'on en finisse ! Son métier, c'était d'être la fille de Philipp Kant – bien rémunéré, à temps plein, sans risque de chômage avec mise à pied ; son métier, c'était d'assister à des assemblées générales dont elle ne connaissait pas l'ordre du jour, de lire des rapports qu'elle n'avait pas rédigés et d'honorer de sa présence des colloques sur des sujets aussi passionnants que *La situation bancaire en Allemagne* ou *La crise économique européenne : enjeux et perspectives.*

— Vous ne voulez pas m'aider un peu ?

— Disons que je suis dans les affaires.

— Et vous êtes ? Vous ne vous êtes pas présentée...

— Juliana Wittgenstein.

— On vous a déjà dit que vous ressembliez à l'actrice Liv Ullmann ?

— Oui ! Tout le temps !

— Vous auriez pu tourner avec Bergman !

Ça me terrifiait... Ce n'était pas l'infidélité à venir qui me révulsait mais cet abandon total, cette soudaine absence de maîtrise alors qu'on lui avait appris à se méfier, à garder la distance, elle connaissait les menaces : les escrocs, les affectifs, la mafia, la presse à scandales, à quinze ans, elle avait été kidnappée – vous ne le saviez pas ? Vous êtes mal informée, j'en étais sûr. Une débutante, ça se voit tout de suite. Peu de gens s'en souviennent mais pour moi, tout est resté intact, les détails, chaque chose à sa place comme la chambre d'un mort. Les souvenirs, ça va, ça vient... ceux-là, dans la chair, inscrits sur les pages sombres de l'histoire des Kant. Un matin, une dizaine de types cagoulés ont fait irruption dans la demeure familiale et ont retenu en otages Juliana et sa mère. D'anciens tortionnaires de la police secrète. Des types massifs avec des yeux de tourbeux. Formés pour persécuter, effrayer, taillader. Arrêtés quelques heures plus tard par la police. L'insouciance, c'était fini. Depuis, elle ne sortait pas sans être accompagnée de deux gardes du corps. Sauf dans cet hôtel plus sécurisé qu'un bunker.

Je la mis en garde : « Juliana, méfiez-vous. »

Il lui raconta qu'il était d'origine allemande. Qu'il habitait à Zurich. Qu'il avait longtemps vécu à Berlin, New York, Londres. Elle voyageait peu, ne supportait pas l'avion, quittait rarement sa ville natale. Il lui parla en italien, en russe, en chinois – elle ne parlait que l'allemand, comprenait l'anglais, « mal », précisa-t-elle. Il la faisait rire, elle qui ne riait jamais, si concentrée, parfaite dans son rôle de fille de, éternellement soumise au contrôle parental, encore à quarante-cinq ans, orpheline, la fille à papa, elle s'esclaffait même, elle détendait la bride alors qu'il eût fallu la maintenir, la serrer davantage.

— Que lisez-vous ?

Il se pencha vers elle, observa la couverture du livre.

— *L'Alchimiste* ? C'est mon livre préféré !

J'eus une pulsion criminelle. Un homme dont le livre préféré était *L'Alchimiste* ne pouvait pas être tout à fait sain d'esprit. Et il se mit à en parler, à en citer des extraits avec emphase à la façon du critique littéraire Marcel Reich-Ranicki présentant son nouveau coup de cœur à la télévision, il y a trouvé ceci, cela, et quelle merveille.

La rencontre, Braun aurait pu la provoquer ailleurs, dans la salle à manger principale, dans un couloir qui menait aux chambres à coucher ou au cœur de l'immense parc avec vue sur les montagnes crayeuses, mais il avait choisi de l'aborder près de la piscine. Lors d'une première rencontre, chacun cherche à paraître sous son meilleur jour, n'est-ce pas ? Regardez-vous : avec votre cache-cœur noué sur la taille, qui cherchez-vous à séduire ? Nous formerions un beau couple mais vous n'êtes pas mon genre. Et ces cheveux longs qui tombent sur vos épaules... ça fait négligé... Attachez-les ! Quoique... j'aime bien cette frange noire qui vous barre le front... Vous ressemblez à ces strip-teaseuses qui se trémoussent dans les bars louches pour quelques dollars glissés dans la culotte en polyamide. Quoi encore ? Dans ma bouche, c'est un compliment. Juliana est assez féminine – oh d'une beauté classique : tailleur-jupe, sandales à petits talons, à bout rond, bien sûr, cheveux coupés au carré, lissés, peu de maquillage, des boucles d'oreilles, souvent, des clips qu'elle achète chez Chanel, rien de plus. Ce jour-là, elle portait une robe noire qui cachait ses genoux calleux, des ballerines plates et un chandail gris anthracite piqué de vert, assorti à ses yeux. Braun lui demanda si elle avait l'intention de se baigner. « Non, il fait trop froid et… » « Allons, l'eau est délicieuse… » « Non. » Juliana ne se baignera pas. Elle déteste son corps. Moi non plus je n'aime pas me montrer en maillot, je suis trop maigre, et même chez moi, quand la métisse du premier degré vient me laver, j'ai un peu honte de me déshabiller, non que je sois pudique… c'est par coquetterie… Mais Braun… Quand il s'est levé… au moment où il a retiré son peignoir, on sentait qu'il avait de l'expérience, qu'il l'avait déjà fait cent fois… On ne voyait que ça, ce corps parfait, musclé, un corps de trapéziste. Sa peau était blanche, lisse, son torse, imberbe. Il y avait quelque chose de féminin en lui, qui excluait la violence. Il se dirigea vers le bassin. Il ne tremblait pas malgré la température très fraîche. Il n'y avait personne dans l'eau. Si j'avais plongé ce jour-là, je serais mort ; lui, rien, il plongea d'un coup, sans hésitation, il nagea avec régularité et constance. Juliana le regardait. Elle faisait semblant de lire mais on sentait le trouble, le désordre intérieur. Lorsqu'il sortit de l'eau, au bout d'une quinzaine de minutes, elle rangea ses affaires. Il prit un grand drap de bain brodé aux initiales de l'hôtel et, en s'essuyant le visage, il s'avança vers elle. Il l'invita à dîner le soir même, à l'hôtel. J'entendais tout de là où j'étais et je jubilais, à l'intérieur, car je connaissais sa réponse – elle devait dîner avec moi, elle avait dit, Karl, ce soir, nous irons en ville. *Oh oui !* elle lui avait dit, *oui, vers 20 heures, au bar de l'hôtel* et à moi, plus tard, *je suis fatiguée, Karl, je dînerai dans ma chambre.* C'est comme ça que tout a commencé.

« Je refuse de me retrouver dans une situation où je devrais me justifier, voire m'excuser d'appartenir à cette famille. »

Axel Kant, au cours d'une conversation téléphonique avec son avocat.

Je les observais, de loin. Je suis un voyeur, j'aime ça, toute ma vie à surveiller, scruter, noter – a fait ceci, a fait cela, j'aurais pu travailler pour les services secrets si je n'avais eu des goûts de riche : séjours dans des palaces, voyages en classe affaires, visites privées dans les plus beaux musées d'Europe suivies de dîners dans des restaurants gastronomiques, oh c'était avant la débâcle, maintenant, un rien me suffit, un verre de vin, un tour dans une librairie, un bordel, et c'est tout.

Herb Braun avait choisi une table à l'écart, à l'abri des regards, un endroit ombreux, éclairé à la bougie. Une heure avant leur arrivée, j'avais demandé au responsable des réservations où se trouvait la table de monsieur Braun. J'y avais placé un petit micro – Juliana, première fortune d'Allemagne, je répète, une espèce à protéger, oh je n'étais pas vraiment dans mon rôle mais ça m'amusait, je m'ennuyais, au bout de tant d'années de cohabitation avec soi, on n'a plus rien à se dire… J'étais là quand Braun a fait irruption dans la salle à manger, peu avant vingt heures, vêtu d'un costume en lin noir et d'une chemise blanche piquée de petits boutons en nacre irisée. De l'endroit où je me trouvais, il ne me voyait pas. Il ne montra aucun signe de nervosité quand Juliana entra dans la salle, vêtue d'une robe en toile grise rehaussée d'une rose en tissu et de petites ballerines bicolores – son uniforme. Son visage était à peine fardé : du mascara, de la poudre beige et un rouge à lèvres transparent qui se fondait avec sa peau pâle. Oh ! la gêne ! Il y avait quelque chose de pathétique dans le visage transfiguré de cette femme qui courait à sa perte, ne le devinait pas, un drame se jouait sans qu'elle en eût conscience, un drame paré des atours de la comédie : il la ferait rire, puis pleurer – la voie d'exécution de l'amour. Juliana fut prise d'un vertige à l'idée qu'un journaliste les photographiât ; bien que sa famille fût d'une discrétion obsessionnelle, elle savait que leurs moindres faits et gestes étaient épiés, analysés, jusque dans les pages des magazines. Les Allemands auraient aimé la voir en couverture du *Spiegel* en combinaison de cuir noir à bord d'une K&S. Ou piéger son frère Axel au bras d'une princesse cocaïnomane, dans la voiture d'un travesti luxembourgeois, à la sortie d'un hôpital psychiatrique. Mais ça ? Ce romantisme petit-bourgeois, cette aridité conjugale, ça les déprimait…

Braun commanda un bon vin, lui conseilla un plat – il connaissait ses goûts. Il lui parla de son expérience professionnelle, lui raconta des récits de guerre, ça la fascinait, ça l'émouvait. L'Etat policier, l'Etat criminel… Les enfants soldats, machettes à la main, qui mutilent et décapitent. Les gangs mafieux composés d'anciens militaires, qui traquent, violent, pillent. Les femmes aux corps éventrés. La mort ? Il ne redoutait pas la sienne mais celle des autres. Parler de la guerre, des disparus, détendait l'atmosphère. On n'était pas dans la légèreté corruptrice, on n'était pas dans la séduction. On cachait son désir sous le masque de la respectabilité sociale et de l'engagement politique – c'était propre. Juliana l'écoutait attentivement, il y avait la guerre entre eux, des conflits lointains et étrangers qui ne les concernaient pas, il y avait des morts, qu'on évoquait avec une gravité artificielle en répétant « c'est terrible » entre deux bouchées d'épinards. C'était un contexte idéal qui lui permettait d'étouffer le désir qui sourdait en elle. Elle mangeait avec appétit tandis qu'il parlait des horreurs qu'il avait vues, elle buvait sans modération – trinquons à notre démocratique Europe ! Le Rwanda, le Darfour ?

— Comment des hommes ont-ils pu commettre de telles atrocités ? demanda Juliana avec une légèreté désarmante.

— Un génocide, dit Braun.

— Je ne comprends pas…

Il y eut un long silence, puis Braun répliqua :

— Pourquoi vouloir à tout prix comprendre ce qui est inexplicable, indescriptible, irracontable ?

— J'aurais aimé créer une fondation pour venir en aide aux victimes du Rwanda.

— Une fondation ? Avec quels fonds ?

Braun cacha mal sa perplexité. Juliana, anéantie par sa gêne et le sang qui montait et la trahissait, baissa la tête – où se cacher ? *Il ne sait pas qui je suis* – cette pensée l'apaisa, elle n'aurait pas à biaiser, composer, manipuler, tous ces comportements artificiels qui lui permettaient de maintenir un écran entre les autres et elle. Elle ne dirait pas : « Je suis la fille de Philipp Kant. » La filiation, tôt ou tard – en payer la note. Juliana n'avouerait rien, elle avait manqué se trahir, elle se ravisa : « J'envisage de récolter des fonds en provenance d'entreprises allemandes. » Quelle candeur politique ! Quelle riposte compassionnelle ! A vous tirer des larmes ! Et ce constat l'excita – il aimait les oies blanches, les filles de bonne famille, les bourgeoises qui organisaient leur vie autour des 3 K : « Kinder, Küche, Kirche », enfants, cuisine, église. Il aimait les femmes frigides, pudiques, qui portaient des dessous en coton sous des chemisiers à col Claudine. Elle aimait les hommes dont l'élocution précieuse, le charme emprunté, l'élégance raffinée confirmaient l'éducation bourgeoise, la pureté des origines. Un produit de l'aristocratie allemande, comme elle. On est entre nous, c'est rassurant.

Il dit : « J'ai connu de grandes épreuves. » Il parla de son père, un industriel allemand qui avait émigré au Brésil dans les années 60, de sa mère, qui était décédée des suites d'une longue maladie, à l'âge de quarante-cinq ans. Juliana pensa que ça pourrait lui arriver… ça ne lui arriverait pas, elle était en excellente santé, une tension de jeune fille, mais elle eut peur de mourir tout à coup sans avoir rien vécu d'excitant, de dangereux, sans avoir été autre chose que la fille de Philipp Kant. Braun voulait tout savoir d'elle : « Que faites-vous ? Où habitez-vous ? Vous aimez cet endroit ? Tout est calme, aseptisé, une petite mort, non ? Et soudain je vous ai vue au bord de cette piscine, votre livre à la main… » Qu'est-ce qu'elle aimait en lui ? Le charme et la discrétion. L'humour et la mélancolie. La culture et la sensualité suggestive. Il séduisait, se pliait, s'adaptait. Ils partageaient les mêmes goûts, les mêmes valeurs, jusqu'à la défense d'un protestantisme un peu austère qui les préservait, pensaient-ils, du chaos. Mais le danger venait d'eux – et d'eux seuls. La définition exacte ! Cherchez !

TROUBLE : Etat, attitude de celui qui manifeste son émotion, son angoisse (rougeur, tremblements, altération de sa voix, décomposition des traits, etc.).

J'aime votre voix… Juliana glissa sa main sous la table de peur qu'il ne la lui caressât – dans l'état d'abandon où elle se trouvait, elle n'eût pas osé la retirer. La capitulation – elle la sentait proche. Pourtant, il ne fit rien. Après le dessert – trois fruits dans une assiette, une tisane où flottait une feuille de menthe –, il prétexta la fatigue, il allait retourner dans sa chambre et sélectionner ses photos, *je suis désolé… demain peut-être.* Elle pensait devoir se refuser à lui, elle s'y préparait mais non, il ne lui demanda rien, *au revoir* ; pas même une invitation à boire un dernier verre. La frustration de ne pas avoir à dire non. Elle était là, presque offerte, dans cet état d'abandon qui annonçait l'amour, elle était là, en manque de lui, l'homme fantasmé, érotisé, déjà, elle eut aimé se laisser aller, le suivre, se donner alors qu'il s'était mentalement éloigné d'elle. *Bonne nuit !* A l'instant du refus, il l'avait possédée.

Vous avez sommeil ? Allongez-vous, moi aussi j'ai des insomnies, toutes les nuits à revivre cette histoire, toutes les nuits à tâter la boîte de somnifères, hop ! dix vingt cachets d'un coup et pour finir où. Cette nuit-là, Juliana non plus ne trouva pas le sommeil. Le feu était là, intact, en elle, il la dévorait et brûlait ce qui avait été construit par elle, jour après jour, cette harmonie conjugale factice, un jouet en plastique que les flammes léchaient et consumaient et dont il ne restait à son réveil qu'une vague douleur frontale. Elle commanda son petit-déjeuner dans sa chambre, ne toucha pas aux croissants, avala quelques gorgées de café sans sucre en lisant le journal. Sur la table de nuit, elle vit la carte de visite de Braun. Elle la prit, la regarda longuement puis la déchira d'un geste sec. Pour vaine qu'elle parût, cette mise à distance de l'objet aimé lui donnait l'illusion de la maîtrise, vous n'avez jamais testé cela, l'éloignement, la passivité, l'indifférence ? Ah, la terreur de l'attachement ! Vous ne savez pas... Quand elle descendit dans le hall de l'hôtel, elle aperçut Braun sur la terrasse... Il fumait une de ces longues et fines cigarettes, d'une manière un peu féminine.

« Il était émouvant, sensible – un homme à protéger. »

Les femmes sont des héroïnes qui pensent sauver les hommes de leurs angoisses existentielles, leurs dérobades, leur goût pour la chasse, la pornographie sentimentale, quel orgueil. Et Braun. Réservé, comme elle, pudique, mystérieux, sans cette complexité névrotique qui caractérisait ses relations avec les hommes qu'elle avait rencontrés jusque-là et en particulier les hommes de sa famille dont l'austérité physique reflétait le despotisme. Il lisait son journal, leva les yeux pour la surprendre. Il y avait du prédateur en lui, une force de captation qui trahissait l'exigence sexuelle, l'érotisation de tous les rapports y compris les plus ordinaires, le désir de maîtriser les gens et les choses ; de la douceur aussi, une forme de connivence immédiate qu'il instaurait naturellement, sans effort. Juliana s'avança mécaniquement comme si son corps lui échappait, elle n'avait plus aucune prise sur ses bras, ses pieds, sa tête, elle s'élançait vers lui avec une légèreté nouvelle, un optimisme naïf – elle l'aimait, déjà. Braun lui adressa un signe de la main pour l'inciter à le rejoindre. Elle marcha jusqu'à lui mais, à sa hauteur, elle flancha – versatilité des sentiments amoureux qui soumet les plus forts aux mains des plus faibles. « Je suis fatiguée, j'ai mal dormi. » Il la fixa : « Moi non plus je n'ai pas dormi... » Il se tut un instant, puis reprit : « Je n'ai pas cessé de penser à vous. » Juliana savait qu'elle devait maintenant partir, apprendre à renoncer, s'en détacher puisque rien n'avait été scellé mais quelque chose en elle résistait, s'accrochait – ah cette aspiration pathétique au bonheur ! Etes-vous heureuse ? Juliana se tenait droite devant lui, rigide, bégaya une excuse incompréhensible, le ridicule de la situation entravait sa fuite : ils éclatèrent d'un rire nerveux. C'était un rire maîtrisé, un rictus social qui détournait le désir comme un enfant auquel on tend un hochet pour qu'il cesse de jouer avec son sexe. « Restez. » Sa voix était ferme, ses doigts serraient son poignet, elle n'opposa aucune résistance, ne détourna pas son regard. « Vous vouliez voir mes photos, je vous les ai apportées, restez, s'il vous plaît. » Cette façon d'exiger, d'ordonner en exerçant une petite pression physique... Moi-même… je n'ai jamais pu repousser une femme qui me traitait mal…

Juliana s'assit à ses côtés, le dos légèrement courbé, saisit les clichés. Ils représentaient un paysage cette fois, un terrain en friche envahi de broussailles. Des étendues verdoyantes piquées de plantes sauvages : espargoute, mauve royale, ortie blanche, camomille allemande, dame-d'onze-heures, mille et une variétés qui semblaient avoir trouvé la terre la plus inhospitalière et s'y être propagées. Au premier plan, on apercevait un panneau blanc rehaussé de rouge sur lequel étaient notés ces mots en lettres noires :

NE PAS ENTRER. DANGER DE MORT

« J'aime ce contraste, murmura-t-il, entre cette image champêtre, paisible, et ce panneau qui annonce un danger invisible, qu'on ne soupçonne pas… C'est un petit paradis situé près de Hanovre, je vous y emmènerai un jour… » Elle rit : « Nous ne nous reverrons jamais ! » « Nous nous reverrons, dit-il. Nous nous reverrons parce que nous ne pouvons plus rien changer au cours des choses. »

« Il est fréquent que nous, êtres humains, endossions la responsabilité de ce dont nous ne sommes en rien coupables. »

Günther Kant, *Mémoires*

L'après-midi, Herb Braun lui proposa une randonnée en montagne, j'adore ça et vous ? Marcher, marcher, l'esprit divague, digresse, il n'y a plus que cet effort, le corps entièrement concentré vers son objectif, et quel paysage, dit Braun, quel sentiment de liberté, allons-y. A cette époque de l'année, des étendues verdorées recouvraient les montagnes, le ciel, quelle pureté, *venez, je vous en prie*. Et Juliana acquiesça d'un rire factice, forcé, alors qu'elle n'attendait plus que cela, l'heure de l'évasion, le moment où ils se retrouveraient seuls. Elle le suivit contre mon gré ; je flairais le danger comme un chien de chasse. Les êtres trop bien élevés, propres sur eux, faut bien qu'ils la cachent quelque part leur merde, on en est tous là. Les types comme moi, ça se voit tout de suite, dès l'échange de regards, le vice, la méchanceté, il n'y a pas à chercher. Mais Braun : une mer étale, une feuille vierge, sa seule présence suffit à poétiser l'existence, on en redemande. S'il avait les cheveux longs, il ressemblerait à Jésus – les personnages messianiques me foutent la trouille, ils annoncent la fin du monde. On ne le connaissait pas, ce Braun, il avait une bonne bouille mais quand même, un kidnappeur, peut-être, la tête pensante d'un gang mafieux, un sbire de terroristes, le représentant d'un syndicat de salariés vengeurs et hystériques, on en connaît. Les grands patrons – tout le monde veut leur peau, désormais. Faut qu'ils crachent. Juliana obéit à sa première intuition : elle avait vu en Braun un aventurier politique, un humanitaire idéaliste, *j'ai confiance en lui*, elle le suivit sans angoisse, *vous voyez le mal partout*, comment lui en vouloir ? Ce qu'elle ressentait pour cet homme, je n'en imaginais pas la portée – discrète, réservée, je l'ai dit, presque renfermée, on ne remarquait pas, au premier abord, le cœur passionné, tendre, la fantasmagorie érotique, le sentimentalisme contenu, tout ce qui précipiterait une mère de famille respectable vers les abîmes d'une liaison destructrice. Elle savait que je ne pouvais pas la suivre : j'étais en miettes. Huit organes se délitaient à l'unisson. A cette époque, je l'accompagnais encore lors de ses déplacements parce qu'elle n'avait pas la force morale de me renvoyer – la retraite, ça me foutait le cafard et je le lui répétais, la mise en quarantaine, ça me tuerait, mais on ne dupait personne, je n'étais pas plus redoutable qu'un tigre empaillé. Alors moi dans les cols escarpés avec mon arthrose – non ! Si je devais crever autant le faire d'une manière politiquement incorrecte, à la Félix Faure, ça fait viril, on s'inscrit dans l'Histoire, on lit son nom dans la presse, un entrefilet ce n'est pas rien… Et puis Braun avait demandé : « Qui est cet homme qui vous accompagne partout ? » – il n'avait pas dit « vieux » par fraternité – et Juliana avait répondu du tac au tac : « C'est mon grand-père », « conseiller spécial » trahissait l'influence… j'étais broyé – j'avais encore deux maîtresses à l'époque, oh des filles tarifées mais quand même, ça fonctionnait. Je n'avais pas de petits-enfants, je n'avais jamais eu de désir d'enfant – oh peut-être une fois, vite, vers quarante ans, comme une envie de pisser –, j'étais hostile à la perpétuation de ma race pour des raisons sociales.

Ce jour-là, elle partit avec lui, enveloppée dans son imperméable bleu marine taille 2, trop large pour elle – cacher quoi ? Je restai à l'hôtel à boire des tisanes aux clous de girofle qui me perforaient l'estomac, je les imaginai, longeant des ruisseaux, empruntant des routes sinueuses que la pluie avait vermiculées, manquant glisser et lui qui la retenait *ne craignez rien, je suis là*. Je le voyais, tendre et rassurant, protecteur et réactif, ils riaient, ça me rendait nerveux, violent, oh contre moi-même – un coup de carabine dans la gorge et... Ah, cette pitié dangereuse dans votre regard, je ne vous envie pas, vous êtes puérile.

C'est ça, prenez vos affaires et partez, j'écrirai moi-même, je l'ai dit à l'éditeur et vous savez ce qu'il m'a répondu ? Vous avez besoin de quelqu'un qui mettra de l'ordre dans vos idées. De l'ordre ! Pourquoi ma tête ne refléterait-elle pas le chaos du siècle ? Il n'y a qu'à m'enregistrer et retranscrire, j'ai tant de choses à dire, à raconter, oh, comme les autres, toujours à parler de vous, j'ai fait ceci, j'ai fait cela, alors qu'on vous demande de vous taire, de rendre des comptes, de témoigner de l'état du monde, d'écrire – vous êtes là pour ça : l'histoire des Kant est celle d'un monde condamné, le monde de l'abstinence et du mensonge, du capitalisme meurtrier et de la connivence, asseyez-vous, et écoutez.

Quand Juliana rentra de sa balade champêtre, j'en étais là. Elle franchit le hall de l'hôtel où je l'attendais depuis des heures, un chien sans maître, elle avait les joues striées de veinules rougeoyantes, ça bouillonnait à l'intérieur comme la lave d'un volcan, son bonheur éclaboussait tout le monde, c'était révoltant. Sa légèreté m'inquiétait. Presque facétieuse – ce n'était pas elle. Elle m'invita à dîner dans un des petits restaurants de la ville – côtes de porc et purée maison, arrosées d'un bon vin, ça réchauffait. Au cours du dîner, elle me montra le cliché que Braun lui avait offert. Il représentait le paysage qu'elle avait aimé, cette nature sauvage, luxuriante. Il ne lui avait pas donné de photos de guerre – corps mutilés, déchiquetés, fragments d'obus – alors qu'il menait une expédition punitive, il voulait sa peau, son cœur, le corps de son peuple, la voulait totalement et éternellement. « C'est beau ! » s'écria-t-elle. « Sublime », répliquai-je alors que je trouvai cette image hideuse. Plus tard, ce cliché ornerait son bureau. Cette déformation critique engendrée par l'état amoureux : pathétique, n'est-ce pas ? Je n'avais rien à lui dire et, à vingt et une heures, on était au lit. Moi, j'y étais, elle, je ne savais pas, avec Braun peut-être, c'est ce que je me disais, quelle angoisse. Une faute professionnelle et c'était la porte. Un enlèvement, pas deux. Je fis la grue dans le couloir qui menait à sa chambre, on me prit deux fois pour le concierge, non, je ne savais pas où trouver un troisième oreiller – j'ai une tête de proxénète ? –, puis j'allai me coucher. Une heure plus tard, on tambourina à ma porte. J'écarquillai un œil, je manquai me fracasser le col du fémur, j'ouvris la porte, elle était là, le visage en larmes, le peignoir de bain entrouvert, dans cet état d'affolement qui préfigurait le pire. Je pensai que Braun était mort dans ses bras, ç'avait toujours été l'angoisse de Philipp Kant, crever pendant l'acte, un arrêt cardiaque dès le premier coït, ça fait mauvais genre, je m'agitai, me contorsionnai, *où est-il ?* Prêt à balancer le cadavre du haut de la montagne, c'était mon rôle après tout, nettoyons, purifions, *où est-il ?* Mais non, c'était autre chose, elle se calma, pâlit, où était le rose qui lui montait aux joues ? Elle venait de recevoir un message de son mari, nous devions rentrer à Berlin par le premier avion. Il était cinq heures du matin, j'avais sommeil, *dépêchez-vous, Karl,* un esclave, vous dis-je. Elle murmura : « Il sait. Il sait tout. Des photos ont été prises qui nous compromettent. On nous voit bien. On ne voit que nous. Je suis perdue, Karl, perdue. » Je ne pouvais pas la prendre dans mes bras, je vous l'ai dit, la tendresse me dégoûte alors je lui ai tapoté l'épaule, doucement, comme ça, ne vous dégagez pas… Elle répétait : « Il sait, il sait. » Je fis ma valise, m'habillai à la hâte et hop, en bas, à la guetter. Une heure plus tard, elle était prête, engoncée dans une veste en toile noire qui cachait son corps, son cou, les pieds plantés dans des bottines à bout rond, soumise à sa discipline, à ses principes, à son code de conduite, elle s'y conformerait désormais, allons-y, dit-elle, nous sommes en retard, nous sommes pressés, partons. Avant de quitter l'hôtel, elle prit soin de laisser un mot d'adieu à Braun rédigé à la va-vite sur une feuille blanche. A côté de son prénom, elle avait noté son numéro de téléphone portable – et pourquoi, j'ai pensé, pourquoi ?

« Pourquoi me sentirais-je coupable ? Je n'étais pas né. »

Axel Kant à sa sœur Juliana,
au cinéma.

Les mots, elle ne les trouva pas ce matin-là. Elle était désolée – ce fut tout ce qu'elle trouva à dire à son mari, dès son arrivée, *je suis désolée*, comme si les excuses privées annulaient la faute et le moment des excuses publiques qui viendrait – et vite. Pendant le trajet, mari et femme s'évitèrent, j'étais assis entre les deux, hochant la tête de gauche à droite comme une marionnette électrique, j'étais nerveux, j'avais envie de fumer, dans ces cas-là, je peux être agressif, je peux tuer. La radio diffusait les *Nocturnes* de Chopin, ça me donnait envie de pleurer, *vous vous sentez bien, Karl ?* J'avais l'impression d'être à la place du mort dans une voiture funéraire, *arrêtez-vous ! Karl fait un malaise.* J'étais là, inspirant, expirant, au bord de la crise cardiaque quand soudain, le mari dit calmement : « J'ai appelé notre avocat. » La pluie éclaboussait la vitre. Juliana ne cilla pas mais on voyait bien que ça débordait. La voiture s'immobilisa un instant. Le chauffeur sortit du véhicule, ouvrit un grand parapluie, s'approcha de la portière. Au moment où son mari s'apprêta à poser le pied sur le trottoir balayé par la pluie, Juliana le saisit par le bras et, d'une voix détachée, articula ces mots avec effort : « Est-ce que tu vas demander le divorce ? »

Il la regarda longuement sans répondre, repoussa son étreinte, il jugeait pathétique son refus d'avouer, d'affronter *ce qui avait été fait*, il exigeait la contrition rédemptrice, les déclarations officielles, la mécanique de la réparation, il participait à l'œuvre d'éclaircissement des faits, coup de projecteur braqué dans les yeux, regardez-les, jugez-la, puisque les médias dévoileraient la vérité. Il s'éloigna sans se retourner. Juliana s'apprêta à le suivre, mais je l'empoignai à mon tour : « Restez ici ! » Dans le rétroviseur, j'avais remarqué qu'un véhicule nous suivait. « Des journalistes sont là, qui vous traquent et vous photographient », lui dis-je, et Juliana ne bougea plus, figea son regard derrière ses lunettes noires.

Depuis quelques mois, ma fonction relevait moins du conseil que de l'assistance à personne en danger. Par moments, je remarquais que

Juliana me considérait comme un père de substitution, un tuteur ; elle m'introduisait davantage dans leur sphère affective et m'éloignait de la sphère économique et juridique. Je jouais le rôle qu'elle m'assignait, j'en étais flatté, au fond, je me pavanais à son bras alors que je savais, je savais depuis toujours, qu'on ne devrait jamais évoquer des liens affectifs une fiche de paye à la main.

Dans la voiture qui roulait à vive allure, Juliana se tenait recroquevillée sur la banquette arrière, à mes côtés. De temps à autre, elle scrutait les ombres qui nous pourchassaient. Elle ne souhaita pas rentrer chez elle et, en une dizaine de minutes, nous fûmes dans ses bureaux de Berlin où l'attendaient ses avocats. Ils étaient au nombre de trois : Goldberg, Handke, Mayer. *Veuillez patienter.* Ils se rassirent comme des poupées, sans sourciller. Au prix où ils étaient payés, ils pouvaient bien attendre une journée entière. Goldberg surtout qui centralisait toutes les affaires juridiques de la famille. Goldberg est un juif allemand – son préféré, une espèce en voie d'extinction, à protéger. En Allemagne, chacun cherche son juif qui déculpabilise et tient chaud. Juliana s'éloigna sans un regard, le corps secoué de légers spasmes, je la suivis mais au seuil de la porte, elle me demanda de rester dans le couloir, de l'attendre, comme les autres, alors je fumai, en dépit des protestations du personnel, je fumai – la seule façon de me calmer. On avait peur de moi, je le sentais, ça m'excitait, un regard et ils tremblaient, je tenais des fiches sur tout le monde, ça m'occupait la tête, on m'insultait, on me critiquait, on pariait sur ma mort, ils me détestaient, Goldberg surtout dont le regard semblait exiger de moi un certificat d'exonération de tout passé nazi, et c'était très bien ainsi, aucun d'entre eux n'osait s'adresser à moi, le bras droit de la patronne, un trublion sadique et hostile – c'est plus fort que moi, quand je suis bien, j'emmerde tout le monde.

Longtemps, Juliana n'a eu confiance qu'en moi. C'était avant que les choses ne tournent mal. Déjà, ce jour-là, *restez dehors, Karl.*

Quelques minutes plus tard, son téléphone sonna : elle reconnut instantanément la voix de Braun, cette voix rauque et hypnotique : « Vous avez été victime d'un prestidigitateur ? Je vous ai laissée hier et hop, vous avez disparu ! » Elle rit : « J'ai dû rentrer plus tôt que prévu. » « Rien de grave, j'espère ? » « Non, non. » Il y eut un long silence, puis il murmura : « Je veux vous revoir. » Elle dit : « Non, c'est impossible, non, oubliezmoi. » Il lui fit parvenir des messages. Lui téléphona cinq, six fois. Sa voix tremblait, elle peinait à cacher son trouble. Est-ce qu'il cesserait de l'appeler si elle consentait à lui accorder un rendez-vous ? *Oui.* Elle le retrouverait au bar d'un petit hôtel de Berlin en fin de journée.

Elle rentra chez elle, plongée dans une sorte de torpeur muette, prit une douche, s'habilla à la hâte, sans séduction, sans force, comme vous avant de venir ici, dites-le, du bleu marine, du gris foncé, se fondre, se cacher des regards imprécatoires, une armée de juges l'attendait dehors, vous attend peut-être, en quelques heures, un drame allait se jouer et plonger sa vie, la vôtre, dans un implacable chaos.

Braun était déjà là quand elle pénétra dans le hall de l'hôtel où elle lui avait donné rendez-vous, pour lui parler, dit-elle, alors qu'elle n'était venue que pour cela : être aimée. Imaginez-la, les yeux dissimulés derrière de grandes lunettes noires, un peu essoufflée, le cherchant du regard, défiant l'obscurité factice qu'elle avait créée pour se cacher, cacher son désir fou aux yeux du monde. Il était vêtu d'un jean et d'une veste en velours, beau et parfumé comme un dandy. Il y avait un érotisme cru, une forme d'audace transgressive dans sa façon de l'accueillir et de se précipiter vers elle comme si elle lui appartenait totalement, dans sa gestuelle précise : frôlements de mains, clignements de l'œil ; il y avait de la manipulation aussi, le jeu de l'acteur qui envoûte sa partenaire, qui en tombe amoureux pour qu'elle s'abandonne sous le regard voyeur du metteur en scène complice qui filme, dirige dans l'ombre. *Embrassez-moi, je deviens fou.* Juliana se dégagea, eut un mouvement de recul : *Ne m'appelez plus, ne vous approchez pas, je vous en prie, nous sommes peut-être surveillés, ne…* Il dit : *Je vous adore, j'ai besoin de vous, je n'arrête pas de penser à vous.* Elle regarda autour d'elle, craignit d'être remarquée. Il avait besoin de la toucher, de respirer son odeur : *Est-ce que vous sentez mon trouble ?* Il approcha sa joue de la sienne – un frôlement à peine perceptible. Elle était dans cet état d'adoration qui figeait les membres et les sens, tétanisée par la force de son désir qui balayait tout.

— J'ai réservé une chambre, montons.

— C'est impossible, je ne suis pas libre.

— La chambre, elle, l'est.

Elle sourit et avant qu'elle pût se rétracter, sur un ton qui n'autorisait aucune opposition, sur un ton où l'on sentait poindre le désir et la contrainte, l'excitation et la violence à venir, il ajouta : « Rejoins-moi. Maintenant. »

« Par le passé, nous nous sommes toujours efforcés de rester en retrait, de ne pas nous placer sous les feux de la rampe, et cela nous a plutôt réussi ! »

Katrin Kant,
à un journaliste allemand.

C'était [illegible]
une [illegible]
[illegible]
avait [illegible]

Katrin [illegible]

[illegible]
champagne, [illegible]
[illegible]
cela [illegible]
[illegible]
avait le sentiment [illegible]
un peu [illegible]
quelque chose [illegible]
[illegible]
une [illegible]
la ville de [illegible]
[illegible]
[illegible]
ne savait que [illegible]

C'était une suite à laquelle on accédait par une entrée secrète, personne ne pouvait les surprendre, Juliana n'aurait qu'à le rejoindre, il avait réservé cette chambre sous un faux nom.

Braun la précéda, commanda une bouteille de champagne, inspecta les lieux, tira légèrement les rideaux pour créer une ambiance plus intime, colla son oreille contre la paroi du mur : à côté, tout était calme – qui pourrait les surprendre ? Il avait le sentiment d'être un enfant manipulé par un père tyrannique et pervers, il obéissait mais quelque chose en lui s'était fêlé, était définitivement perdu : une innocence, le sens de l'illusion, une aptitude à la rêverie – on en est tous là. Dans la salle de bains, penché au-dessus de la vasque en faïence, il rinça longuement son visage à l'eau brûlante, l'inquiétude montait en lui par à-coups, il ne savait pas comment elle réagirait quand elle se retrouverait dans la chambre, avec lui, sous cette lumière tamisée, devant ce lit qu'il avait légèrement défait, il ne savait même pas si elle allait venir, si elle n'allait pas renoncer à la porte de la chambre, rongée par la culpabilité. Il resta un moment à s'observer dans le miroir comme nous le faisons tous avec une fascination malsaine. Il n'imaginait pas la séduire aussi vite, une femme dont la puissance économique occultait tout le reste, une femme hermétique, presque hostile, qu'il faudrait amadouer, forcer peut-être, au risque de l'effrayer, au risque de la perdre, et quelle importance si vous partez ? Il l'attendit dans le petit salon, s'assit sur le canapé, alluma le téléviseur et changea frénétiquement de chaîne jusqu'à ce qu'il l'entendît frapper à la porte. Son pouls s'accéléra tout à coup, il éteignit le téléviseur et lui ouvrit. Elle était là, un peu trop maquillée, voûtée comme un animal traqué, posez ce magnétophone. Il l'étreignit, respira sa nuque, ses cheveux, *détends-toi*. Elle se contracta, étonnamment rigide, prostrée par la peur de se trahir, de regretter, de mal faire, Juliana n'a pas d'expérience des hommes ou si peu, *laisse-toi faire, laisse-toi aller*. Une chaleur nouvelle, menaçante, l'envahissait. Elle plaqua ses mains contre sa poitrine dans une posture défensive, elle ne supportait pas qu'un homme lui touchât la poitrine – et vous ? Il pouvait la rassurer, lui parler, cesser ses caresses – il haïssait la tendresse, comme moi –, au lieu de cela, il la plaqua contre le mur avec une brutalité inouïe et l'embrassa. Pas un mot ne fut échangé.

Dans l'anonymat d'une chambre d'hôtel, l'une des femmes les plus puissantes d'Allemagne se donna à un homme dont elle ne savait rien, qu'elle n'avait vu que deux fois dans sa vie, et qu'elle avait pourtant suivi sans lui poser aucune question, sans avoir obtenu le moindre renseignement, ignorante, inconsciente, sans résistance, violant nos impératifs sécuritaires, sa morale personnelle, ses convictions, elle l'avait suivi parce qu'elle ne pouvait pas lui dire « non », mot abscons, imprononçable, qui limite et restreint, elle avait perdu tout contrôle, toute capacité de jugement, elle était une proie, une poupée de chiffon, une chose molle et sans volonté entièrement commandée par sa matrice, elle était cette femme qui capitulait sans avoir été torturée, violentée, elle se rendait, se soumettait avec une jubilation nouvelle, une excitation guerrière, elle était une machine à aimer, qui hurlait, haletait, et sa voix était un gémissement, un soupir qui gonflait, elle était cette femme résignée, égrotante, à genoux devant lui comme devant un prie-dieu, cherchant la protection, réclamant la servitude, inféodée au pouvoir d'un dieu étranger, cette femme qui se traînait à terre, nue, hirsute, échevelée – voilà pourquoi je déteste l'amour : les papillons redeviennent des larves.

De désir, elle crevait pour l'homme magnifié, prête à passer le reste de ses jours dans l'obédience – mais que comprenez-vous à cette attraction animale, cette comédie érotique ? Ah ! votre façon d'écouter sans m'interrompre... en amour aussi, une fonctionnaire du sexe et rien d'autre. Elle ne pouvait pas lutter contre, mille arguments s'y opposaient, elle ne contrôlait plus ses émotions, ses instincts, elle était coupée de sa réalité intérieure, de son enfance, de ceux qui l'avaient faite, élevée, aimée ; retranchée du monde des professionnels qu'elle côtoyait et dont elle avait oublié les noms, séparée physiquement, mentalement, de son mari qui n'existait plus que de manière elliptique, avait-il jamais existé, amputée de ses enfants, débarrassée des angoisses maternelles, des liens professionnels, familiaux, amicaux, était-elle encore une épouse, une mère, avait-elle un frère, une génitrice, quel était son nom, sans identité la voilà, la femme aimante, amoureuse, aimable, celle qui consent, participe, acquiesce, enroulée, déliée, recroquevillée, enveloppée par lui, par ce corps puissant, mince, musculeux, ce corps qui se mouvait avec l'agilité d'une panthère, qui tressaillait et sautait en elle, et où est le prédateur, pensait-elle, où est-il, il n'y avait plus que cet animal sauvage et doux, tendre et féroce qui la comblait et la blessait, la faisait jouir et la maltraitait sans qu'elle en subît aucun sentiment d'humiliation, aucune douleur, et il la tenait fermement, pourquoi, demandez-vous, pourquoi, taisez-vous, vous êtes là à juger, de la morale plein la bouche. Vous n'avez jamais aimé, comme moi, vous êtes seule, sèche, vous n'avez jamais risqué votre peau, vous ne donnez rien, ouvrez, fermez, la mécanique sexuelle, rien de plus, bravo, vous êtes des nôtres.

Une femme discrète, glaciale, méfiante jusqu'à la paranoïa, qui n'accorde sa confiance qu'à quelques rares personnes, ne se confie pas, une femme qui a été kidnappée, traumatisée, cette femme s'est laissé séduire par Braun et s'est offerte à lui dès le lendemain de leur rencontre et comment, pourquoi, demandez-vous ? Ce que l'attirance sexuelle a de mystérieux, je n'en sais rien mais elle… La frustration cathartique. L'obsession de la transgression. La condamnation des faiblesses humaines. Un protestantisme froid, austère, dont le respect scrupuleux est organisé autour du devoir – le devoir et rien d'autre. Le plaisir sexuel ? On n'est pas là pour ça ! Le sens des responsabilités, oui. L'exécution des tâches, le respect des convenances, la politisation de la vie conjugale, oui. La hiérarchisation des sentiments avec, en haut de la pyramide, la complicité conjugale. Deux partis opposés qui décident de mettre leurs intérêts en commun – la démocratie sentimentale. Mais la sensualité anarchique, non. La sexualité hypnotique, non. Jusqu'à sa rencontre avec Braun. Cet homme a tout fait voler en éclats. Et comment, demandez-vous ? Comment ? Les Kant sont des gens influents, indestructibles, qui ont une faille, ne riez pas, le talon d'Achille des Kant, c'est le désir sexuel. Placez un Kant dans un lit et vous obtiendrez un scandale, une bombe, un retournement historique, une guerre, un crime contre l'humanité. Le lit des Kant est devenu le théâtre de toutes les opérations humaines. Dans leur lit, le monde jouit et meurt. Vous pensez que je suis fou, je suis fou, c'est pourquoi Juliana Kant m'a renvoyé, rentrez chez vous, Karl, vous êtes fatigué, surmené, je suis fou, ils m'ont effacé de leur mémoire familiale, rayé de leur vie, je suis fou alors que je les ai servis, aimés, entourés, protégés, défendus, alors que je les ai aimés, aimés…

Etes-vous réelle ? Suis-je en train de vous parler ? Je perds la tête par moments, depuis que j'ai été agressé en pleine nuit par un homme, un couteau sous la gorge et puis plus rien. Sept jours d'hospitalisation, Juliana n'est jamais venue me rendre visite, elle m'a fait livrer des macarons aux noix – j'y suis allergique. Nous sommes là dans cet hôtel – j'aime Paris, je parle, vous m'écoutez. Comment être sûr que vous transformerez mes paroles en littérature sans les déformer, sans me trahir ? Comment saurez-vous décrire ce premier échange érotique entre Braun et Juliana sans l'avoir vu comme je l'ai vu, avec une certaine excitation et sans doute aussi un peu de dégoût d'être désormais du côté des voyeurs, des inactifs, des retraités du sexe et de l'amour ?

Imaginez-les dans cette grande chambre d'hôtel, enlacés, emboîtés, possédés l'un par l'autre. Elle ne voulait pas dire ces mots à Braun : « Je suis la fille de Philipp Kant », elle se taisait, c'était un instant qui n'engageait pas, qui ne promettait rien, c'est ce qu'elle se répétait tout en sachant qu'elle se mentait à elle-même, depuis le début, elle se sentait attirée, aspirée, happée par cet homme, son visage, ses mains, son corps, elle l'aimait déjà, était-elle aimée, ils étaient seuls au monde, seuls dans cette chambre aux murs beiges, riant, dansant, elle disait, je suis libre, demain, après-demain, toujours, et à elle-même, avec crainte, inquiétude : suis-je *vraiment* aimée ?

« Nous agissons pour le bien de l'entreprise. Nous ne cherchons pas à être aimés. »

Günther Kant à son fils Philipp.

Le lendemain, à l'heure du déjeuner, Braun lui donna rendez-vous au zoo de Berlin, le zoo, quelle idée, un lieu public. Pourtant elle ne dit pas : « Je suis la fille de Philipp Kant, quelqu'un pourrait me reconnaître », elle murmura simplement : « Le zoo, êtes-vous sûr que… » Braun l'interrompit : « Qui pourrions-nous croiser à part des enfants et des animaux ? » Il est original, singulier, pensait-elle, différent des autres. De l'enfance, Juliana n'a connu que les contraintes d'une éducation corsetée à l'excès, et vous ? Du plus loin qu'elle se souvienne, Juliana a toujours été une adulte, une fille responsable, mature, sans fantaisie, sans éclat, la représentation parfaite de ce que ses parents exigeaient d'elle.

Lorsqu'elle arriva devant la lourde grille du zoo, Braun était déjà là, des journaux sous le bras, il lui adressait de grands signes. Un homme l'attendait, l'appelait, Juliana se sentait désirée, était-elle aimée ? Il lui transmettait ce qu'elle n'avait jamais connu, qui n'avait pas de prix, n'était pas négociable – une certaine inclination à la légèreté : un passage secret sur l'enfance. Il prit sa tête entre ses mains, l'embrassa sur la joue d'une façon paternelle, elle baissa les yeux, troublée. Il y avait une tendresse nouvelle dans sa façon de l'aborder, une manifestation physique qui trahissait une évolution affective, songeait Juliana. Alors elle se laissa guider comme une aveugle, elle s'abandonna, suivant son amant, acquiesçant à chacune de ses paroles, riant à ses blagues. Ils s'attardèrent devant les cages comme des enfants indociles et curieux. J'étais là, moi aussi, caché derrière les autruches, je n'étais pas payé pour faire ça et pourtant je la guettais, je ne cherchais pas à la protéger – je les enviais : cette complicité érotique, cette connivence intellectuelle… Pourquoi pas moi ? Le spectacle de leur amour me semblait obscène, pathétique. Je pénétrai dans le bâtiment réservé aux reptiles. C'était l'heure du repas. Les soigneurs glissaient dans les cages de verre des souris vivantes que les reptiles gobaient d'un claquement de mâchoire. Je voyais la forme du rongeur encore vivant qui tressaillait, déformant la peau écailleuse. Cela ne dura que quelques secondes.

Le reptile gisait, repu, indifférent aux cris des enfants terrifiés. Un prédateur, me répétais-je, en sortant du bâtiment et en apercevant Braun qui enlaçait Juliana. Ils étaient assis sur un banc en plein soleil. Les rayons les éblouissaient.

« Je veux tout savoir de toi ! Parle-moi de ta famille ! Quels sont tes goûts ? D'où viens-tu ? Je veux tout savoir ! Tout ! »

Braun embrassa Juliana au milieu des enfants qui se pressaient en hurlant et grimaçant contre la cage des singes, elle se laissa faire, oubliant le danger, la réserve, oubliant tout, écrasée par la puissance d'un désir qu'elle n'avait jamais ressenti. « Parle-moi de tes enfants ! Montre-moi des photos ! Quel âge ont-ils ? » Et il lâcha cette phrase qui anéantirait toutes ses réserves : « Je les aime déjà. »

« J'aï renoncé à l'amour il y a trente ans et depuis je n'ai plus aucun problème cardiaque. »

Karl Fritz à l'éditeur.

J'avais offert à Juliana un exemplaire d'*Adolphe* de Benjamin Constant ainsi que *Madame Bovary* de Flaubert – j'espérais que la littérature la détournerait de Braun, c'était ridicule, rien ne pouvait plus l'éloigner de cet homme, ni les livres, ni la peur de trahir, ni les raisonnements affectifs ou moralisateurs, ni la perspective du chaos, ni la conviction intime qu'ils ne vivraient jamais ensemble, ni mes mises en garde, ni… Comprenez-moi : elle était perdue, perdue pour le monde, et moi avec. Son quotidien, son existence, n'évoluaient plus qu'autour d'une seule et même pensée : était-elle aimée ?

Suis-je aimée ? Elle expertisait l'amour, vérifiait l'authenticité des sentiments – du toc –, réclamait des preuves, et quels risques, quelle mascarade pour ça, quelques heures avec lui, quelques minutes d'une brutalité stupéfiante comme s'ils réglaient leurs comptes – avec qui ? Dans son lit avec la peur, à le désirer, liée comme une louve, nerveuse, à vif, en manque de lui jusqu'à l'heure des révélations sur sa famille, dix jours seulement après leur rencontre : « Il faut que tu le saches maintenant. Je suis la fille de Philipp Kant, le propriétaire de K&S. » Ces initiales, la puissance qu'elles incarnaient. Il savait ce que cela signifiait. Il dit : « Je ne m'en doutais pas. » La légendaire discrétion des Kant. Ne pas s'exposer. Ne pas répondre aux interviews. Comment aurait-il pu savoir ? Il alluma une cigarette, passa sa main sur sa poitrine.

— Je couche avec la femme la plus puissante d'Allemagne, c'est terriblement érotique !

— Est-ce que les choses vont changer entre nous ?

— Oui, totalement ! Maintenant, je vais vouloir à tout prix t'épouser !

« Je voudrais être vue en tant qu'être humain. »

Juliana Kant,
au cours d'une séance d'acupuncture.

La suite est une succession de rendez-vous, un amour caché aux yeux du monde, la routine amoureuse – applaudissez. De Braun, Juliana ne devinait rien, ce souci de discrétion lui convenait, elle ne cherchait pas à le posséder, le contrôler, ils ne vivraient jamais ensemble, elle n'exigeait rien qu'il ne pût lui offrir, rien qui brisât cet édifice fragile qu'ils avaient conçu pour s'aimer – s'aimer et rien d'autre. Elle n'avait pas le sentiment de percer quoi que ce fût de ses goûts, de sa personnalité, pas même lorsqu'ils se retrouvaient dans leur chambre d'hôtel, dans leur lit, Braun restait un étranger jusque dans l'amour – un animal sexuel, et alors ? Il savait qu'elle était mariée, mère de famille, fortunée – c'était assez.

Pour l'anniversaire de leur rencontre – quatre mois déjà qu'ils se retrouvaient en cachette, seuls au monde et moi derrière à surveiller, *je compte sur votre discrétion, Karl* –, Braun l'invita chez lui. Il habitait un loft dans la banlieue de Berlin, un lieu à la décoration dépouillée : une table, un canapé, un lit, un bureau métallique sur lequel s'entassaient des magazines et des pochettes grises. Au mur, des images transgressives, pornographiques, avaient été suspendues selon un ordre rigoureux. Des clichés de guerre aussi, représentant des corps désarticulés, des paysages dévastés par les bombes. Au-dessus du canapé, en grand format, un exemplaire du cliché que Braun avait offert à Juliana. NE PAS ENTRER. DANGER DE MORT. « Tu ne m'as pas offert l'original ? » plaisanta Juliana. Braun était assis en tailleur sur le canapé, vêtu d'un jean et d'un tee-shirt blanc froissé. Un érotisme froid se dégageait de sa personne comme si la distance qu'il instaurait suffisait à susciter le désir. « Déshabille-toi », ordonna-t-il. Juliana s'avança vers lui et, à sa hauteur, se figea. Elle avait honte de dévoiler son corps sous cette lumière crue qui l'aveuglait à la manière d'une torche. « Déshabille-toi », insista Braun. Juliana hésita, resta un moment interdite, puis lui obéit, sans sensualité, mécaniquement, tout en ne quittant pas la photographie du regard. Elle ne portait plus que ses dessous : une combinaison en dentelle crème qu'elle avait achetée la veille. Elle eut envie de pleurer tout à coup : « Ecoute, je ne sais pas ce que je fais ici, je… » Braun se leva, posa sa main sur sa bouche pour la faire taire. Juliana ne bougea pas. Il la serra contre lui, caressa sa nuque, laissa glisser ses doigts le long de ses reins. Il la fit pivoter, se plaqua contre elle. Il la serrait fortement – Juliana ne se dégagea pas. Il souleva sa combinaison et lui murmura à l'oreille : « Je veux tout de toi. » Puis il la lâcha, se dirigea vers l'extrémité de la pièce et ouvrit la fenêtre. Un vent glacial pénétra dans le salon. « J'ai froid », dit Juliana mais Braun ne l'écoutait pas. Il retourna s'asseoir à sa place, sur le canapé. « Regarde la photo, imagine que tu es dans cet endroit et dis-moi ce que tu ressens. » « Je meurs de froid. » Juliana tremblait, sa peau était picotée de rouge. « Ferme, s'il te plaît, ferme cette fenêtre. » Braun lui fit signe de le rejoindre et, quand elle fut à sa hauteur, l'attira sur lui. « Quitte ton mari, je t'aime, je ne peux pas vivre loin de toi » – de la propagande amoureuse. « Je te désire trop. – Jusqu'à quel point m'aimes-tu ? Prouve-le. » « Epouse-moi. »

Alors, elle pensa à tout sacrifier, par amour. Cela vous paraît ridicule, n'est-ce pas ? Qu'une femme de quarante-cinq ans, mariée et mère de trois enfants, décorée de la Croix fédérale du

Mérite, une femme à la tête d'une fortune de plusieurs milliards d'euros dont la notoriété dépassait le cadre de l'Allemagne, qu'une telle incarnation de la perfection féminine pût faire exploser le cocon où elle vivait depuis tant d'années pour une simple passion sexuelle, cela vous laisse incrédule, cela vous révolte même, je le vois bien à votre regard moralisateur qui réprouve et condamne... Cette vie conjugale étouffante, débarrassée des contraintes de la séduction, cette existence morne, mécanique où le devoir préside à toute chose, où rien ne compte que la place sociale, le regard social, cette mise en scène qu'elle maîtrisait parfaitement mais qui détruisait, jour après jour, ce qui restait d'authentique en elle, Juliana n'en supportait plus le cours. Sans-toi-je-ne-peux-pas-vivre-sans-toi-je-ne-suis-rien.

Quitte-le.

« Je ne me sens ni coupable ni responsable. »

Axel Kant à son psychanalyste.

Je suis condamné.

Ils étaient dans une chambre d'hôtel, nus, allongés sur leur lit, après l'amour, quel romantisme, Braun savait choisir son moment, un fin stratège dont la singularité attractive masquait le calcul, la détermination destructrice, il connaissait les gestes qui attendrissaient et capturaient, une façon de caresser le visage de la femme aimée, de poser la voix, je n'ai jamais su, moi, captiver ainsi une femme, la faire mienne, c'est comme ça. Il était aux commandes, rusé, attentif à l'autre, s'enroulant à elle comme une liane. Pourquoi ne se méfiait-elle pas de lui ? Une gueule d'ange, ça voile le reste. La perversion, le vice, l'intention de nuire, on ne voyait rien… rien que ce visage parfait, rieur, avec des éclats d'enfance qui vous sautaient aux yeux comme des fragments d'obus.

Il lui dit calmement : « C'est la dernière fois que je te vois » et avant même qu'elle eût pu évoquer la rupture qu'elle redoutait mais dont elle savait qu'elle adviendrait tôt ou tard, avant même qu'elle eût tenté de le retenir par tous les moyens, la persuasion, le chantage, la déclaration élégiaque, il énonça ces mots en détachant chaque syllabe : « Je vais mourir. » Elle en fut presque soulagée, la séparation physique, elle pourrait la supporter à condition qu'elle ne fût pas le fruit d'une décision unilatérale, imposée et voulue par lui – Juliana ne voulait pas être quittée. Mais sa mort, comment y croire ? Elle ne comprit pas, questionna, harcela, énonça les hypothèses les plus improbables, ne lui laissant pas la possibilité de s'exprimer, comme si cette annonce devenait un jeu, un questionnaire – la seule façon qu'elle eût trouvée de conjurer sa peine. Braun se détourna, il ne pouvait rien lui dire, elle devait l'accepter : il n'avait plus que quelques semaines à vivre, peut-être quelques jours, quelques heures, comment savoir et moi aussi peut-être, finissons-en. Elle dit : « Je vous aime, je t'aime, je ne peux pas vivre sans toi, je mourrai sans toi » – des aveux un peu pathétiques, n'est-ce pas ? Le beau visage de Braun devint mélancolique. Avec une lueur de gravité dans le regard, il répéta qu'il ne pouvait pas se confier. Du bout des lèvres, il concéda qu'il n'était pas malade. Il n'était pas malade mais condamné à une mort prochaine – et impuissant à en interrompre le processus désormais inéluctable, *n'attends plus rien de moi, je suis un homme mort.*

Parle ! Je t'en prie, parle-moi ! Il y avait de la sincérité dans l'acharnement amoureux de cette femme, une forme d'audace sauvage qui trahissait son attachement. *Parle !* Cette injonction le toucha, alors seulement, il commença à raconter. Il faisait frais ce soir-là, les rideaux de leur chambre étaient tirés, ils n'avaient pas allumé le chauffage, la fenêtre était entrouverte, l'air, glacé ; ils se serraient l'un contre l'autre. Moment d'intensité amoureuse comme nous n'en avons jamais connu, nous autres qui n'aimons personne. Il raconta qu'un soir, à New York, en sortant d'une galerie d'art, il roulait trop vite, il n'avait rien bu, quelque chose avait été projeté sur la route qui avait heurté l'avant du véhicule et fait crisser les pneus, un obstacle surgi de nulle part, il ne voyait rien, il avait accéléré, ce devait être un animal, il avait allumé la radio pour couvrir le silence de la nuit, essayant de détourner son attention, n'y parvenant pas, il n'avait plus que cela en tête, cette chose inerte et éventrée au milieu de la route dont il avait perçu la masse opaque à travers le rétroviseur, qu'avait-il renversé ? Un faon ? Un cerf ? Il était rentré chez lui, avait mal dormi. Toute la nuit, il n'avait cessé de penser à cet incident, revivant la scène, en songe. Dans la matinée, il avait reçu un appel d'un inconnu, *Je ne suis pas de la police,* et cet homme à la voix sépulcrale lui avait dit qu'il avait été vu sur cette route, il avait été reconnu, ce n'était pas un animal qui avait débuché, c'était une enfant, une petite fille, dix ans peut-être, dix ans, à peu près, c'est ça.

J'ai renversé la fille du chef de la mafia albanaise.

Sa voix n'était qu'un tremblement, presque un râle, on eut dit qu'il allait étouffer. Juliana frémit. Vérité ? Chantage ? Ses interlocuteurs – dont il ne connaissait pas les noms – affirmaient que l'enfant était à l'hôpital, dans le coma, qu'elle mourrait ou resterait dans un état végétatif, elle mourrait, répétaient-ils, répétait-il à Juliana, par votre faute, ma faute, murmurait-il, la tête entre les mains de Juliana comme si cette étreinte tendre et soudaine le préservait de la menace du crime, vous êtes coupable, je suis responsable, et pourtant, je n'ai rien vu, rien vu venir, je te le promets, et elle lui donna son absolution, en le caressant, devenant sa complice. « Ils me tueront, ils me l'ont dit, ils me tueront. » Une enfant, quelle horreur, songea Juliana.

— Je vais me rendre à la police.

— Mais pourquoi ? Tu n'as rien vu…

— J'ai senti la collision… et… j'ai reçu des photos de l'enfant…

Braun renversa sa tête entre les mains protectrices de Juliana. *Je suis là, mon amour, je t'aime* – toute cette surenchère affective. Juliana s'emporta, enflammée tout à coup, émotive, jusqu'à ce qu'il sortît une lettre de sa poche, un texte de menaces qui énumérait les sévices promis s'il ne coopérait pas : torture, mutilation et meurtre. Il détourna son regard, pris de vertige, il avait peur maintenant, près d'elle. Elle demanda :

— Que veulent-ils ?

Il ne répondit pas.

— Que veulent-ils ?

Même silence obstiné. Il restait figé dans son rôle de martyr sacrifié sur l'autel de la repentance, la réparation. Fier et beau, devant elle, implorante : *Que veulent-ils ?*

— De l'argent. Cinq millions d'euros. En espèces.

— Es-tu vraiment sûr d'avoir renversé cette enfant ?

Braun pâlit, lâcha un « oui » inaudible.

— Que faisait-elle dans la nuit en pleine rue ? Ils te mentent peut-être…

— Ils sortaient d'une salle de fête, elle a couru et…

Juliana caressa le visage de Braun, l'encouragea à parler.

— Ils sont prêts à renoncer aux poursuites si je paye.

— Comment peuvent-ils te réclamer une somme pareille ?

— Je ne sais pas. Oui, comment ? Je ne les possède pas.

— Savent-ils que nous sommes ensemble ?

Il sembla surpris par sa question, ne répondit pas.

— C'est peut-être un piège… S'ils le savent, c'est à moi qu'ils en veulent, ils pensent que je vais payer.

— Non, notre liaison est secrète. Personne ne sait rien.

Elle était rassurée. Le degré de crédibilité de cette histoire rocambolesque ? Peu importe, elle ne voulait pas le perdre. Elle l'aimait, vous comprenez, elle était totalement dépendante de lui, elle l'avait dans la peau, au sens strict, il l'habitait, chacun de ses organes était contaminé par lui, elle ne pouvait pas s'en détacher, s'en séparer ; sans lui, elle était vide et l'argent n'était rien pour elle. Cette fascination malsaine, cette attirance morbide pour Braun, je n'ai pas pu l'anticiper, la prévenir. C'était là, voilà tout. Elle dit qu'elle allait payer. Il refusa son argent : il n'avait jamais rien emprunté à personne, pas même à son père, il était trop fier pour cela, il préférait mourir ou finir en prison le reste de sa vie que de lui être redevable, il ne pourrait jamais lui rendre cet argent. Il était beau, drapé dans sa dignité d'homme fautif. Il assumait sa honte et son crime. Juliana insista : « Laisse-moi payer la rançon. Accepte… Pour moi… » Alors seulement, il accepta. « Pour toi. »

« Ça me heurte quand je suis uniquement jugée par rapport à l'argent. L'argent ne dit rien sur ce que je suis. Cela met un rideau entre les autres et moi. »

Juliana Kant à Herb Braun.

L'opération avait un nom de code cinématographique : *Scorsese.* « Apporte-moi cinq DVD de Scorsese ! » exigeait la voix au bout du fil. Juliana proposa à Braun d'informer la police allemande mais il refusa avec vigueur : « Ils ont des informateurs partout, je suis sur écoute. Nous agirons seuls. » Juliana n'eut aucune difficulté à réunir l'argent : cinq millions d'euros en billets de cinq cents. Je tentai de la dissuader d'agir, cette histoire me semblait suspecte – en vain. Elle n'écoutait plus mes conseils, m'évitait : elle s'émancipait, enfin. Un instant, je songeai à prévenir son frère, puis je renonçai. J'avais toujours gardé le silence au mépris des règles morales. J'étais l'homme d'une famille. Ma loyauté restait sans faille. Je savais beaucoup de choses – oh, pas tout, il restait tant de zones d'ombres, de sujets tabous – mais cette familiarité avec le pouvoir, cette connaissance précise d'une dynastie influente et enviée, me coupaient de mes aspirations profondes : je n'avais existé qu'à travers eux. Depuis l'apparition de Braun, je n'existais plus du tout.

Le rendez-vous avec les maîtres chanteurs fut pris dans le parking de l'hôtel où ils s'étaient revus et aimés. Ils y avaient fait l'amour et se retrouvaient dans un mauvais drame. Dans la chambre, Juliana avait remis à Braun la mallette qui contenait les liasses de billets. Ils étaient là, à quelques dizaines de mètres l'un de l'autre, elle dans sa voiture, lui dans un véhicule de location. Dix minutes s'écoulèrent quand soudain une camionnette blanche stationna. Dans le rétroviseur, un appel de phares aveugla Braun. C'était le signal. Je le vis sortir de la voiture, la mallette à la main, et se diriger vers la camionnette. La fenêtre du conducteur s'ouvrit, un homme cagoulé fit un signe à Braun et, d'un geste vif, s'empara de la mallette. Il jeta aussitôt à terre une enveloppe. L'échange ne dura que quelques secondes. La camionnette prit la fuite dans un écran de fumée. Braun resta un moment immobile, le regard rivé vers l'horizon, comme s'il était choqué, inconscient. Juliana sortit précipitamment du véhicule où elle s'était cachée, enlaça Braun avec tendresse. Puis elle ramassa l'enveloppe, l'ouvrit fébrilement et lut le document qui exonérait son amant de toute responsabilité dans l'accident de la petite fille. Ils s'embrassèrent. Je les observais. Il l'étreignait avec force, pressait sa main sur sa nuque. De loin, ça ressemblait à de l'amour.

« Mon père était un homme droit et responsable. Ce qu'il a fait, il l'a fait pour l'entreprise. »

Juliana Kant à ses avocats.

Florence, les jardins de Boboli, les terrasses des glaciers, les musées et le séjour dans l'hôtel de charme qu'il avait choisi avec soin – le romantisme extraconjugal. Ensemble, dans les ruelles inondées de lumière, les chemins escarpés, ils oubliaient les menaces et la rançon. Je n'accompagnai pas Juliana cette fois-là, j'imaginai – un moment de grâce absolue, partons ensemble. A son retour, Juliana était physiquement transformée, prête à affronter le scandale médiatique dont ses avocats repoussaient sans cesse l'échéance, ça viendrait – et vite. Elle envisageait désormais de se séparer quelque temps de son mari. Depuis qu'il l'avait menacée de divorcer – oh, une fois – parce qu'il craignait que toute information qui entacherait la réputation des Kant ne rejaillît sur lui, depuis ce jour, leurs relations s'étaient distendues, ils se parlaient peu – et pour se nuire. Mais quelques jours plus tard, pour le quarante-cinquième anniversaire de Juliana, son frère, Axel, réunit sa famille dans la belle demeure de Babelsberg. Les amis, les enfants, les frères et sœurs étaient là, oubliant les révélations diffamatoires que la presse publierait bientôt. Même son mari avait fait le déplacement, regrettant ses emportements, cherchant un rapprochement. Au moment où il l'étreignit tendrement – oh une simple pression de l'épaule –, Juliana sut qu'elle ne le quitterait pas. Quelques jours auparavant, il s'était enfin manifesté après avoir trouvé plusieurs lettres de Braun dans lesquelles il évoquait leur « extraordinaire complicité », son amour « irrépressible » pour Juliana et « le désir inouï qui le submergeait ». Il avait également découvert un relevé de facture téléphonique : « Qui est le destinataire de ce numéro que tu composes dix fois par jour ? » « Un collaborateur. » Et il avait eu peur de la perdre, tout à coup, en dépit de ce qu'il savait d'elle. Jamais il n'avait été aussi prévenant. Il avait compris – et avant tout le monde. Perspicacité de celui qu'on abandonne. Et elle était là, devant sa famille, rouge d'émotion, enivrée par le vin qu'ils avaient partagé, elle était là, parmi les siens – comment avait-elle pu songer à les quitter pour un homme dont elle ne savait presque rien, un espion industriel peut-être ? Elle leva son verre à la santé de sa mère, à la mémoire de son père, à l'affection de son mari – elle n'avait pas dit « l'amour » –, à la bienveillance de son frère, à la beauté de ses enfants. Droite, guindée dans sa jupe qui recouvrait ses genoux, cette chemise rose pâle aux manches longues, la tête prise dans un serre-tête en velours bleu marine – une caricature. Ce conformisme bourgeois, ce protestantisme au visage sévère, c'était elle. Cette discrétion, cette rigueur – le mode de vie qu'elle avait choisi et qui lui convenait le mieux. Comment avait-elle pu s'abandonner, se méprendre ? Ah, la corruption sentimentale ! Commença alors l'entreprise de déstabilisation morale, de culpabilisation et d'autoflagellation, des jugements moraux que Juliana s'infligeait comme une punition, des sévices qui réparaient la faute.

Le lendemain, Juliana appela Braun : « Il faut que je te parle, c'est important. » Il ne lui parut pas inquiet, lui donna rendez-vous à l'hôtel. Je dois le revoir pour rompre une fois pour toutes, se répétait-elle, une rupture simple et propre, sans cris, sans atermoiements. Mais quand elle le rejoignit dans leur chambre d'hôtel, quand elle franchit le seuil, vit le lit défait, son corps dans l'embrasure de la porte de la salle de bains, quand elle sentit son parfum, aperçut ses vêtements posés sur la chaise, elle n'avait plus rien de la maîtresse vindicative, rien de l'épouse dévoyée revenue à la loyauté et aux serments éternels ; elle se précipita dans ses bras, corrompue par l'attente, le manque, la force du lien qui s'était noué sans qu'elle en eût pleinement conscience, sans intention délibérée. A nouveau, il la posséda, il la domina ; dans son lit, elle redevenait cette bête avide qui s'ouvrait, prenait – ne donnait rien. Incapable de renoncer à lui, à ce qu'il lui offrait, cette brutalité sexuelle qui la comblait et l'apaisait. Dans le lit de cet homme, elle n'était plus la décisionnaire, la femme puissante et dominatrice, c'était une proie, une victime, qu'on comblait et plaignait. Le désir la sauvait de son quotidien morne, la sexualité la préservait des tourments de l'âge, l'absolvait de sa culpabilité, la faute se diluait. Dans le lit de Braun, Juliana se découvrait une aptitude à la transformation, à l'oubli – au déni. Quel scandale ? Quelle pression ? Quelles vociférations publiques ? Elle n'entendait rien. Elle était cette femme cajoleuse, docile, qui n'aimait rien tant qu'être prise par cet homme, c'était une exécutante, elle n'avait plus aucun pouvoir, elle obéissait aux ordres qu'il lui donnait sans y chercher une dimension morale, elle était tout entière offerte, entre les mains de son amant, des mains puissantes qui saisissaient et prenaient, serraient et caressaient, mais que comprenez-vous à cela ? Dans son lit, elle était cette femme libre et affranchie des conventions sociales, des obligations familiales, elle n'était plus la fille de Philipp Kant mais une maîtresse sans nom, un objet de jouissance et d'abandon qui acquiesçait et devenait chaque jour plus servile, réclamant cette soumission, y trouvant une jouissance intense, se pliant à toutes les volontés de son amant, s'y pliant totalement, ne refusant rien. Mais quand elle le quittait, quand elle sortait de la chambre d'hôtel où elle s'était laissé manipuler, elle sentait monter en elle l'effroi et la honte, une honte puissante, rageuse qui la transformait, elle, l'héritière, la femme d'influence, en une captive effarouchée qui pleurait, cognait contre son ravisseur et sans doute aussi contre elle-même, son impuissance, sa faiblesse, son désir. Elle se sentait coupable d'aimer cet inconnu, ce dieu jaloux, sans clémence ni miséricorde, coupable de trahir son mari, cet homme bon qu'elle affectionnait comme un frère, auquel elle ne se donnait plus que par lassitude, coupable de le tromper, chaque jour, chaque heure, y trouvant du plaisir, excitant le vice, tentatrice, coupable de céder à cet amour hypnotique, coupable d'aimer faire l'amour, d'y penser avant, pendant, après, coupable de perdre la maîtrise d'elle-même.

Nous ne devons plus nous revoir.
Je t'aime.
Je ne peux plus continuer. J'ai un mari, des enfants et…
Je t'aime. Je ne peux pas me passer de toi, je suis fou de toi.
Demain, tu ne m'aimeras plus, demain, un scandale va éclater, ternissant la réputation de ma famille, je ne peux plus te revoir.
Tu ne pourras pas me quitter.
Je te remplacerai.

Elle avait dit ces derniers mots en souriant.

Ce qui s'est passé ensuite, imaginons-le, nous sommes des romanciers, pas des greffiers, écrivez. Il lui demanda de s'agenouiller, ne me regardez pas comme ça – de la littérature, de la fiction, et rien d'autre. Juliana obéit. Elle resta ainsi sans se révolter, sans se plaindre. Elle aimait se sentir possédée par cet homme, renoncer un moment au pouvoir, à la puissance et à tous les attributs que son nom, sa fortune lui octroyaient sans qu'elle le désirât vraiment. Elle songea au questionnaire de Proust qu'un journaliste allemand lui avait soumis et à la question : *Où et à quel moment de votre vie avez-vous été le plus heureuse ?* Elle pouvait répondre désormais : « Ici, au côté de mon amant. » Elle se recroquevilla davantage. Le pendentif que Braun lui avait offert se balançait. Elle attendait qu'il la touchât, qu'il s'approchât mais il resta en retrait, debout, au-dessus d'elle.

« Je suis allée dans une école normale, j'ai reçu une éducation normale, nous sommes des gens normaux. »

Juliana Kant, à une amie,
au cours d'une balade en forêt.

Ma version des faits vous choque ? Je vous l'ai dit : j'invente. Qui pourrait démêler le vrai du faux, la fiction du réel. J'écris, je joue, je suis infidèle aux faits, je fabule, les événements se sont passés tels que je les ai interprétés, et alors ? Les Kant feront relire le texte pas leurs avocats qui traqueront la violation de la vie privée, la diffamation, les atteintes à la dignité humaine, chiffreront le préjudice et nous contacteront pour saisir nos mots. Je suis un menteur, un falsificateur – et pourquoi, demandez-vous, pourquoi chercher à leur nuire, par tous les moyens, la vérité, la fiction, le recours aux faits historiques, à l'affabulation ? Où se situe la frontière entre ce qui relève de la réalité/de mon imagination, de la vôtre ?

Une vengeance ?

Qu'en savez-vous ?

... les faits... rien que les faits... nous y voilà, bien au chaud. Quelques années avant la mort de Philipp Kant, j'ai aimé une femme, oui j'ai aimé, pourquoi pas moi ? C'était une libraire française dont j'avais fait la connaissance au cours d'un vernissage, une femme rousse, au corps osseux, âgée d'une trentaine d'années – mon genre. Elle portait ce soir-là un smoking noir et des escarpins en vernis rouge à hauts talons, ça m'avait donné le vertige. Je lui parlai littérature et la séduisis sans effort, il y a encore des femmes que le sort d'Anna Karénine bouleverse. Elle mangeait peu. Le soir même de notre rencontre, nous eûmes une liaison, qui dura trois mois. Ce qui me charma chez elle en dehors de sa maigreur ? Oh pas grand-chose, son sens de la dérision peut-être et c'était assez pour un homme comme moi. Je la retrouvais trois quatre fois par mois, chez elle, dans le petit appartement parisien qu'elle louait dans le 17e arrondissement. Nous faisions l'amour, nous fumions, je n'avais plus faim – que peut espérer de plus un anorexique amoureux ? Elle me lisait des poèmes, ça m'apaisait – Keats aussi a des vertus anxiolytiques. Au cours du quatrième mois, elle me demanda de quitter les Kant pour vivre avec elle, elle ne supportait plus, disait-elle, ces allers-retours, cette séparation imposée. J'en parlai à Philipp Kant. A l'évocation de cette liaison, il se cabra. C'est impossible, répétait-il. Qu'une personne songeât à l'abandonner lui était insupportable – ça n'arriverait pas. Je proposai ma démission. Il tripla mon salaire – moi aussi, j'avais donc un prix –, et m'attribua une prime annuelle qui annihila mon désir de liberté. Enfin, il me menaça d'une façon qui n'autorisait pas la réplique – j'en savais trop. Je quittai cette femme. Je ne répondis plus à ses appels, à ses lettres. Le jour où elle arriva en Allemagne pour me parler, je lui fis interdire l'accès du domicile des Kant. Je me montrai au bras d'autres femmes. Dans la rue, je fis semblant de ne pas la reconnaître. Je lui envoyai une lettre de rupture, puis d'insultes. Enfin, je l'humiliai publiquement. Comprenez-moi : j'étais fou d'elle. Que dire de plus ? J'ai sacrifié aux Kant la seule chance d'être aimé.

« Comment ai-je pu me fourvoyer ainsi ? »

Juliana Kant à elle-même.

Le lendemain matin, la presse annonça qu'un documentaire qui dévoilait le passé nazi de la famille Kant venait d'être sélectionné au festival du cinéma de Hambourg – le scandale que redoutaient Chris Brenner et la famille Kant éclatait enfin.

L'histoire familiale, les Kant aimeraient bien la réviser. C'est l'objet de ce livre, n'est-ce pas ? La tyrannie du passé. La corruption sentimentale. La fille a fauté là où le père a échoué – le sentiment : l'absolue déroute des Kant.

Pourquoi me regardez-vous comme ça ? Vous avez la tête du procureur de Nuremberg. Que me reprochez-vous encore ? Je vous observe. Depuis ce jour où je vous ai vue je n'ai cessé de penser que je pourrais gouverner l'Allemagne. Ecoutez, enregistrez, transcrivez. Taisez-vous ! Je n'ai besoin de personne pour parler et me souvenir – pour pisser seulement, et encore ! D'une main, je... Plomb, peuple, sang, race, et force, évacuation, foi, volonté, caractère, éternité, cœur, lettres animées, chiffres magiques, noms sacrés, tout est au sol et dans ma tête, tout est là, il n'y a qu'à se servir, et les souvenirs aussi – à vif.

L'histoire, peu de gens la connaissent. Ecrivez ! Ecrivez ! Ça plaira à nos lecteurs, toujours à l'affût d'histoires scabreuses – Leni Riefenstahl en aurait fait un film de propagande !

A l'origine, il y a un cœur lascif. Des obsessions érotiques. Un veuf qui s'ennuie. Au lieu d'aller dans un bordel prendre mille femmes, il erre dans la bonne société pour en épouser une – on y trouve les pires. Au lendemain de la Première Guerre mondiale, l'Allemagne est exsangue – pas la société du grand-père de Juliana, Günther Kant, qui s'est enrichie grâce au commerce d'uniformes. Les drapiers sont devenus les fournisseurs de l'autorité : policiers, employés des chemins de fer. Les belles toiles kaki en drap feldgrau qu'on éclaboussera de sang siglées Kant. Günther profite de la situation économique déclinante due à l'inflation, multiplie les transactions immobilières, rachète des entreprises en difficulté à bas prix avant de les relancer, thésaurise – grippe-sou. Il vient d'ailleurs de prendre le contrôle de BATKA, les piles que vous glissez dans votre magnétophone, c'est lui. Depuis la mort de son épouse, Günther Kant ne se consacre plus qu'à ses affaires – le nouveau maître de l'entreprenariat allemand.

Lors d'un déplacement professionnel, dans un train bondé, Günther Kant rencontre une jeune femme de dix-huit ans, Magda Friedländer. Kant a alors trente-huit ans, il élève seul ses deux enfants, Philipp et Ulrich, âgés respectivement de neuf et onze ans. Kant est chauve, entripaillé, mais il a de l'argent, c'est même sa seule obsession : en gagner toujours plus. Magda est blonde, racée, une beauté discrète, aux manières élégantes, un corps svelte, de grands yeux bleus rehaussés de longs cils blonds, pas trop mon genre, je dois le préciser, je préfère les rousses, les volcaniques, naturelles ou à perruques, la vulgarité m'excite, je n'ai jamais compris comment cette perruche jaunâtre a pu précipiter trois hommes que tout oppose dans le plus grand conflit politique et humain du XXe siècle… Magda vient d'obtenir son baccalauréat et rentre au pensionnat de jeunes filles où sa mère l'a inscrite. Sur cette rencontre, Kant a écrit dans ses mémoires des pages sucrées comme des friandises, attendez, l'exemplaire, là, donnez-moi ça : « *J'avais immédiatement été séduit par la grâce et la pureté qui émanaient de cette jeune femme. Nous discutâmes de théâtre, de voyages, de mes affaires, elle était curieuse et enjouée. Auprès d'elle, je ne vis pas le temps passer* » – le puissant industriel a une âme de midinette. Il l'épate, décrit avec application le confort de ses multiples demeures.

« *Vers une heure du matin, Magda arriva à destination, il fallut se séparer. Je l'aidai à descendre ses bagages à Goslar et parvins à obtenir l'adresse du pensionnat où elle logeait. Pendant le trajet que j'effectuai seul, je ne cessai de penser à elle. Sa candeur, la légèreté de son rire me manquaient déjà. Je n'avais plus qu'une idée en tête : la revoir.* »

Dès son arrivée à l'hôtel, Kant rédige une lettre à Magda, un texte d'un formalisme suranné, au style précieux, tout en courbettes et révérences.

« *Après-demain, sur le chemin du retour, je ferai une halte, vers 15 heures, à Goslar, je viendrai vous rendre visite en me faisant passer pour un ami de votre père... si vous le voulez bien.* » Elle veut bien, Magda, ça l'amuse ce gros bourgeois qui la courtise. Les amis de son père, elle ne les connaît pas. D'ailleurs, elle en a deux, des pères. Sa mère l'a eue avec un Allemand riche et austère dont elle a divorcé très tôt avant de se remarier avec un commerçant juif, Richard Friedländer, un type chaleureux et bon qui donne son nom à Magda les yeux fermés par amour pour la petite – il n'a pas d'autre enfant.

A Goslar, Günther réserve une chambre à l'hôtel et achète deux bouquets d'orchidées : un petit qu'il offre à la directrice de la pension et un autre, immense, pour Magda. « Je suis un ami du père de Magda, je viens voir notre bachelière. » Imaginez-le, avec ses boutons de manchettes en or, sa grosse Mercedes noire avec chauffeur, les bras chargés de fleurs, de chocolats, parfums capiteux, cadeaux pour tous, pensionnaires, personnel, les gavant de petits-fours, de pralines présentées dans de grandes boîtes enrubannées, toujours là à rôder autour de Magda qui joue le jeu : « Oh, bonjour, quelle bonne surprise ! » Günther est amoureux, maladroit comme un jeune premier, il est là, tendre et flatteur, cherchant à l'éblouir, oh l'argent, la position sociale – « Voulez-vous m'épouser ? » Il la veut – et tout de suite, comme on acquiert une nouvelle entreprise. Magda demande un délai de réflexion, il a vingt ans de plus qu'elle, il est déjà père de deux enfants, elle n'a pas commencé ses études, elle n'est pas amoureuse, cet homme pourrait être son père, son oncle, elle ne s'imagine pas dans ses bras, son lit, il ne lui plaît pas, la mèche qu'il plaque sur son crâne pour dissimuler sa calvitie lui donne un air lubrique, elle est indécise, romantique, rêveuse. Elle rentre à Berlin, déterminée à ne jamais retourner au pensionnat, elle l'annonce à sa mère et les voilà reçues dans la demeure de Günther, à Babelsberg, sur le lac de Griebnitz. C'est une grande villa à colombages dont la façade, d'une blancheur immaculée, donne sur un parc immense planté de résineux. Traversant la route pavée qui mène à la demeure, la mère s'émerveille, elle le raconte dans ses mémoires publiés dans un journal allemand, vous ne les avez pas lus non plus ?

« Ciel, comme c'est beau ! – et ce petit chemin ombreux qui mène à la clairière, ces escaliers en bois verni, lustré, qui offrent une perspective d'une beauté inouïe – je suis conquise. »

Oh, comme ils sont désassortis, regardez cette photo : elle, fine, délicate, avec son petit collier de perles blanches et ses cheveux crantés. Lui, à côté, engoncé dans son costume trois-pièces, sa rose ivoire à la boutonnière et ses grosses oreilles décollées, on dirait un boucher de Berlin, un de ceux qui tâtent longuement les plis de la bête qui geint avant de les crocheter d'un coup sec.

Au début de l'été, Günther célèbre son trente-neuvième anniversaire et ses fiançailles avec Magda mais pose deux conditions à leur union : qu'elle embrasse le protestantisme et qu'elle renonce à porter le nom juif de son beau-père. Chez les Kant, on n'épouse pas la fille d'un juif. Ça vous choque ? Je vous parle des années 20, en Allemagne, les juifs n'étaient pas encore à la mode...

Le mariage a lieu quelques mois plus tard. Robe en dentelle de Bruxelles, banquet au Godesberg Hof – tout le tralala. Ulrich et Philipp, les fils de Günther, sont là, parmi les invités. Ses parents ne viendront pas. Officiellement, ils sont à l'étranger, fatigués, sollicités ailleurs, mille excuses. Ils ne consentent pas à cette nouvelle union. Ils sont attachés au souvenir de la première femme de Günther, décédée il y a un an à peine. Et puis cette fille à l'éducation mixte, ça les dégoûte un peu. Une mésalliance. Magda a baigné dans une atmosphère juive, privée de lard et de cochon, impure – on n'en tirera rien de bon. Friedländer non plus n'a pas été convié au mariage de sa fille adoptive en dépit du changement de nom qu'il a reçu comme un coup de poignard. Il n'est ni fatigué ni à l'étranger – il est juif. Günther ne souhaite l'avoir ni sur sa photo de mariage ni dans son entourage. Il exige que sa femme le gomme de sa vie. Qu'elle l'oublie. Le chasse par tous les moyens : l'humiliation, l'exclusion, la destruction des preuves de la filiation. C'est une tare, une tache. Un juif – quelle horreur, la vermine qui rampe et prolifère chez les Kant ! Peu importe qu'il l'ait élevée, adoptée, aimée. Qu'il disparaisse, Friedländer ! Une question d'honneur, une mesure d'hygiène. Magda consent, elle ne veut pas gâcher sa fête, à plusieurs reprises Günther a manqué annuler le mariage. Avec Friedländer, elle pouvait discuter, contredire, se disputer, il lui aura au moins donné ça, le goût de la contradiction, une certaine inclination à l'opposition, au refus. Mais la mère de Magda le veut, ce beau mariage. Entre-temps, elle a divorcé – ce juif lui était devenu inutile. Elle n'en entendra plus parler… jusqu'au jour où elle apprendra qu'il est mort d'une pneumonie dans le camp de concentration de Buchenwald, seul et oublié de tous, quelques mois après son arrivée. C'est le plus beau, Friedländer, dites-vous, votre personnage préféré, le père nourricier jeté aux orties, renié parce que juif, le père oublié, assassiné.

Ah, Friedländer ! Symbole du martyre juif ! Il y a de la tragédie grecque dans le destin de ce père dépossédé de sa progéniture, une forme de prémonition de ce qui adviendra de l'Allemagne. Quand une fille commet un parricide, la Nation entière tue ses Pères. Vous voulez en faire un livre ? Allez-y ! Voilà une belle histoire ! Ecoutez et servez-vous ! Friedländer, il n'y a que lui qui vous intéresse, on vous donne un sujet, vous écrivez sur un autre, quelle trahison. Oh, vous n'êtes qu'une parasite comme tous les écrivains, toujours à… je vous parle d'histoire, de politique, je vous parle d'amour, du Mal, je vous parle de la guerre, en temps de paix, vous ne comprenez rien, vous êtes ignorants, aveuglés par vos biens de consommation que vous agitez comme des hochets, un coup sur la tête et… laissez-moi finir…

Le voyage de noces a lieu en Italie, on n'est pas là pour s'aimer, Günther traque les exploitations industrielles, tâte et renifle la terre, négocie – à la baisse, toujours –, puis impose un retour précipité en Allemagne. Les affaires, encore. La banale histoire de la bourgeoisie gâtée, frustrée : on s'ennuie. Voyages, dentelles et domestiques – Magda trouve le temps long avec le gros Kant qui s'endort pendant les concerts, ronfle comme un ours. N'est pas sortable. N'aime pas la vie mondaine. Evite le contact physique. L'argent ! L'argent ! – et c'est tout. Il la rabroue, la critique : *Tu as vu ta tenue ? Tu as vu ta robe ? Change-toi tout de suite !* Et cette manie de se présenter à la table du petit-déjeuner en déshabillé de soie – il déteste. Il est jaloux et agressif, un autocrate qui rentre en bougonnant, traquant la faute : taches de doigts sur les fenêtres, dîner froid, affaires éparpillées, oubliées çà et là – un tyran domestique : « Une maison doit fonctionner aussi parfaitement qu'une usine. Le personnel domestique ne diffère pas des ouvriers d'un établissement industriel, et c'est toi la directrice. » Magda est une Bovary allemande. Qui veut autre chose. De plus excitant. De plus grand. Günther Kant est d'une pingrerie maladive. Chaque soir, il vérifie les dépenses, Magda tient un livre de comptes, le chiffreur exige des explications, des excuses, coupe les vivres, soustrait, calcule, retranche, divise – et signe : *lu et approuvé*. Kant n'a qu'un idéal : devenir l'homme le plus riche d'Allemagne. L'amour, la sexualité, les plaisirs du quotidien – des accessoires ! Rien ne l'excite plus que de racheter une entreprise concurrente, découvrir un site où il pourra exploiter ses potentialités. Sa femme est un objet décoratif, une sucrerie qu'il s'offre de temps à autre – rien de plus. Du mouvement, un idéal, des utopies politiques, voilà ce dont elle rêve, pas cette petite vie minutée comme un entraînement militaire, sans liberté, sans audace, auprès d'un homme insensible et dur. Elle crève de n'être pas admirée ; touchée, ça lui est bien égal, elle ne le désire pas son gros mari à tête de cochon avec ses oreilles décollées et ses yeux enfoncés dans leurs orbites. Froid, pragmatique, autoritaire, face à elle : enflammée, rêveuse, tendre. Elle ne le supporte plus. Depuis quelque temps, depuis qu'elle s'est rapprochée de son beau-fils, Ulrich, Günther la dégoûte. Trop mou. Trop prévisible. Trop sourcilleux. Et puis il y a ces lettres qu'elle a trouvées dans le bureau de son mari, des missives implorantes, désespérées, envoyées par d'anciennes maîtresses, des putes on dirait, et je le trouve sympathique tout à coup, oh sans tendresse, il les a repoussées ses reines après les avoir consommées et elles ont froid dans les sous-sols où il les a emmurées, oh, Barbe-Bleue ! Ces liaisons, il y a renoncé en se mariant mais quand même, ça fait mauvais genre dans le tiroir de son bureau, au milieu des factures et des notes de frais, ces putes qui appellent au secours et crient « Plus ! ». Les bourgeoises exigent des domestiques et fouillent comme des femmes de ménage. Magda cherche dans les poches de son mari, vide ses poubelles, elle n'est pas jalouse, elle le compromet. Au cas où. Dans un couple, les preuves à charge sont plus utiles que les preuves d'amour. Elle se tait. Dans ces milieux-là, on fait comme si on n'avait rien vu, rien entendu, ça rend les suites conjugales plus agréables. Günther lui propose – et pense-t-il encore sauver son mariage ? – de partir six mois aux Etats-Unis. Magda accepte, confiant les deux enfants de son mari ainsi que ceux qu'elle a pris sous son aile après le décès d'un couple d'amis, à des personnes de confiance, en Allemagne, les oubliant alors qu'ils la réclament – la maternité la comble et l'angoisse. Ses enfants sont des vies extérieures à la sienne sur lesquelles elle a tous les droits. Elle pourrait les tuer mais elle attend, ça viendra. Parricide et infanticide, ça fait beaucoup. C'est ainsi qu'on marque l'Histoire. Elle voyage, Magda. Elle séduit. Sa blondeur naturelle excite les Américains et fait enrager leurs femmes dont l'artificialité physique tente de masquer le vide intérieur. Le neveu de Hoover l'aurait courtisée. Avec un peu d'audace, elle aurait pu passer *de l'autre côté*. Si elle avait eu une liaison avec lui, cette année-là, aurait-elle quitté l'Allemagne pour l'Amérique ? L'avenir de l'humanité tient parfois à un coït manqué.

« Je ne perdrai jamais le respect et l'amour pour mon père. »

Axel Kant à un ami,
au cours d'une partie de golf.

Axel Kahn à un ami,
au cours d'une partie de golf.

Vous m'avez apporté des chocolats ? Reprenez-les, je suis au régime. Que voulez-vous ? Vous m'écoutez, votre petit magnétophone à la main… Savez-vous quel a été le premier cadeau de Joseph Goebbels à Hitler ? Un magnétophone à cassettes. Comme vous maintenant avec votre air de ne pas y toucher, une fanatique de l'objectivité, allons-y.

Au retour de Magda et Günther des Etats-Unis, Ulrich décède des suites d'une appendicite, dans les bras de Magda, c'est mieux ainsi, il l'aimait. Magda prend un amant, s'exhibe en ville, Günther engage un détective et hop, sa femme est sommée de prendre ses cliques et ses claques, bon vent. Elle demande le divorce. Günther veut la laisser crever mais abracadabra, voici les lettres enflammées, passionnées, des putes chez les Kant ? – c'est vulgaire. Il accepte les conditions de sa femme et lui laisse la garde de leur fils, Harald, jusqu'à son quatorzième anniversaire à la condition qu'elle ne se remarie pas. Magda redevient une femme libre et courtisée. Nous sommes dans les années 30. Hitler parade dans les rues. Magda est subjuguée. Le national-socialisme, la communauté du peuple, ça la fait rêver… Elle rencontre Joseph Goebbels, le ministre de la Propagande nazie, celui qui aurait déclaré quelques années auparavant à un camarade : « Il me suffit de voir une croix gammée pour que j'aie aussitôt envie de chier. » Goebbels, son regard démoniaque, son corps maigre, aux os tors. *Et maintenant peuple, lève-toi, et toi, tempête, déchaîne-toi !* Le coup de foudre… Magda devient sa secrétaire particulière. Vous avez lu son *Journal* ? Enfin, vous n'avez rien lu ! Il est amoureux de Magda, il va renoncer à toutes les autres femmes, il se le promet à lui-même, il ne tiendra pas sa parole, multipliant les conquêtes jusqu'à la crise finale… Comment ce nain boiteux, hystérique, cet imposteur au regard d'aigle, déformé par la maladie, la haine, les compromissions, exerçait-il un tel magnétisme ? Je n'ai jamais su l'expliquer… Qu'est-ce qui hypnotisait les femmes qui le rencontraient ? Son militarisme agressif, ce caporalisme décomplexé qui n'était pas sans vertus érotiques ? Ses prophéties noires ? Sa proximité avec Hitler qui le surnommait « le premier satyre du Reich » ? Magda devient son jouet sexuel, il la prend, la manipule, la casse. Mais le père de Magda s'oppose à cette union. Il prédit la chute. Après avoir renié son père adoptif, Magda rompt les ponts avec son géniteur en épousant Goebbels en grande pompe, avec Hitler, en uniforme du parti nazi, pour témoin. Magda trahit et abat ses pères par opportunisme conjugal.

Le jour des noces, au mois de décembre 1931, les mariés sont en noir, comme s'ils présageaient que leur union serait maudite. Un pavillon à croix gammée couvre l'autel où un prêtre bénira le couple. Harald, le fils de Günther Kant, avance lentement au bras de Goebbels, son corps adolescent, chétif, engoncé dans son uniforme des jeunesses hitlériennes, petite cravate nouée autour du cou, la main gauche solidement accrochée à la boucle de sa ceinture, à quoi pense-t-il, le regard fixé vers l'objectif, les lèvres pincées ? Les mariés sont joyeux. Sur leur passage, les hommes font le salut hitlérien, la mère de Magda est épanouie, souriante, elle s'est débarrassée de son juif et se pavane derrière le Führer, elle se sent importante, elle se dit que, peut-être… c'est encore une belle femme… ça l'excite… Hitler suit les mariés, veillant sur cette union, apportant sa bénédiction, son assentiment, son chapeau noir vissé sur la tête. Il sera le mentor de Magda, son protecteur, un père par procuration et son héros jusqu'à sa mort. Visage de Hitler derrière celui de Harald Kant – la transmission. Avec son long corps mince, ses cheveux blonds, ses yeux bleus, Harald est l'incarnation de la perfection aryenne, le représentant idéal de cette Allemagne blanchie, purifiée de la présence juive. Où fêtent-ils leurs noces ? Où accueillent-ils Hitler et toute la mouvance nationale-socialiste ? Dans une salle de mariage ? Un restaurant berlinois ? Un hôtel au charme désuet ? Non. Ils festoient dans la résidence d'été de Günther Kant… Sublime château de brique rouge à la façade percée de fenêtres.

Le soir, légèrement enivré, Hitler va se coucher dans la chambre de Günther Kant, s'endort dans son lit, élabore les plans qui mèneront à la destruction de millions d'hommes, de femmes, d'enfants, vivants et à naître. Ce Günther Kant a du goût, de l'argent, des relations. Il a surtout des entreprises spécialisées dans la fabrication d'uniformes et de matériel militaire. Il ferait un allié idéal… et il est le père de Harald, l'adolescent constituera une bonne monnaie d'échange. Ecrivez, notez. Oh, on peut bien diffamer les morts, je suis vieux, malade, les avocats plaideront trois fois sans frais ; au jour du jugement, je sifflerai mon bourbon au fond de mon lit.

« *J'avais été profondément meurtri de l'union de Magda, mon ex-femme, avec le ministre de la Propagande nazie. Comme son père, je l'avais mise en garde. J'étais convaincu que les nazis, qui ne connaissaient rien à l'économie, allaient précipiter le pays vers la faillite.* »

Est-ce que Günther a consenti à organiser cette fête chez lui ? Oui. Dans ses mémoires, il n'en parle pas. Et même à moi… pas un mot. Jamais. Dans les réunions familiales des Kant, on évoque le cours de la Bourse, les réorganisations industrielles, les plans de licenciements, la guerre, non. *C'est du passé.* Je crois que Günther a compris avant tout le monde l'intérêt qu'il tirerait du remariage de son ex-femme et de l'éviction des industriels juifs. Débarrassé de ses concurrents, il pouvait faire tourner ses usines à plein régime, multipliant les contrats d'exclusivité, rachetant les entreprises les plus florissantes à bas prix, en récupérant d'autres. Regardez cette photo, incroyable, n'est-ce pas ? Elle a été prise en 1934. C'est ma préférée, Günther a tout fait pour la cacher. On y voit bien le regard démoniaque de Hitler. Regardez comme il s'agrippe au bras de Harald en uniforme des jeunesses hitlériennes, sa main est protectrice, aimante, c'est une main qui protège, qui bénit. L'incarnation de l'Allemagne nazie, l'avenir de l'Allemagne, le représentant le plus fidèle de l'idéologie nationale-socialiste, le pur sang aryen, c'est Harald Kant !

« *Magda avait rompu notre contrat de divorce en exigeant de reprendre Harald dont j'avais la garde dans le cas où elle se remarierait. Quelques jours après son mariage avec Goebbels qui eut lieu dans ma résidence d'été, contre mon gré, je fus convoqué au siège de la Gestapo. On me menaça de faire fermer mes usines, de me ruiner si je ne consentais pas à accorder la garde de mon fils à sa mère. Je cédai. Qu'aurais-je dû faire ?* »

Günther place son fils Philipp à la direction du groupe – la production de batteries devient l'activité principale de la famille. Kant est alors incarcéré pour une dette fiscale. Il appelle Magda à l'aide, Goebbels intervient en sa faveur auprès de Goering – Kant est libéré. Etre l'ami de Goering, le plus grand criminel de guerre de l'Allemagne nazie, ça ouvre des portes.

« A cette époque, Magda me demanda d'adhérer au parti nazi et de verser de lourdes contributions. Je refusai catégoriquement. Elle me menaça de ne plus jamais revoir mon fils. »

La prise de pouvoir par les nazis leur offre de nouvelles opportunités économiques. Aryanisation des entreprises. Expropriation. Les juifs sont mis au ban de la société. On les spolie, on les dépouille – donnez-moi ça, c'est à moi, j'aime beaucoup cette table basse et ce canapé, je les ai vus le premier. Qu'ils lâchent leurs actions, ces propriétaires griffus ! On leur prend tout : leurs biens immobiliers, mobiliers, personnels, affectifs, leur corps, leur conscience, tout est recyclable chez le juif. Kant se sert, comme les autres – et bien. Il présente lui-même les batteries qu'il produit à Hitler et devient le premier fournisseur d'uniformes et de matériel militaire.

« C'est avec fierté que nous nous tournons vers le plus grand Allemand de tous les temps, notre Führer bien-aimé ! »

Sans les Kant, père et fils, la guerre ne serait qu'un combat de rue, entre bandes rivales, on tomberait mais pas très loin. Ses accumulateurs alimentent les sous-marins. Kant entreprend de racheter les parts d'une société spécialisée dans la fabrication de batteries militaires mais le patron, un entrepreneur luxembourgeois, refuse. Il est arrêté, transféré au quartier général de la Gestapo du Luxembourg. On le torture, on le cisaille, qu'il crache ses parts. Il refuse de céder. Dans un courrier adressé à Kant, on lui annonce que l'entrepreneur luxembourgeois va être interné dans un camp de travail. Kant fait main basse sur l'entreprise concurrente. Les sous-marins lancent leurs missiles, les avions, leurs bombes. Günther Kant est désormais un homme dont la puissance économique est sans égale. C'est la période faste. On tue à tout-va.

« *Pour moi aussi, la guerre a été terrible, j'ai perdu beaucoup d'argent.* »

« Derrière la réussite de l'entreprise, il y a beaucoup de responsabilités et de travail. »

Katrin Kant à Helmut Kohl,
32e chancelier d'Allemagne,
au cours d'un déjeuner.

La santé [illegible] de [illegible] que la famille Kon[illegible] du monde. [illegible] de jadis. Philipp [illegible] conviction [illegible] lui procure de nouveaux avantages. De la main d'œuvre, surtout.

En qualité de responsable du personnel de l'entreprise, Philipp Kon[illegible] fait une demande de travailleurs forcés car en manquent les usines [illegible] fonctionnement à plein régime. Responsable du personnel, on dirait des ressources humaines aujourd'hui et quelles ressources ! Des millions d'hommes déportés des quatre coins de l'Europe, arrêtés, torturés, des hommes [illegible], déchirés, qui ont résisté à la faim, au froid, au voyage, au deuil, quelles ressources ! Dès leur arrivée dans les camps, dès [illegible] les [illegible] jusqu'au sang, jusqu'à la mort, les tient

La suite est une succession de faits sombres que la famille Kant essaie de dissimuler aux yeux du monde, écrivez, écrivez. L'adhésion du père de Juliana, Philipp Kant, au parti nazi, avec la conviction silencieuse que cette alliance pourrait lui procurer de nouveaux avantages. De la main-d'œuvre, surtout.

En qualité de responsable du personnel de l'entreprise, Philipp Kant fait une demande de travailleurs forcés, on en manque, les usines fonctionnent à plein régime. Responsable du personnel, on dirait des ressources humaines aujourd'hui et quelles ressources ! Des milliers d'hommes déportés des quatre coins de l'Europe, arrêtés, torturés, des hommes hagards, décharnés, qui ont résisté à la faim, au froid, au voyage, au deuil, quelles ressources ! Dès leur arrivée dans les camps, des SS les battent souvent jusqu'au sang, jusqu'à la mort, les trient comme sur le marché aux esclaves de la Rome antique, sélectionnent les plus résistants, vérifient leur denture, leur poids, leur capacité physique, les faibles, au four, à la fosse, qu'ils crèvent, on n'en veut pas. Les autres, du bétail – exhibition morbide sous le regard des dirigeants d'entreprise qui jugent et condamnent. Le personnel dont jouit Philipp Kant : des esclaves fournis par le régime nazi et sa politique ségrégative.

Günther passe un contrat avec les nazis qui prévoit la construction d'un camp de concentration sur les terrains de BATKA, son usine, à Stöcken, près de Hanovre. *Au camp de Stöcken, on meurt en six mois !* ironisent les SS qui gardent le camp. Affamés, maltraités, frappés à coups de gourdins et de fouets en fer, les hommes travaillent sans relâche. Dès qu'un homme meurt, il est aussitôt remplacé par un autre déporté qui mourra à son tour et sera remplacé par un autre déporté qui mourra à son tour et sera remplacé par un autre déporté qui mourra à son tour et sera remplacé par un autre déporté qui mourra à son tour et sera remplacé par un autre déporté qui mourra à son tour et sera remplacé par un autre déporté qui mourra à son tour et sera remplacé par un autre déporté qui mourra à son tour et sera remplacé par un autre déporté qui mourra à son tour et sera remplacé par un autre déporté qui mourra à son tour et sera remplacé par un autre déporté qui mourra à son tour et sera remplacé par un autre déporté qui mourra

« L'après-guerre fut une période terrible. Les Alliés cherchaient des coupables, la dénazification était en marche et avec elle, la chasse aux sorcières. De bons Allemands étaient soudain accusés d'avoir collaboré avec l'ennemi. Des affiches étaient placardées sur les murs des villes en ruine : QUI EST COUPABLE ? Je me réfugiai en Bavière ; Philipp, à Hanovre. Bien qu'innocents, nous fûmes mis sur écoute. En 1946, je fus arrêté et incarcéré quelques mois au camp de prisonniers de Mosbourg. Mais mon dossier fut classé sans suite, il n'y avait aucune preuve contre moi, j'avais fait mon travail honnêtement et c'est tout. »

Günther Kant, *Mémoires*

Alors que s'ouvrirent les procès de Nuremberg, les pièces à conviction contre les Kant, détenues par les Britanniques, ne furent pas remises à la justice. Günther Kant était un homme important, vous comprenez, un rouage essentiel, un personnage incontournable de la machine militaire. Après la fin de la guerre, BATKA disposait de quantités énormes de matières premières et d'un parc de machines en marche. Les Alliés avaient besoin de lui… Ses usines fonctionnaient à plein régime… ils auraient pu les prendre au titre d'indemnités de guerre mais ils ne l'ont pas fait, elles ont été réquisitionnées pour fournir les unités des Alliés, rien de plus. Kant en connaissait tous les rouages, une voiture sans chauffeur, ça ne vaut rien. Dès le 22 mai 1945, les Britanniques autorisent l'usine à reprendre sa production. L'entreprise enregistre un chiffre d'affaires de plus d'un million de Reichsmarks.

Trois ans plus tard, les Américains relâchent Günther Kant qui aura réussi à éviter le tribunal de Nuremberg contrairement aux autres industriels comme Krupp ou Flick.

« *J'avais été victime de persécutions de la part du gouvernement national-socialiste. Le régime fasciste et la guerre ne m'avaient rien rapporté, après la guerre, je n'avais même pas de quoi prendre un avocat.* »

Cette histoire n'est plus un secret pour personne. Vous en aviez entendu parler, n'est-ce pas ? Des journalistes ont tout dévoilé il y a peu, l'affaire a fait grand bruit et puis… pff… le scandale a été étouffé. La légendaire discrétion des Kant. Je ne savais rien quand j'ai rencontré Philipp Kant et puis j'ai su – et après ? J'aurais dû démissionner ? Oui, l'Allemagne est responsable, les Kant sont responsables mais moi, je n'y suis pour rien. La culpabilité, ce n'est pas mon truc. Vous connaissez la phrase ? *Derrière toute grande fortune, il y a un grand crime.*

Berlin, le 30 avril 1945

Harald, mon cher frère, notre père n'a pas la force de t'annoncer le drame dont nous sommes aujourd'hui victimes alors c'est moi qui t'écris, sans forces, sans volonté. Le lendemain de la mort de Hitler, ta mère et son mari se sont donné la mort à l'intérieur même du bunker dans des conditions que je ne souhaite pas te décrire ici. Elle a laissé une lettre d'adieu pour toi à l'aviatrice Hanna Reitsch qui te la transmettra à ton retour.

Je pense à toi, Harald, je sais combien tu dois souffrir en apprenant cela, je pense à toi, je tremble, qui d'autre que moi, ton frère, pourrait te dire l'horreur, car dans sa chute ta mère a entraîné celle de tes six frères et sœurs. Qu'ils reposent en paix.

Ton frère, Philipp

Deux jours avant la diffusion du documentaire, la secrétaire de Juliana réceptionna un paquet : c'est un DVD, dit-elle. L'enveloppe ne mentionnait pas d'expéditeur et, à l'intérieur, elle n'avait trouvé aucun mot. J'avais envie de savoir avant les autres, voyeur, je vous ai dit, alors j'ai demandé « Souhaitez-vous que je le visionne ? » « Non. » Juliana saisit brutalement l'objet, elle voulait être seule pour affronter la honte familiale, seule face aux images de son grand-père, de son père aux côtés de Hitler. La porte claqua. Je restai là, à fumer et faire la gueule.

On entendit un cri. Des pleurs. Puis plus rien. Je me précipitai dans le bureau de Juliana. Elle était assise sur son fauteuil, le visage inondé de larmes, la télécommande dans la main, cherchant à éteindre la télévision, n'y parvenant pas, les images défilaient sur l'écran, scabreuses, obscènes au regard étranger. Le DVD ne contenait pas le documentaire mais des extraits de ses ébats avec Braun. C'était elle cette femme offerte, abandonnée qui gémissait, quelle indécence, c'était elle, ce ne pouvait pas être elle, aguicheuse, sensuelle, érotomane, hystérique, c'était elle et une autre, sur l'écran, et c'étaient ses seins, ses fesses, le déshonneur et la honte, coupez le son, qui était cette femme qui criait et demandait encore, qui, ce n'était pas vous, pas elle, effaçons, il faut tout détruire, pensa-t-elle, brûler l'original et où était la copie, oh cette jouissance, ce ne pouvait pas être elle, la femme sans affects, impavide et dure, tandis que la femme sur l'écran riait et se donnait facilement, sans effort – et quelle audace, arrêtez-vous, elle appuya sur la touche « pause ». Elle vomit, ouvrit la fenêtre pour aérer la pièce qui empestait, elle trembla, s'allongea sur le canapé. Je la trouvais touchante tout à coup. Cette femme qui avait placé sa vie sous contrôle, qui n'avait jamais désorganisé son existence, avait été trompée, manipulée par le seul homme qui avait su gagner sa confiance. Elle avait joué, elle avait perdu – c'était pathétique et bouleversant. « Je crois que vous devriez contacter Braun », dis-je froidement. Juliana cessa de pleurer. Je lui servis un scotch, puis je composai le numéro de Braun et lui tendis le téléphone. Braun répondit aussitôt d'une voix caressante : « Juliana... tu n'as pas perdu de temps... » « Que veux-tu ? » « Sept *DVD de Scorsese* en échange de mon DVD, en espèces, grosses coupures, le tout dans une sacoche. » C'était clair, net et précis, il n'y avait pas à discuter. « Sept *DVD* » – Braun exigeait sept millions d'euros.

— Si tu ne paies pas, j'envoie le DVD à toutes les rédactions.

— Comment peux-tu... Je te hais... Je vais te dénoncer à la police...

— Fais-le et tout le monde visionnera nos ébats...

— Comment veux-tu que je réunisse une telle somme ? Tu es fou... Je ne peux pas les trouver comme ça, c'est impossible !

Braun ne répondit pas. Au bout du fil, il percevait l'affolement de Juliana.

— Je ne pourrai pas réunir autant d'argent.

Il y eut un silence profond, inquiétant, puis une longue inspiration de Braun :

— Avec ce que ta famille a gagné pendant la guerre, je crois qu'elle est en mesure de te procurer cette somme.

Juliana se tut, incapable de maîtriser les battements désordonnés de son cœur.

— Tu es toujours là, Juliana ? demanda Braun.

— Je suppose que l'accident de la fillette, la rançon, c'était ton idée aussi ?

On entendit le rire de Braun, un rire étouffé, sardonique.

— Tu n'es qu'un escroc, continua Juliana. Je ne te donnerai rien. Tu m'entends ? Rien !

— Vraiment ? Ce ne serait pas raisonnable... Tu ne peux pas, Juliana, faire face à un nouveau scandale.

Et il raccrocha.

« Portez plainte, dis-je avec autorité. Si vous lui donnez cet argent, il en réclamera encore, en voudra toujours plus. Jusqu'à quand ? »

Avant qu'il ne soit détruit, j'avais vu le DVD, oh, en cachette, voilà comment je savais tout et mieux que les autres, ça m'avait impressionné et pour tout dire, séduit, ce lâcher-prise. Les informations se succédaient : Braun n'avait jamais été photographe de guerre. Il était vendeur de poulets rôtis dans une entreprise de restauration rapide, un de ceux qui n'oubliaient jamais de verser un peu de graisse chaude sur la chair tendre de la bête, les clientes l'adoraient – oh, si souriant, si aimable. La police conseilla à Juliana de rappeler Braun pour lui dire qu'elle était prête à coopérer. « Promets-moi de ne pas diffuser cette vidéo. » « Oui. » Que valait la promesse d'un traître ?

Les jours qui suivirent la réception du DVD furent les plus terribles de la vie de Juliana. Elle ne parlait plus à personne, restait enfermée dans son bureau, ne répondait pas au téléphone. Pour la première fois, elle avait accordé sa confiance à un homme – et il l'avait trahie.

Je fus chargé de mener les négociations avec Braun qui s'impatientait. Je le jugeais impulsif, dangereux, violent. Mais au-delà de la méfiance instinctive qu'il m'inspirait, son assurance me séduisait. Je l'avais vu troublant, audacieux, dans la connivence amoureuse ; je le découvrais frondeur dans l'adversité, presque rebelle. Il y avait chez lui quelque chose de profondément destructeur, presque d'infantile, qui répondait à mes propres névroses. Je lui expliquai que Juliana ne pouvait réunir une telle somme dans un délai aussi court. Après réflexion, il accepta de baisser ses prétentions et posa une nouvelle condition : Juliana devait lui remettre la somme de cinq millions d'euros dans les quarante-huit heures. Il lui donna rendez-vous sur un terrain vague, dans la banlieue de Berlin. Avant de s'y rendre, sous escorte policière, Juliana avoua tout à son mari.

« Il était attachant, touchant, il ne ressemblait pas aux autres. »

Juliana Kant aux enquêteurs.

Le jour du rendez-vous, Braun était là, au volant d'une voiture de sport, vêtu d'un costume gris à la coupe parfaite. Il sortit du véhicule et s'approcha de Juliana qui serrait fermement la poignée de la sacoche dans sa main. Elle portait une petite robe verte qui contrastait avec son teint hâve. Ils étaient face à face. Une arme pointait entre les doigts de Braun.

— Je savais que tu viendrais.

— Est-ce que j'avais le choix ?

Juliana respira lentement.

— Que vas-tu faire de cet argent ?

Braun eut un sourire ironique.

— Je vais créer une fondation. C'est ce dont tu rêvais, n'est-ce pas, quand je t'ai rencontrée ?

— Une fondation pour les victimes du Rwanda ? Ton altruisme m'épate, très bien… tu fais ce que je n'aurais pu réaliser…

— Et pourquoi ?

Sans réfléchir, Juliana lâcha alors ces mots qu'elle regretta aussitôt d'avoir prononcés : « Si j'avais donné de l'argent pour les victimes du Rwanda, les journalistes m'auraient reproché de ne pas avoir indemnisé les victimes du nazisme. »

Entendant ces paroles, Braun braqua son revolver sur elle, visa la tête. « Arrête ! Arrête ! » Juliana s'effondra à genoux. C'était lui, l'homme qu'elle avait tant aimé, qui la menaçait, la tenait en joue ? Elle ne reconnaissait plus son regard. Ce n'étaient plus les yeux de l'amant, de l'homme amoureux, tendre, passionné, mais ceux d'un fou, d'un criminel. « Pose cette mallette ! Vite ! » Elle obéit. Elle voulait lui poser une question avant de partir, une seule : l'avait-il aimée ? Elle pourrait renoncer à l'argent, pas à la réponse. Elle pleura, s'accrocha à sa jambe pour le faire trébucher, le retenir, l'entraîner avec elle. Il devint nerveux devant cette femme en larmes, secouait sa jambe, il ne savait plus quoi faire, perdit ses moyens. Il lui lança au visage une enveloppe contenant les documents compromettants et les sources : clé, disquettes, vidéos qui avaient servi à la manœuvre. « Il n'y en a pas d'autres, fais-moi confiance. » Ce fut tout ce qu'il trouva à dire : fais-moi confiance, alors qu'il l'avait trahie, volée, dépossédée. Fais-moi confiance. C'est le moment, pensa-t-elle, et d'une voix étranglée par l'émotion, d'une voix brisée, elle lui redemanda s'il l'avait aimée, car comment peut-on mimer l'amour, est-ce que tu m'as aimée, j'ai besoin de le savoir puisque nous ne nous reverrons plus, sa trahison n'expliquait rien, l'argent ! l'argent ! et avant, au temps des promesses ? Il eut un mouvement de recul, elle s'agrippa à lui, répéta : « Est-ce que tu m'as aimée ? » mais au moment où il rangea son arme et s'apprêta à répondre, sept hommes armés surgirent et se précipitèrent sur lui – des policiers appartenant à une unité spéciale. Trois voitures de police pénétrèrent dans le parking, toutes sirènes hurlantes. Braun fut arrêté, menotté. A l'instant où les policiers le poussèrent vers l'intérieur du fourgon, Braun regarda Juliana et d'un hochement de gauche à droite fit non de la tête.

« Il est très difficile de voir ma vie privée étalée comme ça en public mais j'ai pris cette décision pour que justice soit faite et pour toutes les femmes qui pourraient se retrouver dans mon cas. »

Extrait d'une interview
de Juliana Kant.

Braun [illegible]. Une photo de Juliana et lui, [illegible] sur un banc, fut diffusée à la une de [illegible] LA [illegible] Juliana de profil [illegible] regardant l'homme qui parlait [illegible]. Elle avait dû être prise au zoo de Berlin. C'était une image qui reflétait la connivence amoureuse et [illegible] sexuelle, qui violait l'intimité, rompant tous ses efforts de discrétion et [illegible] avec la violence du [illegible] Braun [illegible] pour fraude, [illegible] de fonds et d'extorsion de chantage [illegible] prison. Il eut recours aux services d'un avocat réputé. Ce que redoutait le plus Juliana ? La confrontation avec Braun, les révélations [illegible].

Au cours de l'instruction, Juliana se replia chez elle [illegible] un bloc de [illegible] que nul ne

Braun fut incarcéré à la prison de Berlin. Une photo de Juliana et lui, assis sur un banc, fut diffusée à la une de tous les magazines avec ce titre : LA MILLIARDAIRE ET LE GIGOLO. On y voyait Juliana de profil, souriante, regardant Braun qui parlait, en riant aussi. Il l'enlaçait. Elle avait dû être prise au zoo de Berlin. C'était une image qui reflétait la connivence amoureuse et l'attraction sexuelle, qui violait l'intimité, ruinait tous les efforts de discrétion et dont la douceur contrastait avec la violence du titre. Braun fut mis en examen pour fraude, tentative de fraude et d'extorsion, de chantage ; il risquait jusqu'à neuf ans de prison. Il eut recours aux services d'un avocat réputé. Ce que redoutait le plus Juliana ? La confrontation avec Braun, les révélations tapageuses, intimes.

Au cours de l'instruction, Juliana se replia chez elle – un bloc de marbre que nul ne pouvait débrutir. Dès qu'elle sortait, une meute de photographes armés d'appareils ultrasophistiqués la mitraillait, traquant les yeux décavés, la larme qui a un coût. A sa suite, des journalistes cognaient leurs micros contre des vitres aux verres teintés, réclamaient des confidences, tout ce qui pourrait alimenter la machine à scandale qui dédore et broie. Juliana m'évitait – me reprochait-elle d'avoir été le témoin de son amour ou de ne pas avoir su la protéger ? La révélation du passé nazi de sa famille l'affectait moins que la publicité accordée à son aventure. La seule victime, c'était elle. Le plus grand crime, son adultère.

Seul, dans sa cellule aux murs capitonnés, Herb Braun refusait de s'exprimer, de s'alimenter – il n'avait plus de famille, son père venait de mourir. Il coopérait peu avec son avocat, se montra hostile, rebelle. Il n'émit aucun remords. En prison, il se cadavérisait lentement.

« C'est terrible mais nous n'y pouvons rien : nous tombons toujours amoureux de la mauvaise personne. »

Karl Fritz à Axel Kant.

C'est alors qu'intervint un témoignage inattendu. Pedro Garcia était un homme âgé d'une soixantaine d'années, trapu et velu mais charismatique, magnétique. Avec ses cheveux abondamment fournis, qu'il teignait en noir et gominait, sa façon de s'exprimer en gardant sa main au niveau de sa braguette, il ressemblait à un vieux proxénète, un parrain. Cet Espagnol, propriétaire d'un petit restaurant dans les environs de Tolède, fut présenté comme le complice de Braun puisqu'il était à bord d'un véhicule stationné sur l'aire d'autoroute, à proximité de celui de Braun au moment de l'arrestation. Dans sa voiture, les policiers avaient trouvé un papier sur lequel était noté le nom de Juliana Kant. Au cours de l'enquête, ils précisèrent les liens troubles qui unissaient Braun à Garcia et le rôle que ce dernier avait joué : une sorte de mentor, un gourou qui marcherait pieds nus sur les eaux de la Méditerranée, un rebouteux à l'allure christique, une prise idéale pour les enquêteurs qui traquaient le commando vénal, l'association de malfaiteurs, les séducteurs véreux à gueule d'ange, tous ces parasites qui gravitaient autour des héritières dans les hôtels de luxe où elles s'ennuyaient. Garcia prétendait qu'il n'était pas le complice ou le commanditaire, seulement l'ami de Herb Braun. C'était lui qui, à sa demande, avait filmé ses ébats avec Juliana Kant. Il était caché dans la chambre d'à côté, expliqua-t-il aux enquêteurs, caméra au poing. Il parlait vite et fort comme s'il voulait être entendu au-delà. Il dit qu'il était celui qui connaissait le mieux Herb Braun. Il connaissait sa femme, sa vie. Les films, il y avait collaboré par amitié, il ne savait pas ce que Braun avait l'intention d'en faire. Un jeu sexuel, pensait-il. *Je ne suis pas impliqué dans cette affaire, je ne suis coupable de rien.*

Pedro Garcia fut autorisé à rentrer en Espagne. Quelques semaines plus tard, dans le garage privé de son restaurant, les enquêteurs espagnols trouvèrent des voitures de luxe – Porsche, Jaguar, Mercedes. Ses revenus ne justifiant pas son train de vie, Garcia argua qu'il avait gagné de l'argent au jeu. Il affirma qu'il était le seul à connaître les réelles motivations de Braun. Il se disait prêt à les révéler si les charges qui pesaient contre lui étaient annulées.

« On a mis de la lumière sur quelque chose d'obscur. C'est toujours mieux que si ça prend de la force dans l'obscurité. C'est notre famille… voilà. Cela fait partie de nous et c'est mieux de savoir ce qui s'est passé que de le nier. Mais ce n'est pas à moi de juger. Personne ne peut juger ce que ça signifiait de vivre à l'époque. »

Juliana Kant,
au cours d'une interview.

... la vérité [illegible] jusqu'à l'ivresse — je vous en [illegible] pour m'écouter et [illegible]. Soyez, soyez responsable ! Soyez [illegible] voilà. [illegible] manuscrits des biographes [illegible] par les Kant. Vous avez [illegible] consultés [illegible] La vérité ! La vérité ! [illegible] jamais, dans leur silence, [illegible] vivants...

... la vérité, García la connaissait — et il la lâcha aux enquêteurs. En échange de ses révélations, il ne serait pas inculpé, sans doute relaxé, au pire, condamné à une peine minime. Il sauvait sa peau, et peut-être, celle de Braun — qui n'avouait rien, ne parlait plus. Depuis leur arrestation, les hommes n'avaient pas communiqué. Sur un ton solennel, García raconta une [illegible]

… la vérité, servez-moi à boire, oui, jusqu'à l'ivresse – je vous emmerde, vous êtes payée pour m'écouter et noter, le contrat ne dit rien d'autre, soyez responsable ! Soyez efficace ! Les faits ! Les voilà. Qui contredisent les thèses officielles, les mensonges des biographes corrompus par les Kant. Vous avez acheté ces livres, vous les avez consultés à la bibliothèque ? De la propagande ! La vérité ! La vérité ! Qu'ils la crachent ! Mais jamais, dans leur silence, emmurés vivants…

… la vérité, Garcia la connaissait – et il la lâcha aux enquêteurs. En échange de ses révélations, il ne serait pas extradé, sans doute relaxé, au pire, condamné à une peine minime. Il sauvait sa peau, et peut-être, celle de Braun – qui n'avouait rien, ne parlait plus. Depuis leur arrestation, les hommes n'avaient pas communiqué. Sur un ton solennel, Garcia raconta que Braun n'avait pas agi pour l'appât du gain mais pour se venger. L'argent n'avait jamais été son mobile, pas plus que le désir d'épouser la fille Kant, « il aurait pu l'assassiner froidement, il a préféré la contraindre, l'humilier publiquement ». Aux enquêteurs qui l'écoutaient comme s'ils prenaient la déposition la plus importante de leur vie, il confia que Braun s'était donné six mois pour détruire Juliana Kant, sans violence physique, sans crime... en la séduisant... « Il lui aura fallu finalement six mois et six jours... » La salle était plongée dans un silence monacal. On n'entendait que le cliquetis provoqué par la pression des doigts de l'enquêteur qui s'enfonçaient sur les touches du clavier de l'ordinateur au gré des déclarations de Garcia.

J'ai faim, j'ai chaud, Garcia testait la résistance de ses interlocuteurs – ça l'amusait. Il repoussait le moment des aveux, cherchant à amadouer les policiers qui le cernaient, s'adressaient à lui avec une amabilité complaisante, il les dominait pour la première fois, songea-t-il, il les haïssait, un pourfendeur de l'autorité policière, corruptrice – comme moi. Il pensait à Braun, aux risques qu'il avait pris, à la façon dont il s'était finalement laissé piéger par excès de confiance. L'enquêteur posa sur le bureau la photo de

Juliana et Braun diffusée par la presse. Souriants, absorbés l'un par l'autre, dans cette posture complice qui caractérise les premiers temps de l'amour. « Braun n'a pas agi pour l'argent », insista Garcia. « Oui, bien sûr, répliqua l'enquêteur sur un ton qui trahissait son agacement, il a tenté de lui extorquer dix millions d'euros pour venger une petite humiliation personnelle, quel film ça ferait ! Imaginez la photo avec ce sous-titre : *Il a six mois pour la détruire...* » L'enquêteur déplia le journal. Garcia lut la une :

LA MILLIARDAIRE ET LE GIGOLO

D'un geste brutal, il repoussa le journal. Aussitôt, l'un des policiers se précipita sur lui pour le menotter. « Une petite humiliation ? » répéta Garcia. Et il se mit à rire, d'un petit rire nerveux, grotesque. L'un des policiers rit aussi, on n'entendait plus que cela dans la salle des interrogatoires, ce lieu sombre et glacial qui empestait la sueur et l'urine, ces rires rauques qui fusaient et vous mordaient. Garcia exigea une cigarette. « Tu nous fais perdre notre temps, répliqua l'enquêteur. Tu vas continuer longtemps à protéger ce gigolo ? » A ces mots, Garcia se crispa : « Braun, un gigolo ? La seule pute dans cette affaire, c'est la famille Kant. » Les enquêteurs ne répliquèrent pas, dociles tout à coup – on touchait au but. Ils lui allumèrent une cigarette qu'ils lui glissèrent entre les lèvres. Ils l'observèrent en silence tandis qu'il expirait les volutes de fumée grisâtre qui opacifiaient le lieu. Garcia leur fit signe que les menottes entravaient ses mouvements. L'un des policiers les lui défit mécaniquement comme si ce geste devait aussi libérer la parole. Garcia secoua son poignet gauche et se mit à parler. On n'entendait plus que sa voix, rauque, pénétrante. « Herb Braun, ce n'est pas son vrai nom… il l'a trouvé tout seul un matin, il a changé d'identité… pour changer de destin, c'est ce que je croyais, il s'est inventé une nouvelle vie, vous n'en avez jamais eu le désir ? Changer de nom… fuir… » Les enquêteurs restaient muets, impassibles. « Je voudrais aller aux toilettes », dit Garcia. « Finis d'abord. » « Je ne peux pas. » Il les provoquait depuis le début – et pourquoi ? Le garde fut appelé. « Accompagnez-le aux toilettes. » Dans le couloir, Garcia marcha lentement, en traînant la jambe. Il pensait à Braun, à sa solitude, il avait envie de le revoir, de lui parler. Confirmerait-il sa version ? Avouerait-il ses mobiles ? Il l'imaginait, enfermé dans sa cellule, dans sa douleur, et cette vision le glaça tant qu'il resta figé un moment, au milieu du couloir, devant le garde qui ne le quittait pas des yeux. « Tu y vas maintenant ! On n'a pas que ça à faire ! » Garcia entra dans les toilettes et tira la chasse d'eau, tira si fort que le mécanisme resta dans sa main. Il voulait les faire tous patienter – c'était son seul pouvoir. Quand il sortit, le garde le poussa en avant : « Dépêche-toi. » Garcia l'insulta et avança jusqu'au bureau des enquêteurs, indifférent aux vociférations du garde. Il exigea une nouvelle cigarette. Une fois encore, ils la lui accordèrent. « Vas-y, maintenant. » Garcia regarda fixement l'enquêteur principal : « Herb Braun, ce n'est pas son vrai nom... » « Ça, tu l'as déjà dit... » « Braun s'appelle en réalité Arno Heilbronn. Il est le fils d'Isaac Heilbronn, un travailleur juif exploité par les Kant durant la guerre. » Le téléphone se mit à sonner, l'enquêteur principal répondit, exigea de ne plus être dérangé. Garcia continua d'une voix traînante : « En 1945, après avoir été dépossédé de ses biens, l'industriel Isaac Heilbronn a été déporté au camp de Neuengamme, puis transféré dans le kommando de Stöcken, où il a travaillé pour le compte des usines BATKA, propriété de la famille Kant. Il a travaillé sous les ordres des SS, sous les coups de matraques des SS, sous les coups de barres des SS, sous la responsabilité de Philipp Kant, directeur des ressources humaines qui a réclamé du personnel gratuit, des déportés, des travailleurs, des esclaves, qui a exigé qu'ils soient affectés à la production de l'usine – exploitation, rentabilité, capitalisation –, placés à proximité de l'usine où ils travaillaient sans relâche, affamés, battus, où ils travaillaient jusqu'à ce qu'ils en crèvent ainsi que le prévoyait le règlement : "Cette exploitation doit être épuisante dans le vrai sens du mot afin que le travail puisse atteindre le plus grand rendement." » Garcia montra une photo aux enquêteurs : c'était le cliché que Braun avait envoyé à Juliana et qu'elle avait posé sur son bureau, cette nature qui l'apaisait : « Voilà le camp de Stöcken, aujourd'hui. Vous savez comment les nazis qui gardaient le camp accueillaient les déportés ? Ils les battaient et répétaient : *Au camp de Stöcken, on meurt en six mois.* » Les enquêteurs étaient pâles et silencieux. Ils imaginaient la suite de l'affaire : la médiatisation, l'intervention des associations de préservation de la mémoire, l'inversion des victimes. Braun n'apparaissait plus comme un escroc mais comme un fils vengeur déterminé, après les révélations sur les Kant, à obtenir réparation, indemnisation, excuses publiques. Ils se sentirent accablés quand Garcia conclut : « Arno Heilbronn a agi uniquement pour venger son père. »

Le jour même, les Kant furent informés de la version donnée par Garcia. Ils se réunirent dans les locaux de la société. La grande salle de réunion aux murs recouverts de boiseries était plongée dans la pénombre. Une secrétaire déposa des cafés. D'un geste vif, elle appuya sur l'interrupteur. Une lumière crue, blanche, éblouit Axel Kant. « Eteignez ! » dit-il sèchement. La secrétaire obéit et disparut en claquant la porte. Les Kant échangèrent quelques mots, quelques regards.

Nous ne sommes pas coupables.

Nous ne sommes pas responsables.

Nous n'étions pas nés.

« Nous n'avons rien à voir avec cette histoire. Nous avons un grand problème en Allemagne : nous ne savons pas oublier. Dans la famille, nous avons discuté à maintes reprises de la question. Nous trouvons cela dommage car cela n'aide pas notre pays à aller de l'avant. On revient constamment sur cette époque, on la ressasse, y compris à l'étranger. Il faut maintenant essayer d'OUBLIER. Des événements comparables ont eu lieu dans d'autres pays dans le monde mais plus personne n'en parle et ils n'ont pas cette connotation négative. Chez nous, ils restent très négatifs. »

Axel Kant, à la presse.

Les Kant me licencièrent brutalement. Katrin et son fils Axel m'avaient convoqué dans la grande salle de réunion des locaux de K&S. Près d'eux se tenait Maître Mayer.

Vous avez commis une faute grave.

Vous n'avez pas protégé Juliana.

Vous auriez dû enquêter sur Braun.

Le confondre.

Le dénoncer.

L'évincer.

Vous n'avez plus toute votre tête. Vous parlez trop – et à la presse.

Vous êtes inefficace.

Improductif.

Vieux.

Monsieur Böll vous remplacera.

Vous êtes remplacé.

Je partis le jour même, n'emportant que mes livres. Je m'installai à l'hôtel – oh quelques jours –, puis je louai un petit appartement à Berlin, dans le quartier des Granges. Je lisais, je marchais – c'était tout. Vous m'écoutez ? Je voulais connaître les faits, cela devenait obsessionnel, je me rendais malade, les faits… les faits et rien d'autre. Braun était incarcéré dans la cellule exiguë et crasseuse d'une prison allemande, Juliana avait sans doute réintégré ses luxueux bureaux, son hôtel particulier, ses maisons de famille, ses voitures avec chauffeur : des coupés K&S aux vitres teintées, Bach en fond sonore. La vie avait repris son cours morbide, ils s'étaient aimés, trahis, Braun allait être jugé, et après ? La déposition de Garcia fut reprise dans la presse. Que cherchait-il ? A détourner l'attention des médias ? Des juges ? Rappeler au monde – car les faits étaient connus, oubliés, révélés mais étouffés – qu'un père et son fils, Günther et Philipp Kant, s'étaient enrichis pendant la guerre en ayant recours au travail forcé ? Le souvenir d'Isaac Heilbronn hantait désormais les esprits comme s'il cristallisait la culpabilité allemande, et pourquoi, demandez-vous ? Isaac Heilbronn, le père supposé de Herb Braun, était-il un personnage de fiction issu de l'imagination de Garcia, une invention née de la diffusion du documentaire accablant les Kant, une illusion, un mobile créé de toutes pièces pour attendrir la presse, les juges, sensibiliser l'opinion publique, responsabiliser, culpabiliser l'Allemagne ou un homme qui avait vécu, aimé, un homme qui avait été déporté, exploité, broyé par la machine nazie et qui, à la fin de la guerre, épargné par le sort, dernier survivant d'un monde assassiné, d'une culture sacrifiée, était rentré chez lui, brisé, homme sans identité, sans avenir, un matricule caressant le rêve insensé d'avoir un fils en temps de paix – un fils qui porterait son nom. Les victimes du camp de Stöcken ressurgissaient peu à peu, sombres, terrifiées, comme sorties d'une caverne où elles auraient été retenues captives – des hommes qui allaient mourir, qui allaient mourir d'un jour à l'autre de vieillesse, de saturnisme, de désespoir –, et témoignaient dans la presse, à la télévision, avec crainte, du bout des lèvres, au bord des larmes, des horreurs subies. « La plupart des nôtres sont morts, scandaient-ils, en six mois, oh, rarement plus… » En parallèle du procès pour escroquerie se déroulait un autre procès : celui des Kant et de leur participation aux crimes nazis et aussi improbable que cela parût, le second occultait le premier, le prévenu devenait victime et les parties civiles, coupables d'un crime qu'elles n'avaient pas commis mais dont elles portaient la responsabilité. L'avocat de Braun préparait sa défense : « Nous ne sommes plus au début des années 2000, au cœur de la société consumériste, du capitalisme tapageur, de la démesure financière, de tous ces codes économiques élaborés par des entrepreneurs tels que Günther et Philipp Kant, nous ne sommes pas en présence d'un homme vénal, retors, calculateur, un maître chanteur dont le seul mobile serait l'appât du gain, la corruption, le vol, nous ne sommes pas face à un délinquant aux mœurs coupables, un décadent, mais à un homme sans casier judiciaire, sans histoire, nous ne sommes même pas en présence d'un amant habile, un don juan à la morale entachée, un de ces gigolos, car c'est ainsi que la presse l'a qualifié, ternissant sa réputation et son nom, un de ces hommes qui exercent une pression sexuelle, sentimentale sur leurs victimes pour les faire payer, non… vous êtes ici en présence d'un fils. Ce procès n'est pas celui du chantage et de l'extorsion mais celui d'un fils contre une fille lui demandant de payer pour le crime de son père. Un fils fidèle, aimant, attaché à la mémoire de son père, un fils vengeur, mû par un désir qui ne serait que l'expression de l'amour le plus pur : l'amour filial. »

Braun ne s'était pas exprimé.

Je rencontrai les rares témoins qui vivaient encore : aucun ne se souvenait d'avoir croisé Isaac Heilbronn. Je passais désormais toutes mes journées à rechercher des informations, lisant des témoignages – je ne trouvai rien. J'écrivis une longue lettre à Braun à laquelle il ne répondit pas, sollicitai un rendez-vous au parloir – en vain, et pourquoi, insistez-vous, je vais vous le dire : Une part de moi souhaitait que la version proposée par Garcia fût vraie. Dénoncés, conspués, les Kant suscitaient ma pitié, je n'avais plus besoin de les haïr pour avoir le sentiment d'exister. On les vouait aux gémonies, les traitait d'esclavagistes modernes – cela m'amusait, après tout, je n'avais rien d'autre à faire.

Grâce à l'aide d'un étudiant allemand dont j'avais fait la connaissance au mémorial de la Shoah, je découvris un matin, sur Internet, le témoignage d'un Français qui avait été déporté au camp de Stöcken et qui avait travaillé dans les usines des Kant. Je n'avais lu qu'une partie du texte, sur l'ordinateur, avec difficulté, ma vue était faible. L'autre partie était disponible en version papier, chez l'éditeur. Je commandai aussitôt le livre et le reçus quelques jours plus tard à mon domicile. Il se présentait sous la forme d'un carnet de notes et de dessins. Au récit précis, terrible, de son séjour au camp de Stöcken, l'auteur avait associé des croquis, représentations de ses camarades déportés, morts pour la plupart, des hommes jeunes, aux visages émaciés – de profil, regardez. Sous les portraits, le nom de l'homme, son matricule, la date à laquelle le dessin avait été exécuté, le nom du camp et parfois, oui, ici, en bas du dessin, la date du décès. Il y avait également des croquis de scènes de torture, de cadavres – des images insoutenables. Au milieu du texte, regardez ce dessin : l'usine des Kant, c'était là, à l'intérieur de cet immense bâtiment surmonté d'une cheminée qui crachait sa fumée noirâtre, que les hommes manipulaient le plomb, sans gants, sans protections, exposés à la chaleur des fours dont la température atteignait à l'extérieur 70 degrés, le plomb en fusion qui coulait dans les moules et parfois sur la peau des mains qui brûlait et fondait, lambeaux de chairs noircies, c'était là que des hommes affamés, assoiffés, roués de coups, fabriquaient les missiles qui alimenteraient la machine de guerre allemande, enrichiraient les Kant. Que voulez-vous savoir de plus – lisez-le, je vous le donne. Vers la fin du livre, il y a le portrait d'un homme au nez aquilin, au menton fin. En bas du dessin, vous pourrez lire ces mots : *Isaac, un juif allemand.*

« La famille ne s'exprimera pas. »

Chris Walser,
porte-parole de la famille Kant,
à la presse.

J'attendais le procès avec impatience, le moment où Braun raconterait qu'il avait séduit puis escroqué Juliana Kant pour venger son père. Les juifs vengeurs, belliqueux, c'était nouveau et ça me plaisait. Je pensais à l'avocat de Juliana Kant, Maître Goldberg, à la façon dont il avait réagi en apprenant la version de Garcia. On disait qu'il avait démissionné. Ce ne fut pas lui qui défendit la famille dans l'affaire Kant contre Braun.

Le jour du procès, Juliana ne se présenta pas au tribunal – elle avait pris rendez-vous chez le coiffeur. La tête renversée dans le bac, elle oubliait les faits, l'eau chaude ruisselait sur ses cheveux, le haut de son front – rituel purificatoire qui l'apaisait.

Au même moment, Herb Braun pénétrait dans la salle de la Cour pénale de Berlin, suivi de ses deux geôliers, un homme et une femme, lui, moulé dans un pull-over kaki, elle, dans un blouson de même couleur. On n'aime pas les uniformes, en Allemagne, on n'en fait plus, on fuit tout ce qui pourrait rappeler le rituel militaire et destructeur de l'Allemagne nazie.

La salle d'audience était une petite pièce circulaire aux murs blancs. Herb Braun se tenait droit, derrière son avocat. A quelques mètres, les avocats de la partie civile et le procureur relisaient leurs dossiers. Assis sous une grande croix accrochée au mur, le président du tribunal veillait au bon déroulement du procès. Braun portait un costume trois-pièces noir, une chemise blanche, une cravate bleu marine à pois verts. De fines lunettes cerclaient son regard bleu aux reflets moirés. Il était posé, élégant. Les cent quarante journalistes internationaux accrédités pour l'occasion ne le lâchaient pas du regard, analysant ses moindres faits et gestes. Mais sa coiffure, impeccable et laquée avec soin, reflétait son calme intérieur. D'une voix solennelle, le procureur lut les douze pages d'accusation. Les avocats de la partie civile accumulaient les preuves contre lui : relevé d'empreintes digitales sur les lettres de chantage, missives enflammées envoyées à Juliana. Pas une fois le nom de Garcia ne fut prononcé. Un seul témoin fut entendu – l'un des enquêteurs. Il reconnut que la justice ne savait pas où pouvaient se trouver les vidéos tournées par Braun lors de ses relations intimes avec la plaignante. Ce fut tout.

Chacun attendait la plaidoirie de l'avocat de Braun. L'émotion était palpable. Les journalistes restaient concentrés, prenaient des notes. Soudain, le président demanda à Herb Braun de se lever. Braun regarda son avocat, puis, lentement comme s'il était tiré par un fil invisible, délia son corps. Un léger sourire détendit ses traits. Il ne semblait ni accablé ni anxieux. Son avocat lui fit un signe de la tête. Le président voulut savoir s'il reconnaissait les faits qui lui étaient reprochés. Braun acquiesça d'un hochement de tête. Puis il lui demanda ce qu'il avait à dire pour sa défense. Alors seulement, Braun se mit à parler. Sur un ton monocorde, il présenta ses excuses à la victime et demanda pardon, pardon pour le mal qu'il avait fait, la peine qu'il avait causée. Il y eut des cris de stupéfaction dans la salle. Une femme hurla même : « Traître ! » avant d'être maîtrisée et renvoyée de la salle. Le prévenu était poli, la victime absente, les avocats se donnaient l'accolade. On attendait un procès-fleuve, l'affaire fut réglée en quelques heures. Pendant les délibérations, les journalistes tentaient vainement d'élaborer les versions rocambolesques qui leur permettraient de nourrir leurs chroniques. Je n'étais pas dans la salle mais dans le hall du Palais de justice, un café à la main. Je me sentais mal, j'avais envie de vomir – plus de quarante ans de dévotion pour se retrouver la tête au-dessus de la cuvette.

En sortant de la salle d'audience, les avocats furent assaillis par les journalistes. Les flashs crépitèrent. Je m'étais caché derrière une colonne de marbre. J'entendais, je voyais tout, transparent, j'ai dit.

Herb Braun avait été condamné à six ans de prison. Aucune réduction de peine ne lui avait été accordée puisqu'il n'avait pas révélé où se trouvaient les cinq millions d'euros qu'il avait extorqués lors de la première demande de rançon. Il ne fit pas appel de cette décision et retourna dans la cellule où les Kant l'avaient calfeutré. Juliana s'apprêtait à sortir de chez le coiffeur avec son brushing impeccable et ses lunettes noires quand son avocat lui annonça le verdict par téléphone. Elle l'écouta puis raccrocha brusquement sans avoir prononcé un mot. Sous ses lunettes de soleil, ses yeux étaient baignés de larmes.

« Ce que m'a transmis mon père ? L'honnêteté. »

Juliana Kant à un journaliste.

J'étais convaincu que les Kant avaient acheté le silence de Braun, peut-être même en multipliant par trois ou quatre la somme qu'il avait extorquée la première fois, mais qui était vraiment l'homme qui avait fait tomber Juliana Kant ? Un fils vengeur, un Robin des Bois de la mémoire dont la mission consistait à voler les chefs d'entreprise allemands qui s'étaient enrichis pendant la guerre en collaborant avec les nazis dans le seul but de restituer cet argent aux victimes du nazisme ? Un fils qui, au jour du procès, n'avait pas pu légitimer ses actes par une exception morale : la réparation, une obsession allemande, muselé par son avocat, la partie civile, peut-être même par sa propre conscience, ou n'était-il qu'un escroc habile, retors et calculateur qui coulerait des jours tranquilles sur une plage de Bora Bora au côté de son comparse dont la riposte mémorielle et vengeresse ne visait qu'à travestir leurs aspirations vénales, leur goût pour une vie facile, les filles aux seins siliconés et les voitures de sport nerveuses, des K&S deux-places qui rouleraient jusqu'à 250 km/h ? Garcia avait-il trahi une information que Braun aurait préféré garder secrète ? Et pourquoi ? Une version qui modifiait le cours des événements avait été donnée puis reprise, étouffée. Sous l'emprise de qui ? A quelles fins ? Contre quoi ? Qu'en pensez-vous ? Qu'est-ce qui s'est joué dans ce prétoire ? Qu'auriez-vous fait à ma place ? Que voulait Braun ? Quelles étaient ses relations avec Garcia ? Quel rôle avait joué son complice ? Qui était Isaac, l'Allemand ? D'où venez-vous ? Qu'entend-on par « réparation » ? Quel sens avait ce procès grotesque, cette mascarade judiciaire sans témoins, sans victimes avec, pour seul acteur, Herb Braun, affligé, contrit, demandant pardon, pardon aux victimes tandis que les Kant étouffaient le scandale, ne demandaient pardon à personne *Chaque famille a sa part d'ombre ses secrets mais dans la nôtre il n'y a pas de linge sale à laver il n'est pas question de se retrouver dans une situation gênante où il faudrait se justifier voire s'excuser d'appartenir à cette famille je ne suis responsable ni juridiquement ni moralement il est fréquent que nous êtres humains endossions la responsabilité de ce dont nous ne sommes en rien*

coupables pourquoi me sentirais-je coupable je n'étais pas né je ne me sens ni coupable ni responsable la famille ne s'exprimera pas nous sommes des gens normaux nous n'avons rien à voir avec cette histoire j'ai fait mon travail honnêtement et c'est tout

Depuis, je n'ai pas revu les Kant. J'ai envoyé une lettre à Juliana – je voulais rencontrer les enfants. Elle n'a pas répondu. J'ai téléphoné, deux fois, cinq fois, le petit personnel filtrait les appels, j'étais devenu persona non grata. J'ai reçu quelques affaires, par coursier : des livres que j'avais oubliés, des vêtements éparpillés – sans un mot. J'aurais préféré qu'elle me fasse tuer, un assassinat me semblait moins obscène que cette exécution morale. De Braun non plus on n'entendit plus parler. La nouvelle campagne publicitaire de K&S vient de paraître, vous l'avez vue ? *Le bonheur a désormais un nom : K&S.*

Voilà les faits. Si on s'en tenait à eux et à eux seuls, on se quitterait maintenant pour ne plus jamais se revoir, cette situation vous rend heureuse, mais vous n'en avez pas fini avec l'Allemagne, avec les Kant, avec moi, un livre s'achève, qui s'écrit avec la vie, un autre pourrait commencer sans les contraintes de la véracité, les aspérités du quotidien. C'est la fiction contre la réalité, votre imagination en réponse aux faits. Qui sommes-nous ? Des héritiers du chaos. Certains portent les fautes des pères – et jusqu'à quelle génération ? D'autres réclament réparation, fils vengeurs, rappelant la mémoire des morts. Vous avez raison, l'Histoire s'est souvenue de tous les personnages secondaires : gardes du corps, secrétaires particuliers, amants, chauffeurs, animaux mondains, mais elle a oublié les pères. Isaac Heilbronn est peut-être un père fictif, le saurons-nous un jour ? Je vous l'avoue : j'ai été fasciné par la version du complice de Braun, par l'hypothèse d'une vengeance. Il y avait de la revanche et de la rancœur dans la détermination de ce fils blessé, une forme d'animalité dans l'attaque qui faisait écho à ma propre violence. En dépit de mon appartenance au clan des Kant pendant près d'un demi-siècle, j'étais resté au fond de moi un déclassé, un humilié. Fils d'un ouvrier nazi, j'avais vécu avec ma honte – et mal. J'avais haï mon père et j'enviais les Kant, je les enviais ces fils fiers qui n'avaient pas bu le lait noir de la honte. Ils n'avaient pas retiré de leurs murs les portraits de leurs pères.

Oh, le seul père qui mériterait un livre, c'est Richard Friedländer, le père adoptif de Magda Goebbels, vous avez raison. Sur lui, vous ne trouverez rien, je vous l'ai dit – inventez ! C'est un père qui a existé, qui a aimé et que les Kant ont rejeté, un père réel que l'Histoire a effacé. Günther Kant refuse d'épouser la fille d'un juif, il évince le père, il l'efface – c'est le premier acte, la première décision symbolique, qui le mènera vers la collaboration, l'exploitation, les crimes de guerre. Friedländer, c'est lui qui vous inspire, depuis le début, ce n'est pas moi, n'est-ce pas ? Je l'ai deviné tout de suite à votre façon de questionner. Mes mémoires, vous les écrirez ? Et l'histoire de Friedländer, aussi, associée à la mienne, peut-être. Allez-y, bravez vos réticences, les derniers témoins sont morts ou vont mourir. Après nous, les écrivains de l'interprétation décriront dans la chaleur de leurs bureaux ultramodernes des lieux, des images qu'ils n'ont pas connus. Ils récriront les faits ou diront Je m'en lave les mains. Vous avez peur d'écrire, vous avez peur de vous méprendre, vous demandez si les écrivains ont le droit d'offrir un linceul de mots aux morts, vous dites : « L'obscénité de la fiction, la transgression de la vérité, de la mémoire sacralisée » – vos obsessions. Vous échouerez à dire l'indicible, la littérature est un aveu d'échec, vous écrivez pour dire ce qui vous échappe, ce qui est irreprésentable, ce qui est perdu. Ecrivez ! Et soyez infidèle aux faits – les reconstitutions sont l'affaire de la police, pas des écrivains.

« Il m'est personnellement désagréable et insupportable que l'on me soupçonne d'avoir été élevée par un juif. »

Magda Goebbels
à un journaliste allemand.

« C'est le plus beau, Friedländer, dites-vous, votre personnage préféré, le père nourricier jeté aux orties, renié parce que juif, le père oublié, assassiné. »

Karl Fritz

Berlin, juin 1938

Quelques semaines avant mon trente-neuvième anniversaire, ma fille Magda me fit savoir qu'elle renonçait à mon nom et reprenait le nom de son géniteur au motif que son futur époux, l'industriel allemand Günther Kant, n'épouserait pas la fille d'un juif. Elle me l'avait dit spontanément, sans chercher à mentir, à atténuer la portée de ses propos, comme si sa démarche obéissait à un processus inéluctable et naturel, à l'ordre des choses, en somme, et il me fallait m'y résoudre avec raison, avec calme, sans y chercher une quelconque atteinte à ma personne, sans y voir un antijudaïsme primaire, réactif, mais plutôt un hommage à son père naturel, une façon de lui rendre justice, de lui restituer les droits que l'amour lui avait subtilisés car j'avais aimé sa fille, je l'avais adoptée, et elle me rejetait à présent, non pas pour l'amour d'un homme – pour l'amour, je l'eusse compris et accepté –, ni même pour celui d'un père, non, elle me rejetait par ambition sociale. Elle me repoussait comme on avance ou recule un pion, par stratégie, calcul. Pour gagner.

Il y avait quelque chose de profondément tragique dans cet éloignement, le signe d'un acharnement pathétique de l'Histoire dont l'ensanglantement, le cours arbitraire et criminel, la répétition, semblaient marquer chaque acte de ma vie personnelle : juif, je l'étais de naissance, père, j'avais été choisi – l'élection était une trahison.

Mais je vais trop vite, la peur me bouscule, je n'ai plus de répit, plus de forces, même la rage s'en va déclinant, je ne proteste plus que contre moi-même, mon indifférence coupable, ma capitulation, je n'ai plus de désir, de volonté, mon destin me semble désormais inéluctable, il n'y a rien que je puisse faire, rien que je sois en mesure de tenter, l'étau se referme autour de moi, j'entends la meute aboyante, je serai arrêté aujourd'hui ou demain, je suis harcelé nuit et jour par cette angoisse qui monte en moi et me ronge de l'intérieur sans que je sache quoi faire pour la rendre moins vivace, l'étouffer, la bête qui hurle JUIF, TU N'AS PLUS D'AVENIR.

J'avais vingt-trois ans quand je fis la connaissance de ma première femme, Auguste, la mère de Magda, au début de l'année 1904, quelques mois après son divorce. Je venais alors d'être embauché comme chef de rang dans un restaurant du centre-ville où Auguste avait ses habitudes. J'avais été immédiatement séduit par cette belle femme blonde à la peau laiteuse, au corps mince, dont la voix rauque, presque masculine, trahissait la sensualité tapageuse et sans doute aussi, mais je ne le découvris que plus tard, la brutalité, le désir de domination et un goût maladif pour le pouvoir. J'habitais encore chez mes parents, des commerçants juifs originaires de Berlin, Auguste vivait seule, sa fille avait rejoint son père, en Belgique, pour une courte durée. Deux semaines après notre rencontre, je la demandai en mariage pour une raison qui demeura incompréhensible aux miens : la blondeur de ses cheveux m'apaisait. Il y avait comme une promesse d'innocence, de vie calme, pacifiée, dans cette couleur blanche aux reflets dorés, une invitation à la jeunesse, à l'enfance perdue – une trahison physique. Mes parents manifestèrent leur réprobation : ce qui les choquait, c'était moins le catholicisme offensif de ma future femme que la présence d'une petite fille à ses côtés, une enfant de trois ans que son père naturel avait reconnue tardivement. Ils se plaignaient qu'une charge aussi lourde fût imposée à un homme si jeune. Le caractère soudain de ma décision les portait à croire qu'Auguste était enceinte, et je ne cherchai pas à les assurer du contraire. J'étais bien déterminé à rompre avec la sincérité névrotique qui caractérisait mon éducation : tout se dire, sans rien occulter, sans mentir, cette communion factice, grégaire, confortée par les rituels, rythmée par les fêtes, les anniversaires, tout un cérémonial préservé à travers les siècles, qui, s'il ne me déplaisait pas, n'avait jamais suscité chez moi l'enthousiasme un peu puéril qui animait les miens. La fierté juive, ce cadeau empoisonné, je n'en avais pas été le dépositaire – la honte, non plus. Les mouvements de masse, les pensées collectives, la ghettoïsation des corps et des esprits, j'y avais échappé très tôt, pour survivre. Je n'imaginais pas alors que l'histoire politique m'y ramènerait de force comme un évadé est renvoyé dans sa prison dans l'attente de l'exécution d'une peine capitale.

Je quittai Berlin pour épouser Auguste en Belgique au terme d'une cérémonie houleuse, conflictuelle, entachée d'une méfiance réciproque qui annonçait déjà, sans doute, la guerre intime que nous nous livrerions. Magda, la fille d'Auguste, était au cœur de la discorde. Je décidai de l'adopter, avec le consentement du père biologique qui assista même à notre mariage. Auguste s'y opposa, craignant que ce dernier ne s'en détournât, puis accepta, cédant aux usages belges, peut-être aussi aux supplications de sa fille qui m'aimait, me voulait comme père – une désignation sentimentale contre laquelle il eût été vain de lutter, deux êtres se rencontrent, se reconnaissent et s'aiment, s'imposent de leur plein gré des attaches que la nature n'a pas créées. Je signai les documents administratifs et invitai Magda à déjeuner au restaurant pour fêter la légitimation de nos liens. Cela ne changea rien entre nous. Je l'aimais déjà plus qu'un père.

Dès les premières semaines de mon mariage, je sus qu'il serait voué à l'échec. La nervosité pathologique d'Auguste, ses emportements vifs et inattendus associés à mes brusques accès de mélancolie, provoquaient des drames dont nous étions les acteurs et les victimes pitoyables, nous accusant mutuellement et sans relâche de ne pas être capables de nous aimer sans nous détruire, de nous parler sans hurler. Notre quotidien n'était que disputes et luttes vaines pour déterminer qui de nous deux aurait le pouvoir, qui de nous deux écraserait l'autre. En public, il n'était pas rare qu'elle me critiquât, qu'elle me jugeât avec une violence qui tétanisait nos proches et qui me laissait démuni, prostré dans une passivité coupable – non que je fusse complètement veule mais je savais que viendrait le moment où, en privé, elle se donnerait avec une soumission déconcertante. Nous n'étions jamais aussi proches qu'au cours de ces disputes sauvages où nous en venions aux mains, jamais aussi intimes que dans ces moments de rage où l'érotisme se mêlait à la violence, où la fureur engendrait l'amour et comme je l'aimais alors, comme je la désirais quand, repoussant mes baisers avec une hargne de bête féroce, elle m'injuriait avant de se rendre physiquement, mentalement. Cette femme était un monstre d'ambiguïté et de sang-froid, une servante dure à la tâche dont la rancœur sociale avait contaminé chaque geste. Sous la rudesse, la sensualité. Derrière la rigueur du masque autoritaire, la promesse d'abandon. Sa façon froide, presque virile, de s'éloigner après l'amour, me donnait le sentiment d'être réduit à rien, et j'ai vu par la suite dans cet éloignement qui prenait parfois la forme d'une rupture de nos rapports conjugaux, dans cette attitude glaciale que rien ne venait adoucir, un signe de ce qui adviendrait très vite : la séparation sans formalités. La haine – et puis c'est tout. Pourtant, je ne fis rien pour anticiper la chute, rien pour lui plaire davantage, je savais que tôt ou tard, ce qui l'avait séduite la détournerait de moi, mes qualités deviendraient des tares, mes mots d'amour, des motifs de haine, je l'avais senti d'instinct, au premier regard, et je l'avais suivie, je l'avais aimée, courant à ma perte comme le visiteur d'un zoo se jette dans la fosse aux lions, non par fascination mais parce qu'il veut y mourir sachant qu'il y sera déchiqueté, dévoré, cet amour relevait de la folie. Aucun autre ne me rendait aussi vivant.

(Le sentiment de vulnérabilité qu'occasionne l'amour, la sensation d'être exposé, soumis, attaché à l'autre, la confusion mentale contre laquelle toute tentative de résistance et de raisonnement est vaine – ce n'était pas pour moi.)

Intellectuellement, nous ne partagions rien, il n'y avait que dans un lit que nous parvenions à communiquer. Dans un lit, nous parlions la même langue et je me suis souvent demandé – sans le comprendre – comment deux êtres aussi dissemblables, qui n'avaient pas le même niveau d'instruction, les mêmes origines, pouvaient, lorsqu'ils se retrouvaient enfermés dans une même pièce, ressentir autant d'attirance l'un pour l'autre, être si proches, se posséder et s'aimer d'une façon aussi naturelle, aussi simple. Ce n'était pas tant son corps que sa façon d'en jouer qui me fascinait, une manière singulière de se retenir, de se refuser absolument puis de se donner d'un coup, sans retenue, sans cette pudeur obscène qui vicie si souvent la sexualité et dont Auguste, à la différence des quelques femmes que j'avais connues avant elle, était dépourvue. Elle aimait comme une professionnelle du sexe, mais une professionnelle qu'on aurait maltraitée, violée, battue peut-être – quels crimes vengeait-elle pendant l'amour et quelles fautes occultes expiais-je en tolérant d'être ainsi humilié en public, en privé ? Fallait-il que nous fussions profondément névrosés, accablés par nous-mêmes pour ne pas être capables de nous aimer dans une relative harmonie, pour ne pas jouir de cette union sans passer par ces scènes d'hystérie qui engendraient presque toujours l'intervention de nos voisins et une fois même de la police, cherchant à nous donner en spectacle par la contradiction publique, les cris, le harcèlement moral, cherchant à nous provoquer l'un l'autre et ne trouvant de répit que dans la capitulation réciproque par lassitude, par contrainte. Le chaos nous était nécessaire pour nous aimer et j'enviais ces couples paisibles dont les échanges harmonieux contrastaient avec nos rixes, nous ridiculisant, nous renvoyant à nos faiblesses, nos échecs, à ce qu'il y avait de plus laid en nous. Et il y avait Magda, témoin des crises de sa mère, oh, j'étais plus calme qu'elle, plus soumis, Magda qui prenait systématiquement mon parti, que je considérais comme ma fille et dont l'affection répondait à la mienne, sans faiblir, Magda dont je devinai, au premier regard, qu'elle aurait un destin – je n'imaginais pas qu'il serait funeste.

Qu'est-ce qui m'avait précipité dans les bras de cette femme ? J'étais jeune, plein d'avenir. Au-delà de cette attirance superficielle pour son physique de poupée allemande – et il y avait là de quoi séduire l'homme que j'étais, le juif marginal et railleur qui se vantait de sa germanité, drapé dans sa dignité d'homme libre, et qui ne cherchait qu'à se fondre, disparaître, emprunter une nouvelle identité vidée de la peur et des préjugés raciaux, fût-ce par le mariage –, au-delà de cette fascination érotique, quels éléments m'avaient incité à m'unir à cette femme ? Une inclination pathétique à l'échec, un goût pour le risque amoureux. Pour la perte. Avant Auguste, je n'avais pas connu de vraie passion amoureuse, sa présence, sa seule présence à mes côtés, me rendait fou, fou à lier et si j'avais su, si j'avais pressenti où cette relation me mènerait, aurais-je tenté de changer le cours des choses ?

Nous n'eûmes aucun enfant et je vis dans cette stérilité le signe de mon lien exclusif avec Magda. J'étais son père ; en conséquence, je ne pouvais pas être le père d'un autre enfant. Auguste et moi avions consulté différents médecins, tenté tout ce que la science nous offrait – en vain. Auguste ayant déjà enfanté, elle me fit porter le poids de notre malheur, la responsabilité de notre stérilité. Nous étions alors si soucieux de donner l'image d'une famille recomposée, idéale et ouverte, une famille où cohabitaient des êtres aux convictions différentes – un mariage mixte. Auguste veillait à ce que Magda reçût une éducation catholique mais elle ne s'opposait pas à la pratique d'un judaïsme ouvert dans notre cadre privé. Je respectais les grandes fêtes juives, j'appris à Magda quelques rudiments d'hébreu. A cette époque, elle se lia d'amitié avec Lisa Arlosoroff et avec son frère, Victor, issus d'une famille juive russe qui avait émigré en Allemagne. Victor était un militant sioniste, un de ceux qui avaient fait de Herzl leur nouveau messie et de son livre *L'Etat des juifs*, leur bible. Moi aussi je l'avais lu : « Voici donc, Juifs ! Ce n'est pas un conte de fées. Ce n'est pas une escroquerie. » Des yeux globuleux cerclés de petites lunettes noires, un nez long et busqué, des lèvres charnues, Arlosoroff était laid – d'une laideur électrisante. Aux côtés de Victor et de sa sœur Lisa, Magda militait dans les rangs de mouvements sionistes, réfléchissait à l'avenir de la Palestine, portait une étoile de David autour du cou... Cela m'amusait... Oh, moi, je n'avais pas rejoint les rangs de ces jeunes idéalistes aux corps souples, sculptés par l'effort, qui appelaient à la création d'un foyer juif. Mon foyer, c'était l'Allemagne. Aujourd'hui encore, humilié, rejeté, je n'en ai pas d'autre. Ce fut à cette époque qu'Auguste décida d'envoyer Magda en pension. Chercha-t-elle à éloigner sa fille des Arlosoroff ? Elle n'en dit rien, masqua ses motivations profondes... Il me semblait que cet éloignement soudain manifestait une peur diffuse, qu'elle ne contenait plus : celle de l'influence juive. Cette peur-là rôdait partout, dans notre propre maison, dans notre lit, je ne la pris pas au sérieux, j'interprétais cette nouvelle attitude comme une arme supplémentaire dans la guerre intestine que nous menions, il y avait même une forme de corruption sexuelle : juif, je la dégoûtais – elle m'en désirait davantage.

Sans Magda entre nous, la vie commune devint si difficile que nous songeâmes à nous séparer. Nous faisions désormais chambre à part et, sauf à de rares exceptions, ne nous parlions plus que pour préciser les modalités d'un divorce qui devenait inéluctable. Nous nous aimions pourtant – mais mal, je n'avais pas compris que c'était là ma seule façon d'aimer.

Après son baccalauréat, j'envisageais d'emmener Magda avec moi en voyage, à Paris, peut-être. Je lui écrivais de longues lettres dans lesquelles je lui parlais de ses amis, de ma vie à Berlin – je n'évoquais pas le nom de sa mère que je ne retrouvais plus que pour de rares rapprochements nocturnes (et que j'aimais toujours sans parvenir à le lui dire, comme si notre complicité sexuelle, ce tumulte que le contact de nos corps provoquait encore, exigeait, pour s'affermir, la rupture de tous les autres liens). Mais un événement survint qui bouleversa l'ordre des choses et l'agencement d'un monde que j'avais créé pour elle, pour échapper à la folie de sa mère – à notre passion destructrice. A dix-huit ans, au cours de son année de pensionnat, Magda rencontra un homme de vingt ans son aîné : Günther Kant, un grand industriel allemand, veuf et père de deux enfants, qui exerçait des fonctions au ministère de l'Economie de la République de Weimar. Sur les circonstances de leur rencontre, je ne sais pas grand-chose… Au début de l'été 1920, Magda m'annonça qu'elle allait se marier, sans discussion préalable, sans concertation. Elle l'avait dit froidement, avec une gravité dont je ne soupçonnais pas les raisons latentes. Ce qui pouvait inciter une jeune fille d'une beauté stupéfiante, cérébrale et enjouée, à sacrifier ses études, une passion amoureuse avec un homme de son âge, pour épouser un gros bourgeois austère et tyrannique, je ne l'expliquais pas. Il y avait l'attrait pour l'argent, bien sûr, l'assurance d'être introduite dans la bonne société, mais le rayonnement social de Kant, sa culture, se limitaient à la sphère économique, l'art de la conversation lui était étranger, ce qui nous différenciait totalement et de façon irréversible et qui l'éloignerait de Magda dont j'avais formé l'esprit, que j'avais initiée à la riposte, Magda que ce mariage transformerait en bourgeoise dépressive, Magda réduite à une vie contemplative, larvaire, une vie de frustrations et de renoncements – je savais que tôt ou tard ce compromis infligé à ses aspirations profondes la condamneraient au malheur et à la solitude.

Magda aurait pu épouser Victor Arlosoroff, partir avec lui sur la terre de Palestine fonder le nouvel Etat juif et ramasser les pamplemousses dans un kibboutz du sud de la Galilée. La fermière sioniste avec son fichu blanc sur la tête – ah ce soleil d'Orient ! Au lieu de cela, elle allait épouser un grand bourgeois allemand, protestant et antisémite, dont la première décision conjugale consisterait à évincer le père – le père juif. J'imaginais la scène : Günther Kant et Magda attablés dans un grand restaurant de Berlin, discutant de leur vie future, faisant mille projets et suspendant soudain la réalisation de tous ces rêves à une condition essentielle : ma suppression. Au dessert, elle avait pris sa décision. Magda substitua le nom de son géniteur au mien – sordide tour de passe-passe, rite purificatoire, déjudaïsons-nous ! Elle se convertit au protestantisme puis se maria avec Günther Kant. Je ne fus pas convié au mariage. Je n'y serais pas allé – non que je fusse humilié de cette mise en quarantaine, mais j'avais atteint un état de rage où l'on ne se soucie plus des arrangements sociaux et où la violence intérieure dévore tout, jusqu'au désir de se réjouir – et pourtant la certitude que je ne viendrais pas, certitude confortée par mon silence, ne lui avait pas suffi, elle avait préféré s'entourer de mille précautions, protections, ne m'envoyant pas la carte d'invitation, m'évitant comme si je présentais un danger mortel, une maladie contagieuse, me faisant savoir, par l'intermédiaire de sa mère devenue émissaire de malheur, que ma présence n'était pas souhaitée par son futur mari, ce n'était pas sa faute, elle n'était pas responsable, elle obéissait – c'était tout.

La capacité d'obéissance et de soumission d'une femme à un homme – aujourd'hui d'un peuple, Magda si représentative du sort de l'Allemagne, Magda, incarnation suprême de cette Allemagne cultivée, civilisée, transformée en tyrannie sous l'impulsion d'un homme, l'assujettissement de la fille annonçait la chute morale de la patrie.

Je ne revis plus Magda. Elle avait eu un enfant dont j'appris la naissance par hasard et que je ne rencontrai jamais. Magda ne m'envoya pas de faire-part et je ne lui écrivis pas. Cette vie dont elle m'avait exclu sur les ordres de Günther Kant, ne m'intéressait plus que comme une entité abstraite, un temps qu'il fallait supporter, un vide à combler.

(Je devins invivable.)

Sa mère demanda officiellement le divorce ; je ne m'y opposai pas. J'ai longtemps pensé, je continue à croire, que cette séparation fut moins la conséquence d'un désamour que celle d'un conformisme social et peut-être aussi, mais j'avais peine à me l'avouer, racial. Juif, il fallait me tenir à distance, voire, si c'était possible, m'éviter. On me contournait comme un obstacle, un danger. Je n'étais pas un homme à abattre – c'était pire. Insulté, j'eusse eu le sentiment d'exister un peu. Ils m'avaient effacé de leur vie, gommé pourrait-on dire, comme si je n'y avais jamais tenu un rôle, fût-il mineur, comme si les liens du sang annulaient ceux du cœur.

Mon ex-femme se vit offrir une petite droguerie par son gendre, elle y vendait des paniers en osier, des aiguilles, des clous (je fus pris un jour d'une pulsion terrible : je songeai à lui crever les yeux), et il n'était pas rare que j'y fisse quelques apparitions pour le simple plaisir de la voir tressaillir. J'entrais, j'ôtais mon chapeau, je disais Bonjour Madame, elle répliquait Mademoiselle, son regard devenait noir, menaçant, je demandais à voir les aiguilles, cela ne durait que quelques minutes, le temps de les manipuler, de l'effrayer un peu et je repartais – cela calmait mes nerfs. Elle se pavanait désormais dans les soirées mondaines au bras d'Allemands mafflus et alcooliques. Son opportunisme, sa soif de reconnaissance, la façon brutale dont elle m'avait quitté, dont elle avait dû quitter son premier mari, sans sentimentalisme, sans détour, faisant table rase du passé, reniant ce qui avait été dit et promis, m'avaient anéanti. Magda et sa mère m'apparaissaient comme des femmes vénales, dépossédées du moindre affect, des femmes que l'assurance d'une vie frivole, débarrassée des contingences matérielles, avait rendues cruelles et pathétiques, des femmes que l'attention d'un homme, la perspective d'être protégée des assauts de la vie, n'avaient pas su humaniser. Et pourtant, je ne cessai jamais d'aimer Magda, ne comprenant pas moi-même comment je trouvais encore de quoi nourrir cette affection dans ce rapport de domination qu'elle avait instauré entre nous dès l'enfance, dans cet état de servilité affective qui était le mien et dans lequel je me complaisais avec une félicité coupable. Un autre père eût renié cette période de sa vie, eût ablué le livre familial ; moi, je m'accrochais désespérément à l'illusion que Magda me reviendrait tôt ou tard, qu'elle se souviendrait de mon nom – j'étais pathétique. La fille, puis la mère, m'avaient chassé et je me voyais comme une victime d'une inquisition morale – d'une injustice que nul ne saurait réparer.

(Au début de l'année 1922, je tentai de me tuer.)

Je m'installai dans un petit meublé à Berlin où je vécus seul. Je développai un commerce de conserves. Je dormais, je travaillais – c'était tout. Je fumais beaucoup dans l'espoir de mourir vite. Je n'aspirais à rien. Puis je rencontrai ma nouvelle femme chez des amis communs : je ne répondis pas aux questions qu'elle me posa avec une bienveillance suspecte, refusai de la revoir. Enfin, je lui annonçai que j'étais juif et stérile : je voulais lui déplaire. Elle insista pour m'épouser par masochisme, j'acceptai par politesse. Juif, je lui rendais service en lui donnant une bonne raison de se cacher, elle qui souffrait d'agoraphobie depuis l'enfance. Deux mois plus tard, elle tomba enceinte. Je me haïssais d'avoir réussi avec elle là où j'avais échoué avec Auguste. La joie d'être père était annulée par celle d'avoir été évincé *en tant que père*. Notre enfant naquit au début de l'année 1925. C'était une fille. Je la nommai Hannah en hommage à ma mère. Je serrai l'enfant – mon enfant – contre moi, mais cette petite chose molle et hurlante qui s'agitait dans mes bras n'éveillait chez moi aucun sentiment paternel (toutefois, je ne songeai jamais à l'abandonner).

Je me trouvais dans la rue lorsque j'appris, au printemps 1930, que ma fille Magda était devenue la secrétaire de Joseph Goebbels, le ministre de la Propagande nazie. Ce fut un ancien client qui me l'annonça. Je dissimulai mal la douleur que cette nouvelle provoqua en moi. Dès qu'il se fut éloigné, j'avalai des tranquillisants – trop peu pour mourir.

Mes migraines commencèrent à cette époque. C'étaient des coups violents qui martelaient ma boîte crânienne, y perçaient des trous, me causant des souffrances intenses et des pertes de connaissance. Je restais enfermé dans le noir pendant plusieurs heures, interdisant à ma femme et à ma fille de pénétrer dans ma chambre. Je fumais. Dans ces moments-là où l'accablement succédait à la colère, je pensais à Magda. J'essayais de comprendre par quelle monstrueuse mutation la petite fille blonde et tendre que j'avais le plus aimée au monde, avait choisi de lier son sort à un homme dont l'ambition politique se donnait pour but l'anéantissement de mon peuple, j'essayais de savoir ce qu'était devenue l'enfant que j'avais élevée, serrée contre moi, celle qui m'appelait papa et portait mon nom, de savoir pourquoi elle n'avait jamais cherché à me revoir ni tenté quoi que ce fût pour, sinon me sauver, au moins m'épargner le spectacle de la folie du monde.

Je me rendais complice de son infamie, me demandant ce qui, dans mon attitude, mon éducation, ma façon de penser, de m'exprimer, dans toute la plénitude de mon être, avait pu engendrer le germe d'une haine aussi radicale du juif et l'adhésion à une idéologie qui non seulement prônait notre éviction de la vie sociale, notre affaiblissement moral mais aussi notre destruction, notre mort globale – notre anéantissement. J'avais été un bon chef de rang, un père convenable, un époux décevant, je ne l'avais jamais humiliée, insultée, tenue à l'écart. Je n'avais jamais levé la main sur elle. Je l'avais aimée comme un père. Elle me voyait désormais comme une punaise à écraser, un déchet à éliminer, un sous-homme – et pourquoi ?

Elle était devenue la secrétaire puis la maîtresse de Joseph Goebbels. Pourquoi Auguste me surprit-elle chez moi un beau matin pour m'annoncer cette liaison ? Qu'est-ce qui, dans cette révélation ignoble, l'excitait au point de lui faire renoncer au pacte de séparation totale que nous avions conclu ? C'était sans doute pour elle l'occasion de m'humilier davantage, d'infecter de ses mots les plaies ouvertes et de revendiquer la suprématie de sa personne, de sa nature, sur la mienne, elle disait « ta race » comme elle aurait évoqué celle d'un chien. Je tentai de joindre Magda pour la dissuader de lier sa vie à cet homme – comme l'avait fait avant moi son père biologique – « en vain, me dit Auguste, elle n'écoute personne ». J'imaginais ma fille au bras de ce nazi hystérique, tentant de la disculper, d'atténuer sa responsabilité, invoquant mille excuses : l'attraction érotique, l'ambition sociale, n'y parvenant jamais – comment pardonner à ma fille de se donner à un homme qui avait fait du meurtre de masse l'enjeu de toute une vie, de la ségrégation raciale, le seul programme politique ? Un temps, j'ai pensé que l'excitation du pouvoir, l'enthousiasme criminel qu'avaient suscité Hitler et Goebbels et aussi l'énergie physique, politique, fût-elle démoniaque et corruptrice, que véhiculaient leurs discours hystériques, avaient été pour Magda comme une solution à la platitude de son quotidien avec Kant, comme une réponse à la vie calme, ritualisée, que je lui avais imposée et je m'en voulais alors, je me tenais pour responsable de cet échec, mon éducation avait failli, je ne comprenais rien, la nature humaine, la nature de cette femme-là, me semblait aussi insondable que l'origine du monde : si l'univers avait été créé avec des lettres, il serait détruit avec des mots. La corruption de la langue allemande présageait la barbarie.

Je commençai à découper des extraits d'interviews, des phrases que Magda avait prononcées çà et là. Je devins obsessionnel. Je passais des heures à lire la presse et à traquer le nom de Magda comme s'il pouvait encore être associé à la paix, à la joie, mais c'était toujours au nom de Goebbels qu'il se trouvait accolé – pour son malheur.

A cette époque, je reçus des menaces diverses dont l'une émanait clairement de l'entourage de Goebbels. On me conseillait de veiller à rester à bonne distance de Magda, de ne jamais rappeler que j'avais été son père. Je lui portais préjudice dans son accession au trône hitlérien, je l'encombrais, je souillais son prestige et sa blondeur, la présence juive entachait la biographie familiale. Un jour, en rentrant chez moi, je fus renversé par un véhicule qui roulait à vive allure. Quelques jours plus tard, je trouvai un mot dans ma boîte aux lettres : *Vous ne devriez pas sortir de chez vous.* (Je sortis davantage.)

Puis il y eut ce titre dans la presse, rédigé par les opposants à Goebbels au sein même de son parti :

LE PETIT CHEF NAZI ÉPOUSE UNE JUIVE

J'étais heureux : juive, Magda était ma fille, je retrouvais mes droits sur elle, je redevenais son père.

Magda, ma fille, la fille d'un juif, épousa Joseph Goebbels avec Hitler pour témoin et fêta l'élimination des juifs, fêta la mort programmée de son père. Le mariage eut lieu dans le domaine d'été de son premier mari, Günther Kant. On trinqua à cette union et à la victoire prochaine. On but des vins sucrés dans les verres en cristal estampillés Kant, on but au nazisme et à la grandeur de Hitler. Avec Arlosoroff, Magda aurait bu à la santé des juifs. Avec Goebbels, elle but ce soir-là à leur spoliation. A leur extermination. Le choix d'un homme avait déterminé son destin et sans doute aussi le mien et je pensais qu'en aimant sa mère, en lui sacrifiant tout, j'avais hâté ma chute.

Quelque temps après, mon commerce fut réquisitionné par les nazis. Tous les juifs de mon entourage s'étaient vu déposséder de leurs biens comme s'il s'agissait d'une mesure juste et naturelle. De simples citoyens, nous étions devenus des ennemis à combattre. Je n'avais plus aucun revenu. Un restaurateur accepta de m'engager en tant que plongeur, défiant les lois de Nuremberg. Je passais toutes mes journées et mes soirées à laver la vaisselle, les mains si longtemps immergées dans l'eau bouillante que la peau boursouflée, rougie, s'en détachait par endroits, lambeaux de chair morte dont la désagrégation semblait s'accorder à ma détérioration morale. J'étais terrifié par l'idée d'être dénoncé, arrêté. Je ne dormais plus. J'écrivis une lettre à Magda et sollicitai une rencontre au siège du ministère de la Propagande nazie. Elle ne me répondit pas, si bien que je m'y rendis sans rendez-vous. C'était suicidaire. Je l'étais. « Je suis le père de Magda Goebbels », dis-je au gardien immobilisé devant l'entrée. Le SS qui montait la garde éclata de rire et me gifla. Je sortis alors de ma poche une photo de Magda déguisée en princesse le soir de la fête de Pourim. On me fit patienter dans un bureau. Goebbels s'adressa ainsi, devant moi, à son assistant : « Demandez au juif Friedländer ce qu'il veut. » J'expliquai la raison de ma venue : je ne cherchais pas à revoir Magda mais sollicitais son aide, j'allais être arrêté d'un jour à l'autre, je lui demandai d'intercéder en ma faveur. Goebbels resta de dos et, pour toute réponse, quitta la pièce. J'insistai pour parler à Magda. Deux hommes surgirent, me saisirent brutalement par les bras et me jetèrent dehors. Je roulai dans l'escalier principal et m'ouvris la tempe. Le sang gicla sur le sol. Aussitôt, un agent d'entretien entra, un seau d'eau à la main. Il en renversa le contenu par terre, l'eau emporta le sang, effaça les traces de ma chute. Le sol luisait, nettoyé, purifié. Ce fut tout. Je rentrai chez moi. Personne ne dirait à Magda Goebbels que son père, son père juif, s'était déplacé au siège du ministère de la Propagande, pour la revoir. J'imaginais sa réaction si elle l'apprenait. J'espérais, oh secrètement, je n'en parlais pas à ma femme, à laquelle je n'avais jamais rien dit comme si la révélation de mon passé eut pu faire exploser l'harmonie familiale factice que j'avais su recréer moins par détermination que par conformisme, j'espérais que Magda interviendrait, qu'elle stopperait la folie meurtrière de son mari en effaçant mon nom du livre de la mort, qu'elle ressurgirait dans ma vie pour y reprendre sa place car j'avais été son père, un père aimant et protecteur, un père qu'elle avait renié, oublié, sous la pression d'un homme, par aveuglement politique, et en quoi, me demandais-je, en quoi hurlais-je, ma judéité altérait-elle mon amour pour elle ?